EVERYDAY EVIL

EVERYDAY EVIL

Why Our World Is the Way It Is

MONIQUE LAYTON

TIDEWATER
PRESS

Published by Tidewater Press
New Westminster, BC, Canada
www.tidewaterpress.ca

ISBN 978-1-7751659-6-5 (paperback)
ISBN 978-1-7751659-7-2 (html)

LIBRARY AND ARCHIVES CANADA CATALOGUING IN PUBLICATION

Title: Everyday evil : why our world is the way it is / Monique Layton.
Names: Layton, Monique, 1930- author.
Identifiers: Canadiana (print) 20190177357 | Canadiana (ebook) 20190177381 |
    ISBN 9781775165965 (softcover) | ISBN 9781775165972 (HTML)
Subjects: LCSH: Social ethics. | LCSH: Social values. | LCSH: Moral conditions. |
    LCSH: Good and evil. | LCSH: Evil, Non-resistance to. | LCSH: Ethics.
Classification: LCC HM665 .L39 2019 | DDC 170—dc23

Back cover quote: Aldous Huxley, *The Devils of Loudun* (1952)

www.moniquelayton.com

Printed in Canada

This book is dedicated to the memory of my European parents who survived two global wars and lived in a different world, Etienne (1903-1960) and Simone (1905-2014), and to my twenty-first-century Canadian great-grandchildren, Alexander, Lana, Henry, Benjamin, Juliette, Lilith Alexandra and those yet to come, who will bear witness to the future and whose generation will be responsible for shaping it.

Contents

PREFACE

TWICE IN MY LIFE, I SAW a face that I felt personified evil. The first was when, changing television channels, I switched mid-play to *Othello* and saw Iago speaking softly into the Moor's ear. In the closeness of the screen, the actor's face looked so unbearably and creepily venomous, almost forcing us to participate in his betrayal, that I had to turn the TV off. The second time was while waiting with my husband to cross the street beside three teenagers, a boy and two girls. The boy was whispering to one of the girls, looking at us while doing so. I felt a sense of absolute revulsion—the boy's face could only have been described as evil, even if one had not known a second earlier what evil might look like.

The following day, I went to the offices of the British Columbia Police Commission, whose reports were available to the public, and asked whether they had done any studies on juvenile delinquency and prostitution. They had not but, since I was a PhD student in anthropology at the time, they thought I would be qualified to prepare one myself. The report, albeit with a different focus, came out in 1974 with some fanfare but also some controversy–it had been published with many names blacked out, thus raising suspicion. By then I knew more about bad luck, poor judgement, poverty, naïveté and ignorance, but I was none the wiser about evil.

On the verge of entering the tenth decade of my life, I am still reflecting on the nature of good and evil. With age and the narrowing of my horizon, such questions puzzle me all the more as I can see the time when their answers will no longer affect me. But they still do, and I wonder, perhaps with more curiosity than generosity, why we are not kinder to each other and to ourselves. We have but one world, one life. Yet, it is not love and compassion that rule us, but anger and greed. And, according to some, we are doomed from birth to be so afflicted.

An act of courageous rescue reported in the press a few years ago prompted me to consider the motivations of heroism—particularly everyday acts of bravery, often accompanied by heartfelt denials by their performers that these were heroic actions and only what 'anyone' would have done in the same circumstance. Heroic rescuers often mention that they acted entirely 'by instinct' and without thought.

Contemplating heroism but never having been in a position to be tested on it myself, I looked into my own heart and read a confusing message. I had little doubt that, by instinct, I too would dive into the river, crawl to the edge of the cliff and even perhaps ignore my fear of fire, falling unthinking into heroism—but only if I did not give myself time for reflection.

Reflection might bring a few attendant anxieties: paralyzing fear of danger and pain; hope that others (younger, fitter, more effective) might step in ahead of me to do what must be done; and, lurking almost beyond my consciousness, I could half-perceive the rejection of responsibility, craven selfishness, even cowardice and incipient shame. Other rescuers would be more effective than I and so I would put my conscience at rest and merely encourage from the shore those heroically diving into the freezing waters in my stead. Self-interest, far more than a desire for more efficiency and speed in saving drowning children, was the guiding principle behind my non-heroic hesitation.

In this process of reflection, my interest shifted from the nature of heroism to the consideration of the sly process of self-deceit and self-preservation I could see at work in myself in this imagined scenario. Would I know the right thing to do, the ethical choice, the one that I wished others would do unto me? Without a doubt. Yet, my heart (figuratively speaking, for my real heart has no crises or qualms of its own and is only concerned with keeping on beating), my other heart was a battleground. So is everyone else's. And not just when heroism is called for, but also in our everyday actions, their motivations and the choices we make. Contemplating the nature of self-interest caught my curiosity and caused me to wonder more widely about the concepts of good and evil and how they affect our daily lives.

For the next year and a half, this curiosity guided my reading and prompting me to explore topics and events that illustrate the various degrees of nastiness performed by our species; acts that contain some unsavoury, malevolent or even criminal element in their conception and intent, their execution or performance, or in their consequences—sometimes all at once. I chose to focus on a western perspective, drawing information from the four countries I know best: Canada, France, the United Kingdom and the United States.

Having spent years as a student studying medieval society, comparative literature and cultural anthropology, I had not anticipated many revelations in my exploration of evil deeds. After the wars of religion, the Crusades, the Marquis de Sade and his successors, the pitiless hierarchy known in every society, and other common and nefarious activities I had discovered through my previous readings, I believed that this topic of evil thoughts and deeds would only need a few more sources and slightly different approaches than the ones I had already explored some forty years earlier, when one of my theses examined the hidden 'masks of Satan' in André Gide's works. I should have known better.

Mine has been a life deprived of extreme events, and by nature I am not unduly inclined to originality or excessive introspection. While I sometimes use words that a Catholic might use to express thoughts of utter dismay, they are not backed by faith. My mother was an agnostic Frenchwoman brought up in an anticlerical middle-class home where respectability was of the utmost importance. My father, from an impoverished but well-born Hungarian family, was educated by Jesuits until he ran way to join the French Foreign Legion; he prized good manners above all, which he may have taken as the most appropriate form of morality. I was educated at a convent school in Casablanca and grew up in an Arab country under the influence of *Inch'Allah* (God willing) and *Mektoub* (it is written) and so I think of myself as a fatalist. Years in post-war France exposed me to further influences: humanism, existentialism and the philosophy of the absurd. Later in England, I worked at a psychiatric hospital where scenes of violence were offset by seeing gentle old men still sitting, every Sunday for twenty years, by the side of raving women who no longer knew them.

From this mishmash of influences grew my belief that we are born with the possibility of doing both good and evil deeds and that personal choice (even if our decisions may be preordained, which I do not see as a contradiction) is still our rule of conduct and that our acts are the measure by which we should be judged.

At the beginning of my research for this book, this was my guiding assumption—that it was within each of us to decide upon our actions, having weighed the pros and cons. By the end, I concluded that all the good actions mankind performs may weigh extremely little against the depths of aberration that generally constitute human conduct.

Yet, we still yearn for a generous and compassionate society; craving and nostalgia for such goodness are also parts of our nature. Some languages even have a word that refers to neither good nor evil, but conveys a desire for something other than our present circumstances: the Portuguese say *saudade* to express a soul's longing; the Japanese phrase *mono no aware* alludes to the pathos of things, the infringement of sadness that intensifies experience; and the Welsh say *hiraeth* to express an unformulated nostalgia for a place. This is a feeling we all recognize, even if our language does not have a word for it: a yearning to go beyond ourselves, to escape our feet of clay.

In *Gulliver's Travels*, Jonathan Swift described the kind of utopian society we strive for:

> Friendship and benevolence are the two principal virtues among the [people] and these were not confined to particular objects, but universal to the whole race, for a stranger from the remotest parts is equally treated with the newest neighbour and where ever he goes, looks upon himself at home.

More than two hundred years later, Swift's vision remains unrealized. This book explores examples of evil-doing to try to understand why such a world remains elusive.

CHAPTER ONE

ON HUMAN NATURE

A VIDEO RECORDED BY A SURVEILLANCE camera in 2015 was widely circulated on the internet—a scene in the Paris Metro, probably late at night, showing a man sleeping on a bench, very likely drunk. A young man appears on the screen, sits beside the sleeping man, pokes him a little to check on his alertness, steals something from his pocket and leaves. The drunk then half wakes up, stumbles around, and falls onto the tracks. The platform seems empty, save for a third man standing in the foreground, a passive witness to the drunk's fall, who looks on for about three seconds, then turns around and walks away. A train pulls into the station and a few people gather, ready to board. Suddenly, the thief is seen running back to the scene. He jumps onto the tracks, pulls the drunk safely back and, assisted by the others, lifts him onto the platform.

Only one of these three men acted naturally as we might expect—the drunk, who confused and half-awake, goes too close to the edge of the platform and falls over the side. We see the thief, in the space of minutes, choose to do both evil and good; his moral compass elastic enough to plan petty theft and spontaneously rush into heroic rescue. The spectator's role is more problematic. By doing nothing he had no effect on the situation, yet his inaction deeply offends our notion of what 'good' behaviour should be in such a case.

The video only lasts a couple of minutes, but the shock we experience in watching it is intense. In this wordless vignette, we see acts of good and evil, ambiguous intentions, responsibility and consequences, dangerous disruption and order restored, and, ultimately, the exercise of free will.

GOOD AND EVIL

Perhaps since the onset of reason, men and women have been perturbed by the complexity of their natures and their contradictory impulses. Philosophers have variously argued that the opposition of good and evil creates a form of harmony and continuity; that happiness can be found in the desire to do good; that there is in fact no moral rule by which mankind should be bound; that anyone is free to determine their own moral codes. Most believe humans prefer good over evil and encourage self-improvement. Basic philosophical positions range from seeing good and evil as either absolute and innate, or social and situational. The French philosopher Jean-Paul Sartre, on the other hand, believed that the perception of evil is consensually shared and, at the same time, individually intuitive:

> The only immediate and universal sign available for recognizing Evil is that it is detestable. Not detestable to this one or that one, but to everyone, hence to the evildoer himself. I shall know unmistakably that an action is evil when the very idea that I might commit it horrifies me.[1]

Mythology, religion, philosophy and literature have attempted to formulate both questions and answers concerning the impulses of good and evil that motivate our thoughts and actions. Anthropology, a comparatively new discipline with less didactic objectives, introduced another dichotomy—purity and pollution, that we may less specifically perceive as order and dissonance, where order refers to a congruent environment in which a particular culture thrives and dissonance to whatever disturbs the equilibrium to which that culture aspires. In this context, purity relates to wellness, while pollution implies danger.

Greeks philosophers provided the basis of our current thinking.

---

1. Jean-Paul Sartre, *Saint Genet. Actor and Martyr* (New York: George Braziller, 1963), 152-53.

The three most influential—Socrates, his student Aristotle and Plato—all saw a connection between good and happiness, evil and unhappiness. Socrates believed in man's essential goodness and saw ignorance as the source of evil deeds—given the choice and the knowledge, man would rather do good. Plato thought that being able to distinguish between good and evil was innate and that good could win over evil through sermons and meditation, leading to a life of good behaviour and happiness. For Aristotle, whose influence extended well into the Middle Ages, reason was at the source of all behaviour, and happiness was to be found in harmony with nature. He believed good men were consistently good and bad men could change their ways.

A different view, also fundamental to Western thought, was espoused by the fourth-century theologian St. Augustine who believed that the 'original sin' of Adam and Eve (eating from the Tree of Knowledge of Good and Evil) was transmitted to all their descendants and that salvation could only come from the grace of God. In the myth of the Garden of Eden, we succumbed to the Serpent's temptation and our innate quest for knowledge became our curse. But the question of motivation remains. Did we even know we were looking for something when we ate the forbidden fruit? Did we actually, as God accused us, want to "be as gods, knowing good and evil?" Or did Adam simply follow the lead of someone he trusted? And do we, who came after, deserve punishment—even the innocent newborn whose souls have not even had time to conceive of evil and sin? Some believe in a *felix culpa*, where the cruelty of being branded with original sin is far outweighed by the delights of an eventual redemption and the promise of resurrection. Others must find comfort elsewhere.

Religion, the theoretical fount of truth for its believers, actually roils the waters even further. Historian Yuval Noah Harari, in his book *Sapiens: A Brief History of Humankind*, considers what happened when polytheism gave way to monotheism. If there is a single

God, the world should be an orderly place, all things obeying the same laws. How then does mankind accept the presence of wickedness, discord and the lack of order? If evil exists as separate from God, as dualism posits, then the world is governed by two opposing forces. But dualism has its own drawbacks. "While solving the Problem of Evil, it is unnerved by the Problem of Order...If Good and Evil battle for control of the world, who enforces the laws governing this cosmic war?" He concludes, "Monotheism explains order, but is mystified by evil. Dualism explains evil, but is puzzled by order." Man, he says, is also burdened with the possibility of free will. If it really exists, man is then allowed to choose evil—the choice is real and the option valid.

On the eve of the Renaissance, medieval thinkers started looking at evil in a new way, reducing it to worldly temptation and equating good with spirituality. Johan Huizinga the great twentieth-century medievalist historian, described this shift: "In the Middle Ages, the choice lay, in principle, between God and the world, between contempt and eager acceptance, at the peril of one's soul, of all that makes up the beauty and the charm of earthly life. All terrestrial beauty bore the stain of sin."[2]

Soon the seductions of the world and the temptation of evil were differentiated again. Between the Renaissance and the culmination of the Age of Enlightenment in the late eighteenth century, a flourishing of Western philosophers added their reflections on the never-ending confrontation of good and evil fighting for the conquest of the human soul. Exceptional among them was the political philosopher and Florentine exile Niccoló Machiavelli, whose book, *The Prince,* radically abandoned the principles, mainly derived from Plato and Aristotle, that social justice and human happiness were the foundations of an ideal state. Instead, he advised those wanting to establish and maintain power to focus on an entirely pragmatic approach devoid of ethical

---

2. J. Huizinga, *The Waning of the Middle Ages* (Garden City, NY: Doubleday Anchor Books, 1954), 40.

considerations, seemingly promoting a governing philosophy that justified the ends, whatever the means.

Many others (but not all) continued to believe that good and evil were inherent human traits. In Germany, Gottfried Leibnitz coined the word 'theodicy' (justifying God) to explain the problem of evil and how a good and almighty God could permit its existence. The third Earl of Shaftsbury proposed that mankind's essence was to be good and that a proper sense of morality could be obtained through spontaneous emotions. His work influenced the French Encyclopedists, particularly Denis Diderot, whose *Essai sur le mérite et la vertu* gave rise to the notion of the Noble Savage, an eighteenth-century conceit that saw civilization as the corrupter of mankind.

In the nineteenth century, Arthur Schopenhauer had a grimmer view of mankind's struggle, seeing the will to live as the greatest source of evil, as it competes with every other emotion. As the survival instinct pits men against one another, good can only be accomplished through self-sacrifice. A little earlier, Immanuel Kant and Johann Fichte believed that good was associated with seeking pleasure and evil with fleeing pain, essentially an egoistic process.

We all feel the pull of our inner contradictions, perhaps seeing in them as well a conflict between our natural disposition and the *modus vivendi* culture imposes on us. Our selfish nature, bent on individual or small group survival, struggles against the veneer of civilization that requires surrendering personal preference for the good of the whole. Philosophers, behavioural psychologists, and political theorists have all addressed this subject and most conclude that when preferred traits are arbitrarily allocated to some members of a society, the group swiftly divides into two antagonistic sides, independent of other characteristics.

In a well-known 1968 experiment, primary school teacher Jane Elliott divided her students into a blue-eyed group and a brown-eyed group. When she arbitrarily assigned power to the brown-eyes, they almost instantly became antagonistic and condescending toward the blue-eyes; the ones deemed better or stronger immediately start lording it over those felt to be weaker and less desirable.

Literature is as concerned as philosophy with the nature of good and evil thoughts and the motivation for good and evil actions. Being more accessible, though often derived from formal philosophical stances, literary works have helped shape our conception of a moral world. William Golding's deeply upsetting book, *The Lord of the Flies* (1954), explored our inner impulses towards the contradictory poles of morality and immorality. Golding built an unpleasantly plausible graduation of small details that traced a return to an earlier, lawless environment where survival through dominance and the allocation of arbitrary privileges were the only rules. Coming out of the chaos of World War II, the book was shockingly significant. We saw how easily we could revert to more basic instincts if our individual survival could not be accomplished within the social constructs imposed over time for the good of all.

Robert Louis Stevenson's *The Strange Case of Dr. Jekyll and Mr. Hyde* (1886) and Oscar Wilde's *The Picture of Dorian Gray* (1891) went further than any other novels in attempting to elucidate the dual nature of man. Stevenson did so by cleaving the two distinct entities within the same person, one personifying good, the other absolute evil, thus making it theoretically easier to isolate evil and destroy it. The first encounter with Mr. Hyde, narrated at the beginning of the book by Mr. Utterson, involves an act of apparently gratuitous evil:

> All at once, I saw two figures: one little man who was stomping along eastward at a good walk, and the other a girl of maybe eight or ten who was running as hard as she was able down a cross street. Well, sir, the two ran into one another naturally enough at the corner, and then came the horrible part of the thing; for the man trampled calmly over the child's body and left her screaming on the ground. It sounds nothing to hear, but it was hellish to see. It wasn't like a man; it was like some

damned Juggernaut. I gave a few hallos, took to my heels, col-
lared my gentleman, and brought him back to where there was
already quite a group about the screaming child. He was perfectly cool and made no resistance, but he gave me one look, so
ugly that it brought out the sweat on me like running.

In *Dorian Gray*, Wilde's belief that "youth is the one thing worth
having" involves his hero in a destructive and demonic trade-off—a
portrait of himself where he is shown in all his youth and beauty will
take on the degradations of sin and ageing and become "ignoble,
hideous, and uncouth," while his physical self can pursue unscathed
a real, self-indulgent and hedonistic life. "Eternal youth, infinite
passion, pleasures subtle and secret, wild joys and wilder sins—he
was to have all these things. The portrait was to bear the burden of
his shame: that was all." However, it seems easier said than done, for
man may not be able to escape after all, despite the promise of Lord
Henry Wotton, Dorian's seducer, "Be always searching for new sensations. Be afraid of nothing." Finally seeing the portrait of Dorian
he first painted, the artist is appalled.

> "My God! If it is true, and this is what you have done with your
> life, why, you must be worse even than those who talk against
> you fancy you to be!"... Through some strange quickening of
> inner life the leprosies of sin were slowly eating the thing away.
> The rotting of a corpse in a watery grave was not so fearful.

Dorian Gray must die to destroy the last evidence of his evil deeds;
no more than Mr. Hyde will he escape the consequences of his acts.

Today we might see the characters of Jekyll and Hyde, and Dorian
Gray and his portrait, as signs of a schizophrenic personality. The
complexity of the human mind was in the air when these books
were written. Sigmund Freud would bring it to the forefront as he
expounded on his theories of the opposites, Eros (the life instinct)
and Thanatos (the death instinct), that animate the human spirit, and
the conflicting elements that struggle to constitute its identity: the id
(instinct), the ego (reality) and the superego (morality).

ORDER AND DISSONANCE

The thief–hero of the Paris Metro almost simultaneously commits both good and evil acts. According to psychoanalyst Julia Kristeva, it is this contradiction that we find upsetting:

> It is not the lack of cleanliness or health that causes abjection but what disturbs identity, system, order. What does not respect borders, positions, rules. The in-between, the ambiguous, the composite. The traitor, the liar, the criminal with a good conscience, the shameless rapist, the killer who claims he is a savior.[3]

It is in human nature to organize and classify. Indeed, it is the only way we can experience our surroundings, as including some elements and eliminating others help us understand our environment. We do so in what anthropologist Mary Douglas describes a "chaos of shifting impressions." Our senses do not simply register what they see, smell, hear, or feel. They also lead the brain to form impressions, create associations and select what we wish to retain, usually preferring sensations and feelings that confirm an established mental schema. So powerful are classification systems that almost every culture is uncomfortable with unclear categories.

In *Purity and Danger. An Analysis of Concept of Pollution and Taboo*, first published in 1966, Douglas suggests that confounded expectations are sometimes at the source of our distaste. For instance, we define as dirt something that may be merely out of place: ketchup on a blouse, shoes on a table, toothbrushes in the dining room, outdoors things inside and vice-versa. Kristeva agrees that disorder (a break in categorization) leads to the disgust we might experience with whatever occupies a liminal position and argues that the main reason we find blood, sweat, sperm, vomit and excrement objectionable is that they belong both inside and outside the body.

To organize and maintain order in a world that would otherwise be incoherent, cultures offer various sets of guiding principles, among which are hygiene (including diet) and etiquette (notably

---

3. Julia Kristeva, *Powers of Horror. An Essay on Abjection* (New York: Columbia University Press, 1982), 4. The word 'abjection' is used here to mean 'rejection, being cast off.'.

table manners). Both come into play when considering, for instance, how specific and opposite physical functions have been attributed to the hands. Eating has historically been strictly associated with the pure right hand and defecating with the polluted and profane left hand (in Latin the word 'sinister' merely means 'on the left side'). So strong is the attachment to an apparently irrational symbolism that some traditional societies continue to feel abhorrence when the left hand performs actions that were normally the purview of the right. Many modern Arabs, for instance, would still be upset at seeing someone using their left hand to take food from a communal dish.

Hygiene aside, in a world organized around normatively clean right-handedness, being left-handed was disruptive. From antiquity to today, left-handed people were and are forced to adapt to a right-handed world. Romans dining on couches could only lean on their left elbows in a proper party configuration, leaving the right hand free to handle food; Greek hoplite soldiers formed a phalanx of solidly overlapping shields held in their left hands, leaving left-handed soldiers awkwardly clasping their swords in their right ones. Today, this quirk of nature is no longer a cause of danger or a source of embarrassment, but it still goes against the common grain.

Idiosyncratic dietary laws reflect cultural notions of purity, pollution, and the fear of contamination deriving from the latter. Many cultures classify animals that are fit for eating according to rules that are exclusively specific to that culture and would be meaningless to others. Douglas uses the Lele, a small group still living in the Congo, as an example. Animals were deemed acceptable as food depending on a taxonomy separating day animals from night animals, and animals that lived above (in the air or up in the trees) from those that lived below (on land or in the water). Lele men could only eat certain animals or animal parts, women ate others and children others still. The Lele also considered that animals that lived within the human circle could not be eaten. This included dogs and chickens, but also unwanted companions such as rats and lizards.

Such dietary categorization would be meaningless to us. We are more familiar with the Jewish and Muslim decree that the pig is one of the 'abominable things,' described and listed in Leviticus 11 and Deuteronomy 14, which man may not eat. To be acceptable, an animal must both have a hoof cloven in two and chew the cud. Thus, the pig, whose foot is cloven but does not chew the cud, is unclean. Animals with the opposite disposition (with uncloven hooves but chewing the cud) such as the camel, the rock badger, and the hare, also fall outside the rules and should not be eaten.

Social scientists vary in their understanding of purity and pollution and the order and dissonance they generate as much as philosophers and novelists disagree about the nature of good and evil. For Douglas, the rules for dealing with purity, pollution, and the avoidance of danger are ways of organizing our world. "Ideas about separating, purifying, demarcating and punishing transgressions have as their main function to impose a system on an inherently untidy experience." She concluded that, unlike moral rules, pollution rules are unequivocal. They are theoretically more rigid since they do not depend on intention or on a "nice balancing of rights and duties." One does not argue with a taboo.

This untidy experience is one of life in general, but it may sometimes peak during periods of rapid cultural transformation. History has shown that the breakdown of ordinary social and cultural controls often leads to especially disruptive periods when all hell breaks loose. For instance, the French Revolution and abolition of royalty included a short period known as the Terror (1793–94), the forming of the American nation included the aberrant American Civil War (1861–1865) and the creation of a long-lasting Communist regime in China also brought on the dreadful Cultural Revolution (1966-76). These events all occurred in a sort of vacuum of authority, at a time when the social and philosophical orders were already disrupted and societies had not yet re-created themselves. However, excessive behaviours tend to self-regulate and these extreme and fearful movements died of their own accord; a semblance of order could then be re-established, albeit within a system that was still flawed.

INTENT AND CONSEQUENCE

The behaviour of the thief in the Paris Metro is, to say the least, ambiguous. Having robbed a helpless victim, he acted promptly to save his life, perhaps assuaging his conscience in so doing, as he may have wondered about his own part in the accident and its potentially fatal consequences.

Obviously, causing the man to fall and endanger his life was not the thief's intention. Yet his two consecutive actions force us to consider the matter of responsibility and, eventually, of possible retribution. A single act can have very different outcomes—a shove, for instance, could result in either a minor bruise or a serious fall with enduring or even fatal consequences. In such a case, the intent and action are the same, but should the responsibility be deemed greater in the case of fatal consequences? In Canada, the law is clear: if a victim died after being pushed (inadvertently or deliberately) the offender would be charged with manslaughter.

When only a twist of fate intervenes to change a petty gesture into a life-threatening situation, should retribution be commensurate with the damage done or should it only reflect the intention behind the deed? If intentions determine whether an act is taken to be good or evil, what of its consequences, and should their magnitude affect the deed? Lawmakers are naturally concerned with such questions and, in Canada, the Criminal Code clearly states that a sentence must be "proportionate to the gravity of the offence and the degree of responsibility of the offender."

These questions have naturally also absorbed philosophers, particularly in the second half of the medieval period. Pierre Abélard for instance, believed that only the intent made an act either good or evil—suggesting that an evil deed committed with good intentions was not sinful. Thomas Aquinas, while agreeing that intention was of the utmost importance, rejected the merit of evil deeds backed by good intentions. For him, good deeds had to be done with good intentions and the knowledge that they would also bring good. His views were even more extreme, as he considered that the very absence of good was enough to create evil.

With the Renaissance philosophers of the seventeenth century came the notion of relativity. Thomas Hobbes believed that good and evil were not absolute but varied with individuals and occasions, while René Descartes argued that mankind was incapable of discerning between the two and was often led astray by desires and feelings. Baruch Spinoza also considered good and evil to be relative and human knowledge too incomplete to form an opinion. Yet, since mankind's only tool was reason, people should consider that, on the whole, what furthered their wellbeing was good and what impeded it was evil.

The same questions of good and evil, intent and consequence, are at the heart of the oral, and later written, tradition of fairy tales. Unlike myths, which attempt to address the existential issues of entire cultures—Where do we come from? Why do we die? Why are there illnesses?— fairy tales focus on individual actions and quests. They introduce the notion of unfavourable fates to be overcome, they instil fear (dragons, evil queens, dark forests, unexpected obstacles) but they also reassure since, unlike myths, they usually end in a satisfactory manner. Through them, many children come to an understanding of innocence, evil, unfairness, justice and retaliation. The unfairness of fate is one of the least bearable evils to befall the heroes of fairy tales, and it satisfies our sense of justice to see that no one in these tales escapes the consequences of their actions. Yet, in fairy tales, if not always in life, redemption is often possible, alleviating the doom of evil.

Later authors too have explored issues of intent, particularly Charles Dickens who, mixing comic and threatening elements in an unparalleled manner, provided us with an enormous gallery of virtuous and villainous characters. Inherent to Dickens' approach is the notion of true gentility and honesty of purpose. Any deviance from either, even if well disguised, marks the character as a villain; any evidence of character shows him a good man. At the two poles, we find the repulsive dwarfish wife-beater Daniel Quipp (*The Old Curiosity Shop*, 1841) and the socially aspiring, smarmy, creepy, writhing Uriah Heap, set against the true nobility of character of the humble Ham (*David Copperfield*, 1850) who, a rope tied to his waist, swims out into the storm to attempt the rescue of a man seen struggling on a sinking schooner, dying in the attempt.

The gulf between intent and consequence becomes infinitely wider when we move from individual to collective actions. Two seventeenth-century English philosophers, Richard Cumberland and Francis Hutcheson, believed that the morality of individual actions should be determined by their impact on society, aiming to the greater good and using Western Europe as the only model of civilization.

Yet, history is rife with examples of discriminatory behaviour (the creation of religious castes, social classes, hereditary elites), each with its own attempt at social, political, economic or religious justification. Others did not seem to need justification: slavery, for instance, since it was generally seen as socially and politically acceptable in the white cultures where it thrived for over three centuries, creating immense private fortunes in its wake. Colonization could be rationalized through the language of religion, morality and good intent, expounded by the missionaries, legislators, colonial civil servants, teachers and traders who collectively destroyed entire traditional societies. Yet, it must be assumed that, among those who participated in such activities, some meant well and could then have found validation in the writings of Immanuel Kant, who argued that only intention mattered—a deed performed with good intention was good even if it led to disastrous consequences. Should these people then be exempt from individual guilt for causing so much suffering to those who stood outside the small group the system was intended to benefit?

CONSCIENCE AND REDEMPTION

Once, the likes of Jack the Ripper and other shadowy serial killers who viciously attacked women and innocent children were deemed to be mysterious monsters, their horrible actions incomprehensible. At some point, it was even thought that the criminals' facial features were so revealing as to identify them at once for the deviants they were. Phrenology, as it was known, believed there was an almost perfect concordance between the shape of the skull and the capacity of the brain within, and that an individual's character could be predicted from the size and shape of his head. Various protuberances were seen as signs of specific aspects of personality and assumed an importance of a purely fanciful nature. Today, we know that unimaginable crimes are performed by people like us, killing their neighbours in Rwanda and in Bosnia, or shoving Jews into boxcars on station platforms all over Europe. When evil becomes so commonplace, we lose our ability to recognize it.

In this context, the example of Reserve Police Battalion 101 is telling. In 1942, these soldiers were ordinary Germans, seemingly not predisposed to committing atrocities and murder. Yet, when given their orders to round up Polish Jews, select the fit young men for work camps, and shoot the others—men, women, children— only twelve out of five hundred opted out of the dreadful task. The others obeyed their orders, eventually becoming immune to the effect of killing and being totally corrupted by it. When, after the war, they were arrested, they mostly stood out through their feeling of self-pity. They believed that obeying orders would, and should, protect them from any sense of responsibility.

The philosopher Hannah Arendt was profoundly affected by the events of World War II. Her 1945 essay, *Organized Guilt and Universal Responsibility*, includes quotes from an interview with an official at the Majdanek concentration camp who admitted to having gassed and buried people alive. When asked, "Do you know the Russians will hang you?" the man broke down in tears and answered, "Why should they? What have I done?" His confusion seems genuine.

FREE WILL AND RESPONSIBILITY

Those who merely obey orders have rejected the fearful gift of free will. Fyodor Dostoevsky demonstrates in *The Brothers Karamazov* the impossible burden of moral freedom. In the Parable of the Grand Inquisitor, he shows Christ being arrested and sentenced to burn at the stake for having offered mankind the possibility of free choice. The Inquisitor's main argument is that "man prefers peace, and even death, to the freedom of choice in the knowledge of good and evil." He believes that men "in their simplicity and natural unruliness" cannot understand freedom, and in fact fear and dread it. Instead they will be given "the three powers alone able to conquer and hold captive for ever the conscience of these impotent rebels for their happiness—those forces are miracle, mystery, and authority."

Twentieth-century dictators such as Hitler, Mao, Mussolini and Stalin followed the same argument. They took away the possibility of free will and replaced it with blind obedience and, through fear or brainwashing, made new virtues of past sins: treacherous denunciation, unjustified expropriation, imprisonment without cause and even murder. 'I only obeyed orders' is an excuse that would come to haunt us at the end of the second millennium of our era, an excuse many found acceptable within that particular context.

It is often convenient to blame outside forces for our misdeeds. How could we possibly not fall when fate is against us? Shakespeare wrote magnificently about wrong decisions, unexpected consequences, turmoils of the heart, murders most foul, and the most chilling example of moral treachery and personal betrayal in the psychopathic Iago, creating archetypes in so doing. In addition, he

21

developed in *King Lear* the character of Edmund, a man attempting to justify and rationalize evil behaviour by blaming it on circumstances and destiny, thus releasing him from true responsibility:

> This is the excellent foppery of the world, that, when we are sick in fortune—often the surfeit of our own behaviour—we make guilty of our disasters the sun, the moon and the stars: as if we were villains by necessity; fools by heavenly compulsion; knaves, thieves and treachers, by spherical predominance; drunkards, liars and adulterers, by an enforced obedience of planetary influence; and all that we are evil in, by a divine thrusting on: an admirable evasion of whoremaster man, to lay his goatish disposition to the charge of a star! My father compounded with my mother under the dragon's tail, and my nativity was under Ursa Major; so that it follows I am rough and lecherous.

The model transmitted to us from ancient, medieval and Renaissance thinkers includes the notions of right and wrong, the possibility of free will, and personal responsibility. But at the end of the nineteenth century one philosopher rejected common understanding when he wrote, "You have your way. I have my way. As for the right way, the correct way, and the only way, it does not exist." Friedrich Nietzsche, in his influential *Beyond Good and Evil* (1886), portrayed moral concepts such as truth, good, and evil as essentially shifting and flexible notions. He distinguished between pre-moral societies (the old order) that judge actions through their consequences, and moral (modern) ones that judge actions through motives. In such a world, 'free spirits' stand outside the norms and are praiseworthy for defying regulated morality based on fear. Thus, hierarchies are created, giving precedence to those who are not afraid to seek independence from the common rule. They are seen as 'good,' in contrast with those who do not and are deemed 'bad.' The purpose of societies should then be to nurture such singular individuals—creating in its extreme form a 'good' master race ruling over 'bad' subjects.

The Nazi party eagerly adopted this ideology, seeing it as an apt philosophical context for totalitarianism. The philosopher Nietzsche, the musician Richard Wagner, and the poet Johan Wolfgang von Goethe unwittingly became the tripodal foundation of the essence of Nazism through their ardent demonstrations of a superior sort of man who fit the Nazis' own Aryan ambitions. In *Twilight of the Idols* (1889), Nietzsche particularly admired Goethe for conceiving "of a human being who would be strong...A man for whom there is no longer anything that is forbidden—unless it be *weakness*, whether called vice or virtue." And so was created a man without responsibility, a man without a conscience.

Nazism and the Holocaust, and the need for a renewed sense of responsibility, became the crucial moral test of the twentieth century. Hannah Arendt, struck by the "banality of evil" on display during the 1961 trial of Nazi Adolf Eichmann, wrote, "The problem of evil will be the fundamental question of postwar intellectual life in Europe— as death became the fundamental question after the last war."

CRIME AND PUNISHMENT

The most famous literary exploration of conscience occurs in Dostoevsky's *Crime and Punishment* (1866). The gist of the novel concerns the unleashing of man's unsuspected possibilities and the attendant consequences. Raskolnikov, an impoverished student, formulates a plan for murder, wondering, "How could such an atrocious thing come into my mind? What filthy things my heart is capable of." He eventually commits a double murder, is tormented, gives himself up and confesses, is sentenced, and eventually finds salvation.

Dostoevsky goes much deeper in *The Brothers Karamazov*. Whether the question is 'Are we our brothers' keepers?' or 'In the absence of God is everything permitted?' he argues the answer must be the assumption of responsibility for one's actions. "The acknowledgement of one's own conscience" is the only effective punishment for doing wrong.

Themes of intention, free will, personal responsibility, and retribution are the foundation of the whole genre of mystery novels, which are based on growing suspicions and the interpretation of clues, the slow build-up of an atmosphere where evil deeds and thoughts are shown to make sense to their perpetrators, the detection and investigation of crimes, their motivations, and their punishment.

The Norse Noir sub-genre coming out of Scandinavia also serves a contemporary need to identify the sources and forms of evil in society. The quintet of contributing nations (Sweden, Norway, Finland, Denmark and Iceland) have different histories, languages, geographies, and political convictions but share a reputation for happy, privileged and comfortable lifestyles. Yet, their mystery novels go against the cliché of a well-ordered Scandinavian way of life, intent on equality and social justice, to expose the cracks in their societies: rape and deep-seated misogyny in Stieg Larsson's *Millenium* trilogy; failed immigration policies, conflicting customs and beliefs in Henning Mankell's *Faceless Killers*. Mankell's protagonist, Detective Kurt Wallander, voices the general concern: "Something has happened that should not have," adding, "Not here." He later evokes a telling nostalgia for an illusionary model, "We live as if we were in mourning for a lost paradise."[4]

However, most mystery novels do not attempt to illustrate serious societal flaws and conclude with the apprehension of the perpetrator and a suitable punishment. This is seen as 'paying one's debts to society,' a judicial and penal concept that does not guarantee remorse or redemption, or any extension of conscience. This distinction is clearly understood by Anne Perry, a successful writer of mystery novels who, at the age of fifteen, under her birth name of Juliet Hulme, helped a girlfriend kill the girl's mother, and served five-and-a-half years in prison. When fellow mystery writer Ian

---

4. Two painful events shattered the Scandinavian sense of rightful wellbeing: the assassination of the Swedish Prime Minister Olaf Palme in 1986, as he walked unguarded on his way to a movie theatre; and the horrific attack on ordinary people in Norway by Anders Behring in 2011, killing eight and wounding 209; and later at a youth camp, where he executed sixty-nine young people, wounding another 110. For many Swedes, the last blow came with the 2018 elections when the formerly despised Swedish Democratic Party, known for its neo-Nazi roots, had its best showing ever, gathering 17.6 percent of the votes.

Rankin asked how she came to terms with her role in the murder, her answer was direct—it was only when she accepted her guilt that she felt free of it.

This can only be achieved through a personal journey. Our justice system on its own is not capable of fostering in offenders an understanding of the impact of their crimes and the responsibility for having committed them. Other societies have developed their own wisdom and rules for a balanced life that do not obsess, as we do, with finding culprits, assigning blame and administering punishment. They seek instead personal improvement through meditation and purification for those responsible for harm done. The restorative justice system operating in Canada and Australia, for instance, attempts to mediate between the victim and the offender when dealing with First Nations and Aboriginal people. It is organized in the form of 'sentencing circles' that involve a judge, members of the community, the offender (who has pleaded guilty to acknowledge his or her responsibility) and the victim. Every aspect of the crime is discussed in the circle, whose members eventually set goals for the offender to achieve before sentencing. The circle reconvenes a few weeks or months later to review progress and assess the likelihood of the offender's eventual redemption. Based on the community's recommendation, the judge then passes a sentence that may include no jail time if it appears the offender has honestly accepted his responsibility.

OUR WESTERN MODEL SEEKS TO BALANCE good and evil, crime and punishment—a form of ledger-book mentality that suits our mercantile history and the evolution of our culture. Good and evil guide our morality; purity and pollution, coupled with our innate need to establish and maintain order, inform our behaviour.

In harsh times, when we must acknowledge the depth of our flaws and wonder at our motivations, we may seek more subtle and nuanced guidance. Literary and philosophical trends may then emerge to which we can adhere while looking for answers. Thus the period of the two world wars that witnessed modern Europe's moral bankruptcy gave rise to such writers as Herman Hesse *(Siddhartha, Steppenwolf)* and Franz Kafka *(The Metamorphosis, The Trial)* who, faced with an incomprehensible world, led the way in voyages of self-discovery and the possibility of other and more complex realities.

Independently from their historical context, generations of thinkers have struggled with issues of good and evil actions, the need for order and harmony, the importance of intent and the role of conscience. More than answers, they have provided questions to guide our thinking. Some of these are asked afresh by a contemporary Koranic scholar, Imam Amin Ahsan Islahi, who reviewed how Western philosophers and religious thinkers have interpreted the nature of good and evil. These questions address what this Eastern scholar views as fundamental to their approach:

- Are good and evil absolute, or are they related to time and place, and does our thinking about them change when they are taken out of their original context?
- Are good and evil innate parts of mankind, and how can we discern one from the other?
- Have good and evil, if independent from our nature, been infused in the human soul by the same creator, or is there a separate entity that created each one, raising the possibility of a supreme satanic force of perhaps comparable power to the force of good?
- If the knowledge of good and evil is instinctive, how can we interpret the variance of their manifestations across various human groups?

Around 1482, Botticelli painted 'Pallas and the Centaur,' where the centaur, half-human and half-animal, supposedly represents the uncontrolled side of human nature. Pallas stands by, equipped with a halberd, a symbol of the ability to discern right from wrong. She deals gently with the half-beast man—perhaps guiding him toward good. Were that it was that simple.

CHAPTER TWO

US AND THEM

IN THE SPRING OF 2018, MUCH of the world was horrified by the spectacle of young children being separated from their parents and apparently detained in makeshift wire cages. The crisis arose when the administration of US President Donald Trump, alarmed by the influx of immigrants illegally crossing the border from Mexico, announced a new zero tolerance policy that would criminally prosecute any adult caught trying to enter the US illegally. As children could not be jailed along with their parents, families were separated; children became "unaccompanied alien minors" and wards of the state. Such an unprecedented influx overwhelmed an already strained system and resulted in a rash of newly constructed and wholly inadequate holding facilities. The images were particularly shocking in a country whose iconic Statue of Liberty still proclaims: Give me your tired, your poor, /Your huddled masses yearning to breathe free.

Media coverage was greeted with widespread disbelief that a democratic country could decide to break families apart with no justification. Yet the state was simply asserting its power to decide who— literally—was 'in' and who was 'out.' This explicit notion of exclusion is so entrenched in the world at large that many disciplines or theories (sociology, anthropology, history, genetics, eugenics, physiology, religion, psychology, economics) have been brought into play to validate it. Ordinary citizens (with little power and even less status) can only stand by and witness events, their isolated voices initially counting for very little.

HIERARCHIES

They kept them away. Never let them come near.
And that's how they treated them year after year.

These verses describe how Dr. Seuss' Star-Belly Sneetches treated their inferior Plain-Belly counterparts, a story that has introduced generations of children to the fate of outcasts. However, in the end, young children's innate sense of fairness is satisfied when all Sneetches eventually accept each other as equals—an unlikely outcome in human experience.

Power and hierarchies are intrinsically connected. In several traditional cultures, the name of one's own group is the very word used to designate 'man.' Those outside the group cannot use the same word to describe themselves, and so, in a sense, are denied their humanity. Having one group designated as non-human allows behaviours that would otherwise be unthinkable.

Among their many contradictions, human beings often promote lofty notions of equality, while actively dividing the world into Us and Them. Differentiation leads to hierarchies and, in the 1970s, French anthropologist Louis Dumont, examining the religious caste system of India, dubbed *Homo hierarchicus* as the creator of this divided universe, in opposition to *Homo aequalis,* the theoretical ideal of Western society.

We know humans categorize in order to make sense of an environment that would otherwise seem chaotic. While categories vary from culture to culture, those intended to sustain a system where moral values and the social environment complement one another are universally favoured because they promote order and facilitate survival. To ensure social cohesion, mankind has consistently developed ways to include desirable people within their groups while excluding undesirable ones. Some exclusions are deemed legitimate and intended to support the welfare of all (prisons, leper colonies), while others are meant to preserve cultural purity (isolation for menstruating women).

Many, however, are or were morally indefensible displays of raw power. Exclusion is punishment *par excellence* in all cultures: religious excommunication, political exile, shunning, solitary confinement, exclusion from tribal life and high school cliques all seek to deprive their victims of essential economic or social supports.

The balance of and the desire for orderliness and peace is fragile. This fragility becomes even more evident when its constituent categories (social, political, religious, racial) are deemed to be under attack and entrenched interests are called upon to reinforce existing hierarchies. They often do so by introducing concepts of good and evil to inflame supporters. Not surprisingly, one voice then predominates: male (over female), white (over black or brown), rich (over poor), colonist (over native), believer (over pagan). The order of dominance does not happen by accident—it is carefully constructed and supported by a variety of social, legal and physical mechanisms.

SOCIAL BARRIERS

Historian Fernand Braudel, in his 1982 work *Civilization & Capitalism, 15th-18th Century,* speaks of the universality of social hierarchies, a term he prefers to social strata, categories or even classes. He believes every society has them, "whether externalized or not, that is consciously or not, in terms of permanent class struggle. This is true of *all societies.*"

There are many ways of differentiating Them from Us. In Britain, for instance, accent and vocabulary were once the incontrovertible delineation between the upper classes (referred to as U) and the non-upper classes (non-U). Such modes of expression revealed all that mattered to determine someone's social standing and acceptability. These distinctions, while subtle, were unmistakable for people in the know, superseding regional accents and personal idiosyncrasies. Such distinctions were naturally imposed by the upper class, which could also change them at will. As the code was presumably unknown to the Non-U, its secrecy gave it exclusionary value.

English author Nancy Mitford, who first thought social class "too intimate a topic" for publication, relented in an article in the magazine *Encounter* (1955) and, betraying the U side, cited some examples. In *Family Britain 1951–1957*, David Kynaston lists a number of pairings, the first word being the one favoured by the non-U while the second is used by the upper classes: cycle/bike, dinner (referring to the noontime meal)/lunch, greens/vegetables, mental/mad, toilet/lavatory or loo, lounge/sitting room, dentures/false teeth, sweet/pudding, glasses/spectacles. Who could make fun of the Sneetches and their belly stars when the British sense of superiority derived from knowing whether penning letters should be done on 'writing paper' or on 'note paper'?

There was a time in British society when such choices were significant. It has since been washed over by the combined influence of non-U celebrities (notably the Beatles, with their working class Liverpudlian accent), immigrants with their own speech patterns and vocabularies, more standard education, a mixed and sometimes foreign workforce, and the influence of television. But snobbish acknowledgements of social inequality have merely shifted to other symbols, and social climbers attempting to penetrate the fortress must keep on their toes.

Symbolic distinctions are also shown through insignia that denote rank, in the military and elsewhere. In eighteenth-century France, there was concern that unworthy characters might fake their rank through expensive displays of unmerited symbols. To avoid such calamitous social confusion, it was suggested that the king should confer a blue ribbon upon the highest-ranking couples, a red one to lesser-ranking noblemen, that military men should wear their uniforms and servants their liveries. According to Braudel, this would "reduce the humble to the impossibility of being confused with the great," although, in truth, the confusion would naturally be superficial—real luxury and commanding power are always on one side, poverty and obedience on the other, and neither need help in proving themselves. Braudel also cites an early Italian text that showed the difference to be critical and readily acknowledged: "One section of humanity is ill-treated to death so that the other can stuff itself to bursting point."

To be effective, symbolic distinctions must be merited. So attached are we to their authenticity that faking them is always deemed invidious. When Canadian Franck Gervais impersonated a military veteran (an act covered under Section 419 of the Criminal Code of Canada) during Remembrance Day ceremonies in 2014, he was widely condemned, but most particularly for wearing medals he had not earned.

Hierarchical thinking has led to a number of symbolic systems related to social classes dominated by an 'establishment.' There are also subdivisions within classifications, each with their own symbols, wardrobe, customs and vocabulary. From beatniks to hippies, yuppies to hipsters, jocks to techies, we continue to find ways of discriminating between Them outside the privileged group and Us well inside it. George Orwell in *Down and Out in Paris and London*, describes with exquisite minutiae the hierarchies among those serving in expensive hotels and restaurants in the Paris of the 1930s, revealing respective duties, privileges, salaries and tips, races and nationalities, food allowed and its service, modes of dress, permitted facial hair, expected types of pilfering for all staff, from the manager who has his own dining room to those in the *cafeterie*, "the very dregs of the hotel, despised and *tutoied* by everyone."

Further examples of this discrimination may be less formally structured but exist in a variety of settings, such as the 'pink ghetto' over which looms a 'glass ceiling,' specifically targeting women's professional advancement and socio-economic equality with men, in spite of some recent improvements.

LEGAL BARRIERS

When social conventions are not enough, modes of exclusion find a way of being artificially reinforced. Such has been the case against Jews throughout history, made to identify themselves by both Christian or Islamic decrees. In the eighth and ninth centuries, Islam required that two yellow badges be worn by both Jewish men and women, one on the headgear, the other hanging from the neck. The Synod of Narbonne in 1227 described the yellow oval badge Jews were to wear precisely—it was to measure one finger in width and one half of a palm in height. In 1215, Pope Innocent III decreed that both Jews and Saracens be made recognizable through their garments, lest the men have relations with Christian women unaware of their identity. More recently, of course, the Nazi regime required that all Jews wear a piece of yellow cloth shaped like the star of David.

This was only the beginning. The Nazis became even more militant and aggressive, creating categories of 'enemies' from people who were neither violent opponents of the regime nor insurrectionists who could legitimately be incarcerated. These groups owed their outcast status to the fact that the "regime has defined them as such, due to some characteristics—appearance, 'race,' class, political identification, religion—that the regime perceives as intolerable or threatening."[1]

Without going to the extremes reached in Germany, the pattern is common. In South Africa, for instance, exclusion became institutionalized when, under the influence of the National Party intent on controlling the country's economic and social systems, apartheid laws were enacted in 1948. They favoured white domination and formalized racial discrimination with its attendant segregation, curfews and work restrictions. In the United States, the Jim Crow Laws had a similar effect on blacks living in the south.

Few discriminatory systems are as rigidly complex as the Hindu caste system in India, said to be around 3,000 years old. It constitutes a hierarchical structure that assembles groups according to their karma (work) and dharma (religious duty). Deemed to be the basis for an orderly society, it consists of four classes believed

1. David Stone, *Concentration Camps* (Oxford: Oxford University Press, 2017), 6.

to be issued from various parts of Brahma's body and encompassing all occupations: the Brahmins (priests, teachers, intellectuals), the Kshatriyas (warriors and rulers), the Vaishyas (farmers and merchants) and the Shudras (involved in the most menial occupations). Outside this system are the Dalits, also known as the Untouchables.

These four basic categories are further divided into some 3,000 castes and about 25,000 sub-castes, rendering the system extremely complex. It is maintained through strict regulations addressing all aspects of life, such as marriage, residence and food, particularly in rural communities where traditions are seldom challenged. It is far more difficult to maintain the integrity of the system in cities where many different castes are forced to live side by side but this propinquity does not lead to integration; in fact, identification and caste appurtenance are always revealed by a person's last name, making it all the more difficult to ignore.

The hierarchical structure bestows many privileges on the upper castes and maintains a stratification from which it is almost impossible to escape, in spite of some notable efforts for improvement on the part of the Dalits, whose status is otherwise dismal. Cultural practices remain well-entrenched, even though the modern Indian constitution has officially banned discrimination on the basis of caste, allocating quotas in government jobs and schools to which some caste members did not previously have access. In 1989, the quotas were further extended to include those known as the OBCs (Other Backward Classes) of uncertain status. As recently as 2015, violent protests by several communities demanding to be recognized as OBCs with access to the quotas have shaken the status quo. While pressure is mounting to allay some of the more discriminatory measures of the caste system, many suspect that politics back the systems since various castes usually vote as blocs and are thus actively solicited by politicians.

Those at the bottom of the social ladder, be they Hindu Untouchables, Soweto Blacks, urban poor, the homeless, or victims of Jim Crow Laws, occupy a recognized place in society, necessitated by what Dumont describes as "the principle by which the elements of a whole are ranked in relation to the whole." The powerful need the powerless in order to be properly graded and find their place in the order of things—'we' would not exist without 'them.' The powerful, when they find the system does not sufficiently maintain their status or validate their claims of superiority, may create apocryphal hierarchies leading to extraordinary excesses, notably eugenics and sterilization.

Eugenics, a movement promoted in Britain by Sir Francis Galton in the 1880s, sought to improve humans through selective breeding focused on the enhancement of positive traits. It was an old notion, until then applied to plants and animals. The movement spread to other parts of the world, being transformed in so doing. In America, for example, it was a small step from eugenics to enforced sterilization. The movement, rather than promoting and encouraging positive traits, focused on avoiding and ultimately eliminating negative ones. The initial definitions of undesirability broadened to include physical disability, mental impairment, low birth, poverty and illiteracy.

A Model Sterilization Law, drafted by Harry Laughlin and published in 1914, served as a basis for laws that were initially enacted in twelve states with widespread popular support, particularly in the 1920s, targeting the "socially inadequate," those "maintained wholly and in part by public expense." These included the "feeble-minded, insane, criminalistic, epileptic, inebriate, diseased, blind, deaf, deformed; and dependent" including "orphans, ne'er-do-wells, tramps, the homeless and paupers," as well as the sexually promiscuous and morally delinquent.

Eventually, eighteen states passed compulsory sterilization laws based on the same model. By 1924, about 3,000 people had been involuntarily sterilized in America, the vast majority in California. But it was in Virginia, with the Carrie Buck case, that the workings of the law were laid bare. Carrie Buck, a seventeen-year-old girl from Charlottesville, Virginia, was the first person to be sterilized on the basis of two arguments: being pregnant out of wedlock (having been raped by the nephew of her foster parents) and having an institutionalized mother. Doctors at the institution where Buck resided decided to use her case to determine whether forced sterilization of "defective persons" whose reproduction represented "a menace to society" would survive a legal challenge. After a sham hearing, where Buck received only token representation, the institution's Board of Governors approved the procedure. Buck's state guardian, unaffiliated with the institution, protested on her behalf, arguing that due process and the Equal Protection Clause of the 14th Amendment were being violated, but failed to convince both the Virginia State and Federal Supreme courts.

The Supreme Court ruling in the case of Buck v. Bell had far greater import than the sterilization of one young woman (later proven to have been based on false arguments): some 8,300 Virginians underwent the same procedure. With even greater consequences, the German Nazis used the Laughlin's sterilization law as a model for their own Law for the Prevention of Defective Progeny, providing the legal basis for sterilizing more than 350,000 people. A proud Harry Laughlin was awarded an honorary degree from the University of Heidelberg in 1936, recognizing his work in "the science of racial cleansing."

Having proven its effectiveness, involuntary sterilization was extended to include repeat offenders and, by 1942, thirteen states had enacted laws to this effect. Later, it was further extended to the mentally ill and the developmentally disabled, right through the mid-1970s. Altogether, thirty-three states had statutes allowing the involuntary sterilization of more than 60,000 Americans. The Supreme Court still has not expressly overturned Buck v. Bell.

The pattern and timeline were similar in Canada, where the same principle was also applied to indigenous women. In 1928, Alberta enacted legislation leading to the sterilization of an estimated 2,800 women, most of them aboriginal. In British Columbia, the law passed in 1933 resulted in the sterilization of 400 people. The sexual sterilization law was not repealed in Canada until 1972; some argue it still persists as 'family planning,' targeting men and women whose children would likely become charges of the government. It is still the focus of active litigation—in 2017, sixty indigenous women filed a class action lawsuit alleging forced sterilization in Saskatchewan thirty years ago, claiming they had undergone the procedure under duress, or that they had been assured tubal ligation was reversible. Many have equated the enforced sterilization of aboriginal women to a form of genocide, covered by the United Nations convention on the prevention and punishment of genocide.

PHYSICAL BARRIERS

Belonging to a group provides identity, strength and cohesion, so it is natural for members to strive for its survival. There is nothing nefarious in the desire for self-protection, but erecting barriers is always seen as a hostile act by outsiders. With the rise of urbanization, walls surrounded whole cities in Mesopotamia as early as 4,500 BCE. The larger the group, the more complex the means of protection and the stronger the desire for control, a familiar pattern even today.

In a disorderly world where definitions may become confused, physical barriers are primitive attempts at establishing or restoring order, with all things well in their places. Whatever their official purpose, the delineation of barriers (reflecting physical and mental divisions) generally reveals the conviction required to separate internal and external categories, an important survival concept.

Walls

Walls are intended to provide defence, protection, and privacy; to keep dangerous outsiders out and inhabitants safely in. In extraordinary circumstances, walls have been used to separate whole countries, consuming enormous amounts of time and resources. These walls, wherever they are found (China, England, Berlin, Israel, potentially the United States), even as they physically sit at the border between countries, have never been built by common accord in the spirit of 'good fences making good neighbours'—the stronger and defensive nation is the one paying for it, building it and manning it.

The author A.G. de Voisin, visiting the Great Wall of China (as Europeans had named it), described in *Ecrit en Chine* (1909) the "monstrous splendor" of the Juyong (or Jiayuguan) Pass, even as parts of it were reduced to mere mud wall and a few gates:

> It imposes, it astonishes, it fires the imagination. It is a long poem in brick and stone, composed by human hands, its meanderings following the contours of the living landscape in its abrupt twists and turns, as if it were part of Nature... From the time when Huangdi linked those fragments that had already been built, from the days when he could condemn to death a careless workman who left the tiniest breach in his work, one barely large enough to hold a nail, from the day when this massive thing was complete, it took twenty-one centuries to destroy just a few sections of it.

The Wall, made from earth, stones, wood, and bricks, is over 21,000 kilometres (around 13,200 miles) long. It was built over more than 1,000 years, beginning in the fifth century BCE, and winds across China, cutting through deserts and around mountains before reaching the sea. The first emperor, Qin Shi Huangdi, gave the order to build a wall against the Mongols; at his death the construction slowed down. When Genghis Khan broke through the wall, the need for a stronger deterrent became evident and the construction started again in earnest. Between 1368 and 1644, the Ming Emperors built the sections through the Jiayuguan Pass, the Gobi Desert, across the Yellow River, past the city now known as Beijing and to Shanhaiguan in the east. Construction on the Wall then ceased, except for restoring parts of it, a project started in 1984 by Deng Xiaoping, then China's leader. The Wall included far more than an actual wall: there were passes or strongholds guarded by gates that were used for trading; blockhouses, or outposts consisting of towers, usually found in the more remote areas; signal towers, to keep communication between outposts; wall platforms (another form of watchtower) kept level with the wall; and garrison towns for off-duty soldiers.

In 1987, the Great Wall of China was designated a UNESCO World Heritage Site, in recognition of the human genius for engineering and the feat of imagination required to conceive such a project. The distances, the means of construction, the available resources and the number of people involved simply beggar the imagination. That so much effort should be exercised to keep people out is extraordinary, especially as a large number of the very people the Wall was supposed to protect were killed during its construction; frequent death sentences were issued to incompetent, lazy, or exhausted workmen. The twelfth-century poet Lu Yu saw both the Wall and its hetacomb:

> The Wall is being built, with raucous cries and groans;
> The Moon and Milky Way seem low in comparison.
> But if the white bones of the dead were not removed,
> They would rise as high as the top of the Great Wall.
> (*Songs of the Frontiers*)

The ancient bones of the dead have been found among the ruins of some Wall segments, embedded in their foundations. The human reality seems to have been lost behind the "monstrous wonder" and the dream of exclusion.

Hadrian's Wall was also designated as a UNESCO World Heritage Site in 1987, one of the Frontiers of the Roman Empire. Unlike their Chinese counterparts, Roman soldiers built their wall. In fact, historian Adrian Goldsworthy surmises that the wall's primary purpose may be been to occupy the 35,000 soldiers stationed in Britain, while also separating the Romans from Iron Age barbarians (Picts and Caledonians). Little is known about what actual threat they posed the Romans, although raiding seems to have occurred from the second to the fourth centuries CE.

A more modest affair than the Great Wall of China, if only in topographical terms, the 117-kilometre (73 mile) wall was built over a decade to protect the northern border of the Roman Province of Britain, running between the North Sea and the Irish Sea. Made of turf, timber, and earth in some sections, and of stone in others, the wall also featured a twenty-foot wide moat, the *vallum*. As emperors succeeded emperors in the complicated history of the Roman Empire, Hadrian's Wall gradually closed down but remained more or less continuously manned up to the fifth century.

Walls stand as monuments to a mode of thinking we might think obsolete, were it not for the ones standing today, or being planned for. Among the former, the Israeli West Bank Wall, built in the early 2000s, defines the Green Line created by the 1949 armistice agreements following the Arab-Israeli War of 1948. The Israeli claim it protects Israel from Palestinian attacks. The Palestinians, on whose land it is built, consider it a form of apartheid.

Segregated Communities

In 1205, Pope Innocent III proclaimed that the special status of Jews as Christ-killers doomed them to servitude, leading Thomas Aquinas to conclude that, since Jews were the slaves of the Church, it could also claim their possessions. In theory, the Jews had some rights: they should not be condemned without trial; their synagogues and cemeteries should not be desecrated; their property should not be robbed with impunity. In reality, they had little recourse should any derogation occur. Their main value to society was as moneylenders, a particularly useful trade to assist kings always short of cash; they depended on the same kings for their protection. The common man, as explained by historian Barbara Tuchman, viewed the Jews as "rapacious, merciless monsters, symbols of the new force of money that was changing old ways and dissolving old ties."

In the twelfth and thirteenth centuries, the rise of powerful Christian banking houses (notably in Florence) and the advent of the Inquisition left the Jews in far more precarious circumstances. They were blamed for causing the Black Death and for poisoning wells. Throughout Europe, growing hostility and multiple decrees led to their greater isolation; expulsion and persecution generally went hand-in-hand with seizure of Jewish property. Various parties, such as the flagellants (a self-flagellating group that appeared in a sudden frenzy during the Plague, going from town to town and claiming to intercede with God for humankind) took it upon themselves to attack the Jews directly and, in several German cities, Jews were slaughtered by the hundreds. At Worms, in March 1349, some four hundred Jews chose to burn themselves in their houses rather than be killed by them. As Tuchman shrewdly observed, "Authorities in most places tried at first to protect the Jews, but succumbed to popular pressure, not without an eye to potential forfeit of Jewish property."

In this hostile environment, Jews felt more secure in their own separate quarters, the walled-in mellahs or ghettos, well apart from their Christian and Muslim neighbours. The mellahs were specific to Morocco and, while imposed by the Arabs, were relatively autonomous enclaves created for Jews who had been expelled from the Iberian Peninsula during the Reconquista after 1492. Usually located near a royal compound, they provided the Jews with protection against riots and offered the Arabs some control over the Jewish community, their taxes and their numbers. The Jews provided a valuable boost to the local economy, and a form of *modus vivendi* more or less succeeded in accommodating both faiths. This had been partly true in Spain and was again true of Morocco, where Jews generated a very active trade. By the mid-1800s, Mogador (now Essaouira) was in the extraordinary position, unique in the Arab world, of having more

Jews than Arabs. Historian Martin Gilbert, who studied the history of Jews in the Islamic world, claimed that they often found greater opportunities, respect, and recognition there than under Christian rulers. However, it is also true that they have been subjected to dreadful treatment under Islamic rule as well, notably in Fes, where several thousand Jews were massacred in 1465.

Like the mellahs, ghettos (perhaps derived from the Italian *getto* or foundry, since the first ghetto was established on the site of a foundry in Venice in 1516) were separate quarters allocated to Jews where they could both be controlled and offered protection to lead an ordinary life and freely practise their religious observances. Among the ghettos that have marked history, one stands out precisely because it was different from the well-established pattern—the one in Warsaw, a short-lived anomaly in the long line of ghettos harbouring European Jews. Rather than being a place of safety and common reassurance, it was a place of danger and death, built to destroy rather than protect.

The Jews had lived in Poland since the thirteenth century. Many Jews participated in Polish life (attending Polish schools and universities, practising professions, regarding Polish as their second mother tongue) while leading a rich intellectual life of their own, with Jewish schools, newspapers, theatres and sports organizations. However, beginning in the mid-1930s, anti-Semitic propaganda led to the segregation of Jewish university students, street demonstrations and the ransacking of Jewish shops. On September 21, 1939, three weeks after the German invasion of Poland, the Jews were ordered into separate residential districts. Many were deported from the cities to fifteen newly created ghettos in northern and western Poland; the largest one in Lódz had a population of 160,000. All were ordered to wear the yellow star of David on their back, chest or left arm.

The Germans built a separate ghetto in Warsaw, which they called the *Wohnbezirk*, the Jewish residential district. This Warsaw ghetto bore no resemblance to traditional ghettos, consisting of approximately 1,000 acres and surrounded by a ten-foot-high wall and a parapet of barbed wire. Some 500,000 Jews were left there to survive, often as many as thirteen people to a room and many without a roof. More than half of them had no means of earning a living.

In spite of the horrendous conditions, a spirit of resistance rose behind its wall. The Jewish resisters saw themselves as part as an all-Polish resistance movement. During 1941, there were thirty major underground publications in the ghetto, written in Yiddish, Hebrew and Polish. There was also significant assistance given by Polish citizens from outside the ghetto, notably the Warsaw tramway workers who provided food when they could and in some cases smuggled out Jewish children.

The ghetto had actually become nothing other than a large concentration camp, where 96,000 Jews died, 45,000 of them from hunger. The Governor of Warsaw, Ludwig Fischer, said, "The Jews will die of hunger and privation, and of the Jewish question only a cemetery will remain." The sentiment was shared by another German governor, Hans Frank: "It is not necessary to dwell on the fact that we are sentencing the Jews to death. If the Jews do not die of starvation, it will be necessary to step up anti-Jewish measures, and let us hope that, too, will come to pass."

It came to pass in July 1942, when Heinrich Himmler ordered the destruction of the Warsaw Ghetto and the deportation of its inhabitants to the death camp of Treblinka. They were to be transported by groups of 6,000 every day. Eventually, between 265,000 and 300,000 (the numbers vary with different sources) were thus deported by the SS, assisted by the Polish police. Opposition to the deportation by Polish groups, mostly the Polish Workers' Party, was severely punished.

The deportation to Treblinka left behind some 35,000 people in the ghetto, mainly workers employed by Germans together with their families, and another 25,000 hiding illegally. Armed with

Molotov cocktails, some machine guns and a few pistols, they rose to oppose the German tanks coming to liquidate the remnants of the population. On April 19, 1943, the Germans were forced to retreat in the face of this unexpected resistance, but they returned soon afterwards with flamethrowers and hand grenades. In spite of the mismatched forces, the resistance went on until May 8, 1943. General Stroop signalled the German victory by blowing up the Great Synagogue in Warsaw and saying, "The Jewish Residential District is no more."

Concentration Camps

Holocaust historian Dan Stone defines a concentration camp as "an isolated, circumscribed site with fixed structures designed to incarcerate civilians." It is the specific objective of incarceration that distinguishes camps from other forms of segregation. Such camps certainly existed before the Third Reich gave them their unique stamp. Isolating groups seen as dangerous already had a long history. For instance, camps were created in Saint-Domingue (now Haiti) by the French under Napoleon to contain groups of insurgent slaves seeking independence in the aftermath of the French Revolution, which had inspired a movement toward emancipation; the British established colonial compounds in South Africa during the Boer Wars; Franco opened camps during the Spanish Civil War; and so on. Wherever we turn in history, we see palisades, compounds or barbed wires and people confined behind them. The image is universal and omnipresent, seemingly the first line of defence against potential or real agitators—both indigenous and foreign.

The Nazis first established their camps prior to World War II, and these expanded over the next decade. There were essentially two types of camps, although some had dual functions and others evolved from one designation to the other: the concentration camps where prisoners were often used as workforce for local industries (sometimes described as *Vernichtungdurch Arbeit,* annihilation

43

through labour); and the death camps, symbolized by the gas chambers and chimneys.

While Jews were the primary target, other despised groups were included: criminals, cripples, the chronically ill—those normally protected by Christian values. The Nazis deemed them enemies of the Party and 'out-groups' outside the 'master Aryan race' and began to eliminate them. When the camps were freed in 1945, unforgettable newsreels revealed "piles of corpses, mass graves with hundreds of dead people, their emaciated arms and legs entangled, half-dead survivors, barely able to stand, staring into the camera, bewildered, sick, and starved."[2]

However, Nazi concentration camps, often the focus of our attention, do not stand alone in the history of radical imprisonment; the Russian gulags can hold their own in the cruel narrative of state-driven civilian incarceration. The term gulag referred to a system of administrative institutions created in 1921 until Solzhenitsyn coined the expression 'gulag archipelago' to include prisons, punishment colonies, corrective labour camps, agricultural colonies and 'special settlements.'

There appear to have been ideological differences between the camps. In *Hope and Memory: Reflections on the Twentieth Century* (2005) Tzvetan Todorov wrote that "the Soviets sacrificed human lives as if they were worthless, but the Nazis were overcome by a 'murder madness.'" He explains:

> Ironically, it was the Soviets whose theoretical framework stressed social and historical processes, who allowed "natural selection" to run its course: in the gulag, hunger, cold, and sickness drove the weak to the wall. The Nazis, on the other hand, who claimed to believe in the pseudo-Darwinian doctrine of "the survival of the fittest," used "artificial selection" at Auschwitz and also at Ravensbrück: the SS, their doctors, and guards, decided on which prisoners should die and which should be saved.

---

2. Christian Goeschel and Nikolaus Wachsmann *The Nazi Concentration Camps 1933-1939.* (Lincoln and London: University of Nebraska Press, 2012) ix.

To the millions of unwanted individuals selected for elimination, it mattered little whether the process of selection was natural or artificial. Ideologies may have differed and even conflicted, but the outcome was the same for the victims. Todorov quotes a survivor of both camp systems: "It is hard to know which is less humanitarian—gassing people in five minutes or taking three months to crush them with hunger."

For the guards in the camps, however, relying on natural fitness was a (theoretically) lighter burden on their souls than active participation in murder. But what determined true guilt was the individual decision to obey, whatever the dangers involved in resistance, and the remarkable elasticity of the human conscience.

Reservations and Reserves

In some cases, segregating groups was merely a matter of expediency in pursuit of agricultural or economic goals. Across North America, it was deemed good politics to remove the original inhabitants to spaces specifically reserved for them (hence the terms reservations and reserves). In the United States, when President Andrew Jackson pushed an Indian Removal Bill in 1830, fiercely debated in Congress but finally passed in the Senate, his intentions were clear—removing some three dozen native tribes standing in the way of the settlers' rights to clear the land, build homes and grow cotton. He validated his views in his annual address to Congress in 1833, saying of Indians, "They have neither the intelligence, the industry, the moral habits, nor the desire of improvement which are essential to any favorable change in their condition. Established in the midst of another and a superior race… they must necessarily yield to the force of circumstances and ere long disappear."

The passage of the Indian Removal Act of 1830 marked a systematic and forcible displacement of tribes to designated areas for the convenience of the colonists. They were known as the Five Civilized Tribes (Cherokee, Chickasaw, Choctaw, Creek and Seminole) and

were displaced to west of the Mississippi River and the newly constituted Indian reservations. The removal of some 16,500 Cherokee
in 1838 was particularly cruel and, in what came to be known as
the Trail of Tears, about 4,000 of them were marched over 1,900
kilometres (1,200 miles) of rough terrain and perished on the way
from exhaustion, cold and hunger.

In 1868, President Ulysses S. Grant's 'peace policy' reorganized
the Indian Service and substituted members of religious institutions as supervisors for the previous government officials. This was
a common practice for colonialist powers from Africa to Oceania
to South America, blending the greed for land with pious hopes for
the salvation of native souls. American natives were not as willing as
others to be subdued, removed and saved, and were soon involved
in wars and massacres.

In Canada, the fate of aboriginal people fell immediately into the
hands of the Church. As early as 1637, missionaries were entrusted
in New France with lands intended for their Indian charges, with
the intention of settling the latter and introducing them to agriculture while also converting them to Christianity. These first initiatives
became the models for the establishment of later reserves in Canada.

Gradually, European newcomers became more numerous and
required more land, selecting the more fertile spreads for themselves
and eventually occupying the traditional territories of aboriginal
people. The next step was the creation of separate settlements for the
latter, either on Crown land ceded by the government or on private
lands purchased by the government to be used as reserves. The practice
spread across the country but, as the administration of reserves was not
overseen by a single authority, the system varied among regions.

The Indian Act was elaborated over time through separate pieces
of colonial legislation (the Gradual Civilization Act of 1857 and the
Gradual Enfranchisement Act of 1869, eventually consolidated into
the Indian Act of 1876, with many later changes) where the reserves,
often still entrusted into the practical care of missionaries, were said

"to be held for the use and benefit of Indians." In effect—and we see that Jewish ghettos were far more liberal institutions than aboriginal reserves—the government controlled most aspect of native life, ruling on the matter of status and overseeing land, resources, education, band administration and so on.

Prime Minister John A. Macdonald validated the concept in 1887, explaining that "the great aim of our legislation has been to do away with the tribal system and assimilate the Indian people in all respects with the other inhabitants of the Dominion as speedily as they are fit to change." It was an improvement in tone from President Jackson's views on the same matter, but how isolating people in reserves was going to achieve this goal was not clearly specified. It was likely understood that conversion to Christianity and, eventually, education in residential schools would be suitable and achievable means.

WALLS PROVIDE A SOLID VISUAL IMPACT and their intent is clear. However, effective barriers can be symbolic as well as physical, such as the one formed on January 1, 2019, by five million Indian women standing side by side over 620 kilometres to demand the right to worship at Kerala's Sabarimala Temple, where women of child bearing age are not permitted to enter because of the god's mythological celibacy. But these, while significant, are rare and often speak of helplessness rather than power.

Establishing power, on the other hand, is the key to all other cases of exclusion and inclusion. Throughout history, groups have sought dominance by relying on self-righteousness and displays of power. In such cases, acts that were once deemed immoral or even criminal become inherent to the new dominant culture and the new morality constitutes an organizing principle to institute a new rule of law. Outsiders dominated by a new order they cannot understand can only fall by the wayside, having lost all relevance. They perished by the millions in the last century.

We are all at a loss to understand the magnitude of gulags and death camps, and wonder that they could have existed in a world similar to our own. Arthur Koestler's *Darkness at Noon* (1940) was *de rigueur* reading after World War II because he addressed this dilemma—the discrepancy between belief in a noble cause and the frailty of its human manifestation. His hero, Rubashov, is a loyal and respected Bolshevik who becomes torn when he compares his idealistic commitment to the actions performed in the name of the Party he loved. How could he possibly reconcile mass executions and the deaths of millions of people with the future Utopian society he had been promised? The Holocaust and its attendant deviance will always be the twentieth century's unresolved conundrum and remains the question asked today, as we sense the profound divide between our moral aspirations and the realities of our lives.

Walls are the epitome of physical demarcation, but the effort and cost involved in building them often seems disproportionate to the situations they attempted to remedy, particularly when their main function is to assert power and dominance. The Great Wall of China and Hadrian's Wall were recognized and protected as UNESCO monuments, celebrating grandiose accomplishments of human effort, notwithstanding their human cost. Such was not the fate of the camps. Some have disappeared, leaving few traces, except for a malefic aura that must surely permeate their former grounds. Others have become museums with a triple mission: keeping alive the memory of those who suffered and died in them; bearing testimony to the lengths to which organized human evil can lead; and as warning that it could strike again at any time, whatever our individual vigilance might be. Yet, an informal French survey in 2018 found that ten percent of the respondents had not heard of the Holocaust and twenty percent were not sure when it had taken place.

Today, concentration camps have become a metaphor for the way of life of millions of us, from the refugee camps throughout Africa, the containment centres of Guantánamo Bay and other prison camps, the restrictions of the Gaza Strip and similar lands, as well as *favelas* and shanty towns the world over.

Dan Stone, writing on concentration camps, argues that, even if this abomination was one of the hallmarks of the twentieth century, states have powers that can partially compensate for the harm done: they can also "nurture populations through education, health programmes and access to welfare in the way that creates critically engaged citizens rather than downtrodden, suspiciously regarded subjects." However, he notes that such benefits apply to very few and concludes, "those of us who are more fortunate—who live in places where a vestige of the post-war democratic settlement still survives—might do well to watch our backs."

While the division between 'us' and 'them' may sound like an abstraction whose main purpose is to outline theoretical discrepancies, the facts are only too real—according to Credit Suisse's Global Wealth Report (2017), less than one percent of the world's population holds 46 percent of the world's wealth. In such an equation, the larger numbers, despite their individual powerlessness, represent both a threat and a rebuke to the continuing dominance of the few.

CHAPTER THREE

BEYOND THE WHITE MAN'S BURDEN

IT ONLY TOOK NINETY SECONDS FOR the Savar Building in Rana Plaza in the Dhaka District of Bangladesh to collapse on April 24, 2013. "Deep cracks had appeared in the eight-storey building outside Dhaka the day before. That morning, workers who had been producing clothes sourced by major international brands had begged not to be sent inside. Managers would not relent. More than 2,000 people filed in. Some time before 9am, floors began to vanish and workers started falling."[3]

In that minute and a half, 1,134 people died—the deadliest ever such disaster in garment factories. Before that date, about seventy-one garment workers died every year in fires or building collapses in the garment manufacturing districts of Bangladesh. Since then, the numbers have decreased to seventeen annually. This notable, but still dubious, improvement occurred when the eyes of the world finally turned to the conditions of workers employed in sweat shops. The European and American companies for whom the clothes were being manufactured claimed ignorance of these conditions until they were faced with what unions have called a "mass industrial homicide."

Being forced to work under obviously unsafe conditions at the risk of losing the only job available, however long the hours and however badly paid—this is the face of contemporary forced labour, the modern face of slavery. It is not accidental that the garment industry in London, Paris, New York, and Milan is not involved in

---

3. Michael Safi and Dominic Rushe, 'Rana Plaza, five years on: safety of workers hands in balance in Bangladesh,' *The Guardian*, April 24, 2018.

clothing the poorest Bangladeshi, Pakistani or Filipino. We may be past the days of official colonialism, but economics still direct the flow of commerce in the old familiar direction.

SLAVERY

European interests in what we call today the developing world are not new. They flourished between the sixteenth and the twentieth centuries as two distinct types of exploitation—the slave trade and colonialism, the former seen as a legitimate commercial activity, the latter felt to be a moral duty. Slavery, the more egregious version, focused on three continents: Africa, which provided the raw material; Europe, in charge of acquisition and transportation; and America, the consumer and beneficiary of an unwilling work force. Its parallel, colonialism, had a farther reach. Both relied on concepts of elitism, religious fervour, military and technological superiority, and greed and hypocrisy put to the service of self-interest.

In 1899, Rudyard Kipling, Britain's imperial poet, published 'The White Man's Burden: The United States and The Philippine Islands.' Although the expression may be familiar, the poem is little known today. It urges the white man to take up his noble burden by exiling the best among them to serve the needs of their colonized people, these "new-caught, sullen peoples, / half-devil and half-child." His task is "In patience to abide, / To veil the threat of terror/ And check the show of pride; / By open speech and simple, / An hundred times made plain / To seek another's profit, /And work another's gain." Duty-bound to take up his civilizing burden, the white man will "Fill full the mouth of Famine / and bid the sickness cease." Yet, he must be prepared for disappointment as he faces the inadequacies of his subjects: "Watch sloth and heathen Folly / Bring all your hopes to nought." He is warned that his reward will only be "The blame of those ye better, / The hate of those ye guard, / The cry of hosts ye humour" at the hands of "The silent, sullen peoples." All this constitutes a hard task for the white man for these will be his "…thankless years, / cold, edged with dear-bought wisdom." Such is the price of colonialism, but the white man must forge ahead.

Some reacted strongly against the poem, notably Mark Twain, who recognized the missionary spirit that animated it as a front for imperialism. Indeed, the idea was not new, having been expressed with less pomp by Richard Hakluyt to Sir Walter Raleigh in 1595, "For to posterity no greater glory can be handed down than to conquer the barbarian, to recall the savage and the pagan to civility, to draw the ignorant within the orbit of reason." Such sentiments, often sincere and motivated by religious proselytism, also provided a convenient justification for Europeans to exploit the rest of the world. High-minded white governments could raise the people of other countries and races to their level; in fact, it was their duty as Christians and their responsibility as civilized nations to do so. At the same time, their own societies found it highly profitable and grew rich in the process.

The earliest, and most direct, form of exploitation was the slave trade. European conscience could remain scrupulously clear as there was no opprobrium attached to the outright ownership of other human beings. Slave labour was an ancient commodity that many cultures had relied on for personal use and economic welfare. It flourished in Ancient Rome, a highly practical culture and a model for later European nations in many ways, where it relied on an extensive and complex system. Slaves' sweat and toil were the source of many aristocratic fortunes—Saint Melania the Younger, for instance, was said to own over 8,000 slaves, 2,400 of them in one estate alone. Even the middle class enjoyed the possession of slaves, as it denoted a certain level of respectability. Everyone, including prostitutes and even slaves themselves of a better class, could and did own slaves.

In the Americas, the legitimate slave trade began with the Africans' first arrival with Spanish settlers in Santo Domingo in

1501. Ironically, this new trade derived from Spain's royal prohibition on enslaving indigenous American peoples, already decimated by the introduction of new diseases. The Iberians then looked to Africa for their work force.

In 1562, Elizabeth I leased the carrack *Jesus de Lübeck* to John Hawkins (variously a naval commander, administrator, merchant, navigator, shipbuilder, privateer, and successful slave trader) to transport Africans to the Spanish colonies of Santo Domingo and Venezuela. The "good ship Jesus" became the first ship entirely devoted to the trafficking of slaves. In 1567, Hawkins captured the *Madre de Deus* with four hundred slaves on board and decided to run her himself. As a reward for his services to the Crown and his contribution to the Royal purse, Hawkins eventually received a crest which he proudly flew on the *Jesus de Lübeck*—it featured a black man bound by a cord.

Many private fortunes were built on the slave trade and the prosperity of many English cities derived from it. Far from being secretive, the trade received a seal of royal approval in 1660 when the Royal Adventurers into Africa (later becoming the Royal African Company) received a charter to run the ivory and slave trades from the Gold Coast. Plymouth and London were hubs in the mid-seventeenth century, but Liverpool and Bristol—safe from enemy privateers and away from the Customs in London—later dominated the trade.

While goods from Africa (gold, ivory, and particularly slaves, known as 'black ivory') were eagerly sought after, it would be an error to blame the trade exclusively on Europeans, since the control usually remained in African hands. Slave labour was long indigenous to Asia and Africa and constituted a substantial element of the workforce. The Congolese king Nzinga (renamed João upon becoming a Christian) and his successors were particularly active in this trade. In 1540, King Afonso of Congo wrote to King João III of Portugal, "Put all the Guinea countries on one side and only Congo on the other, and you will find that Congo renders more than all the others put together…No king in all these parts esteems Portuguese goods as much as we do. We favor the trade, sustain it, open markets, roads, and markets where the pieces [prime male slaves] are traded."

By the 1740s, many seafaring European nations were engaged in the busy traffic of human beings, but Great Britain was the world's leader in this extremely lucrative commerce. Ships of all nationalities en route for the Americas and the Caribbean carried slaves to the New World or mixed cargoes of slaves with other equally profitable merchandise; it was easy to outfit a ship for the slave trade by simply building bulwarks to segregate decks and equipping platforms with shackles.

It may be difficult to understand how slavery could continue in the Age of Enlightenment, a time when more liberal notions on the human condition were forcefully emerging. Indeed, many were strongly opposed to it, and the nineteenth century saw a general awakening of anti-slavery sentiments. A British slave ship, the *Zong*, came to public attention in 1781, its captain accused of having thrown overboard 132 sick and dying slaves, who could not be sold in their condition, in order to collect their cargo insurance instead. Two Spanish slave ships based in Cuba later became the subjects of well-documented court trials: the *Antelope* in 1820 and *La Amistad* in 1839. A number of treaties and acts were introduced, starting with one arising from the French Revolution in 1794, finally confirmed by the abolition of slavery in France in 1848, as well as the Slavery Abolition Act of 1833 passed by the British Parliament. In the US, a federal Act Prohibiting Importation of Slaves was passed in 1807, but the abolition of slavery had to wait until the end of the Civil War in 1865.

For most westerners, slavery is closely associated with North America, where it has played a unique ethical, social, and commercial role. Beginning with the 1619 arrival of twenty African slaves in Jamestown, Virginia, the number of slaves eventually grew to several millions as they replaced, to great advantage, the indentured

55

European servants who had previously provided free labour. Initially brought in to work mostly on tobacco and rice plantations, two events, both occurring in the late eighteenth century, modified the nature of slave work: the exhaustion of the land used to grow tobacco and the 1793 invention of the cotton gin mill by Eli Whitney. By the mid-1850s, cotton production employed about half of the four million slaves then living in the United States. They ranged from the few who could read and write and held responsible positions within the household on the cotton plantations to those who toiled in the fields.

Deplorable working and living conditions led to occasional slave rebellions, the most violent being the 1831 revolt led by Nat Turner. Eventually overpowered by the militia, it resulted in the murder of sixty white people and about 120 slaves. The treatment of slaves in the south led to a growing abolitionist movement in the north, reflected in articles in the newspaper *The Liberator* and the novel *Uncle Tom's Cabin*. Another significant ally in the liberation of slaves was the creation of the Underground Railroad, starting in the early nineteenth century. It consisted of a network of secret routes and safe houses, set up by people sympathetic to the abolition of slavery, that permitted runaway slaves to reach safety and freedom in the northern states or Canada.

The intense sentiments animating both sides came to a boil with John Brown's 1859 raid on the federal armory at Harper's Ferry. Leading a small group that included five black men, Brown hoped to arm local slaves and start a liberation movement. The uprising was quelled by local militia backed by troops under the command of Robert E Lee. In 1862, President Lincoln issued his preliminary Emancipation Proclamation, but it wasn't until the end of the Civil War three years later that the 13th Amendment was adopted by Congress, ending slavery in the United States.

However, the Amendment did not miraculously bring racial harmony. The introduction of the Jim Crow Laws effectively segregated black people from the white population—there was officially free-dom but no equality. The name 'Jim Crow' goes back to the 1820s and a character played by a song-and-dance man, dressed as a plantation slave and doing his wheeling and dancing routine. The performances gradually grew more derogatory and racially abusive and, when the southern states implemented a series of racial segrega-tion laws (1878), they became known as the Jim Crow Laws. Where they prevailed, notably in the southern states, they imposed legal punishment on those who consorted with black people. Marriage between blacks and whites was forbidden, and access by blacks to most facilities (restaurants, hotels, hospitals, transportation, schools, cinemas) was restricted. Attempts to modify the Jim Crow Laws were opposed by the white-dominated Congress until the twentieth cen-tury, when they were repealed by President Lyndon Johnson's Civil Rights Act of 1964 and the Voting Rights Act of 1965.

COLONIALISM

As the slave trade was coming to an end, the technology of the Industrial Revolution was creating new opportunities for exploi-tation and conquest. While several European empires had been colonizing in the Americas, Africa and Asia since the 1500s, the nineteenth century saw the world being divided among the powers of Europe. At the Berlin Conference of 1884–85, most of Africa was parcelled out among half a dozen European countries, formalizing what was known as the Scramble for Africa, as the 'advanced' and strong nations laid claim to the 'backward' and weak.

This elitist interpretation of colonized populations was already firmly entrenched in the minds of the early colonizers of the 'back-ward' indigenous populations of North America, as explained by Canadian historian Bruce Trigger:

> Europeans never interpreted native American societies without
> preconceptions. Even the first European explorers sought to make
> sense of what they saw in terms of diverse and often contradictory

medieval speculations about what the inhabitants of far-off regions of the world might be like...The debate whether Native Americans represented the childhood of mankind or the product of degeneration was to continue into the nineteenth century.[4]

Indigenous North American nations, whose way of life was mostly seen as primitive and immoral, needed to be converted to Christianity and taught to live as Europeans. Moreover, they did not appear to cultivate their lands properly, an adequate excuse—not exclusive to North America—for seizing their territory.

Some concerns over the rightful ownership and use of conquered lands emerged during the early days of discovery and colonization. James Douglas, the 14th Earl of Morton and president of the Royal Society, had been shocked by the violence of some of the initial meetings with native populations of Oceania and had urged James Cook and Joseph Banks in particular to check the excesses of their men, reminding them that the natives were "the natural and in the strictest sense of the word, the legal possessors of the several regions they inhabit."

James Cook's contemporary, the French navigator and explorer Lapérouse, who died in Oceania, wondered, "What right have Europeans to lands their inhabitants have worked with the sweat of their brows and which for centuries have been the burial place of their ancestors? The real task of explorers was to complete the survey of the Globe, not to add to the possession of their rulers." His remark is particularly significant as it outlines the conflict between the quest for scientific knowledge illustrated by the exploration of lands unknown to Europeans, with their wealth of natural curiosities, and the quick and greedy grasp of trade and administration over those same lands.

It seems historically inevitable that the European 'discoverers' of new peoples and lands must immediately be followed by missionaries to desecrate the native populations' religions and save their souls, by traders to take advantage of their natural resources, and

4. Bruce G. Trigger, *Natives and Newcomers: Canada's 'Heroic Age' Reconsidered* (Kingston and Montreal: McGill-Queen's University Press; Manchester: Manchester University Press, 1986), 21

by administrators to ruin their social structures. These combined actions and the fatal consequences of the diseases brought in by the newcomers usually decimated the local populations and destroyed their cultures.

Since historical records were mostly one-sided and written by the colonizers, and the oral literatures of the oppressed peoples only appeared in print in the twentieth century, we must turn to the original words of white observers who witnessed the effects of the devastation, misunderstanding and despair brought on by colonization. James Cook, for instance, wrote after his first voyage to Tahiti in 1769:

> We debauch their Morals already prone to vice and we introduce among them wants and perhaps which they never had before knew, and to which serves only to disturb that happy tranquillity they and their Fore fathers had enjoy'd.... Let him tell me what the Natives of the whole extent of America have gained by the commerce they had had with the Europeans.

George Hamilton, surgeon on the *Pandora* in 1788, regretted what he could see happening. "Happy would it have been for these people had they never been visited by the Europeans; for, to our shame be it spoken, disease and gun powder is all the benefit they have ever received from us, in return for their hospitality and kindness."

The French encyclopedist Diderot borrowed the voice of an elderly Tahitian to address Europeans in 1772. "This country is yours! And why? Because you set foot on it? If a Tahitian landed one day on your shores and carved on one of your stones or on the bark of one of your trees: This country belongs to the natives of Tahiti, what would you think?... Leave us to our way of life... we do not want to trade what you call our innocence for your useless lights."

Unfortunately, the more prevalent view was that expressed by Charles Darwin in 1837. An otherwise radical thinker, he shared with many of his contemporaries an inability to see beyond his own cultural bias to appreciate the inner workings of traditional societies.

In *The Voyage of the Beagle* (1839) he defended the work of the missionaries in Oceania:

> They forget, or will not remember, that human sacrifices, and the power of an idolatrous priesthood—a system of profligacy unparalleled in any other part of the world—infanticide, a consequence of that system—bloody wars, where the conquerors spared neither women nor children—that all these have been abolished; and that dishonesty, intemperance, and licentiousness have been greatly reduced by the introduction of Christianity.

Historians suggest that some empires, at the least, provided stability by constraining violent ethnic and religious antagonisms, which often flared up again after the regions regained their independence. However, foreign domination was naturally seen differently by local populations and, generally speaking, the patterns and aftermaths of colonization were the same everywhere: plundering of natural resources using native workers (Africa, South America), expropriation of native lands by white farmers (Africa, America), suppression of religious or social practices (the potlatch of North America, the dances of Polynesia), isolation into territorial reserves (North America, Australia), separating children from their parents (residential schools in Canada, Australia)—some overt, others more subtle, but all intended to destroy the old ways and instil a sense of 'civilization' among native populations.

Empire-building requires a country to be superbly confident in its superiority, a notion reinforced by the supposed inferiority of the populations it dominates, particularly when this sentiment is confirmed by racial differences. Historian Krishan Kumar, who explores the nature and impact of great empires (Roman, Ottoman, Habsburg, Russian, British and French) comments that England and France were in the unique position of having colonial empires located entirely overseas (America, India, Africa, Oceania) and dealt with populations totally different from their own in terms of race, religions, customs and history. When the differences were of a lesser nature, such as with the Roman Empire, integration of the native populations could be more easily achieved through an effective administrative approach. The Roman Emperor Caracalla, for example, issued an edict in 212 CE that enfranchised the colonized, declaring that all free men in the empire had theoretical citizenship of Rome.

The case of modern European empires spreading their grasp far and wide across the globe was different. Historian Fernand Braudel's view of hierarchical differences among cultures in terms of development, supported by colonialists, is at odds with the more common understanding of what constitutes a culture: the sum of a people's practices and social organization expressed through a complex system of knowledge, beliefs, art, morals, laws and customs. Some systems may be more or less complex than others, but none are actually inferior or superior; they are just different and adapted to intrinsic needs and circumstances. The consequence of colonization, as expounded by the White Man's Burden, is that alien cultural modes supplant those that would have naturally evolved. Braudel cites the sixteenth century conquest of Mexico and Peru by the Spaniards—the mismatching of cultures did not lead the 'inferior' one to evolve into the 'superior' one, but created a deep social and moral sense of disorder with profound consequences. Ironically, this violent outcome is the unavowed purpose of the supposedly benevolent White Man's Burden.

In *An Area of Darkness* (1964), V.S. Naipul's semi-autobiographical account of his first visit to India, the Trinidadian writer disdainfully said, "While dominating India [the British] expressed their contempt for it, and projected England; and Indians were forced into a nationalism which in the beginning was like a mimicry of the British."

It takes time for each cultural environment to adapt. In the case of Africa, where the oppressive presence of Britain and France was most keenly felt, integration in the face of apparently insurmountable cultural differences would have taken far longer than the brief African colonial period lasted (1876–1915).

It is not surprising that Western education facilitated the creation of an opposite movement. In the early 1930s, three overseas students met in Paris: Aimé Césaire from Martinique, Léopold Sédar Senghor from Senegal, and Léon Gontran Damas from Guiana. Their intent was to promote the self-affirmation of black people and the values arising from a specific and different civilization. They founded a journal, *L'Etudiant noir,* in 1934 and created the concept and movement of *Négritude.* This is Aimé Césaire's definition:

> Négritude... is a way of living history within history: the history of a community whose experience appears to be ... unique, with its deportation of populations, its transfer of people from one continent to another, its distant memories of old beliefs, its fragments of murdered cultures. How can we not believe that all this, which has its own coherence, constitutes a heritage?

For Senghor, a poet and politician, all blacks share a biological make-up (their race), an outer appearance (the colour of their skin), and an inner being (their spirit, their very essence). He naturally rejected the notion that the African is inherently inferior to the white man, establishing the concept of négritude as a major weapon against colonialism.

Césaire, a respected poet, writer and politician, finally put to rest the sanctimonious proselytizing and crusading of the White Man's Burden when he wrote his *Discourse sur le colonialisme* in 1955:

> And I say that between *colonization* and *civilization* there is an infinite distance; that out of all the colonial expeditions that have been undertaken, out of all the colonial statutes that have been drawn up, out of all the memoranda that have been dispatched by all the ministries, there could not come a single human value. First we must study how colonization works to *decivilize* the colonizer, to *brutalize* him in the true sense of the word, to degrade him, to awaken him to buried instincts, to covetousness, violence, race hatred, and moral relativism; and we must show that each time a head is cut off or an eye put out in Vietnam and in France they accept the fact, each time a

little girl is raped and in France they accept the fact, each time a Madagascan is tortured and in France they accept the fact, civilization acquires another dead weight, a universal regression takes place, a gangrene sets in, a center of infection begins to spread; and that at the end of all these treaties that have been violated, all these lies that have been propagated, all these punitive expeditions that have been tolerated, all these prisoners who have been tied up and 'interrogated,' all these patriots who have been tortured, at the end of all the racial pride that has been encouraged, all the boastfulness that has been displayed, a poison has been instilled into the veins of Europe and, slowly but surely, the continent proceeds toward *savagery*.

Independently from this group, Frantz Fanon, born in Martinique, published in 1961 the seminal *Les damnés de la terre* (translated into English as *The Wretched of the Earth*, 1963), whose impact on civil rights, anti-colonialism and black consciousness movements was felt around the world. He articulated thoughts that few among the peoples just liberating themselves from the European hold had heard before.

Let us not lose time in useless laments and sickening mimicry, let us leave this Europe which never stops talking of man yet massacres him at every one of its street corners, at every corner of the world. For centuries it has stifled virtually the whole of humanity in the name of a so-called 'spiritual adventure.'

The opening sentences of *The Wretched of the Earth* must have sounded like a thunderclap: "National liberation, national reawakening, restoration of the nation to the people or the Commonwealth, whatever the name used, whatever the latest expression, decolonization is always a violent event." Ironically, Fanon died in America ("that country of lynchers"), having anonymously sought there the only treatment then available for his leukemia.

History has proven Fanon correct—the national reawakening and the severance of ties from colonizers have generally been violent. The real unravelling of European empires started with India in 1947, followed in 1954 by French Indochina (now Vietnam).

Within two decades, the European empires (British, French, Dutch, Belgian, and Portuguese) were gone; some fifty new independent nations, arising from this dissolution, joined the United Nations between 1960 and 1980.

GLOBALIZATION

During the summer of 2018, two wealthy white men met in Palm Beach, Florida, to negotiate the merger of their two companies. The house where they met belongs to one of the men, whose business is headquartered in Toronto. The other man lives in Mauritius in the Indian Ocean and owns homes in Wyoming and London, while his business headquarters are in Jersey in the Channel Island. Although the men's lives are anchored in these various locations, the focus of their discussion was faraway Africa—where the merger of Barrick Gold and Rangold Resources was intended to improve the mining of African gold. It is natural to assume that the mine workers are mostly Africans and that the majority of the investors are not. Time will tell whether the benefits of creating local jobs resulting in a growing economy are a fair trade for the foreigners' returns on their investments in the exploitation of natural resources—or whether this is simply another form of the previous colonization model. Is the economic advantage foreign investments may provide worth the cultural interference that changing modes may inflict on the population, its social structure and its traditions?

Colonialism in its previous overt form has officially ceased, and the Scramble for Africa would now seem obscene. However, a new international intervention into local affairs appears to be entirely acceptable as it is usually worded as an argument for sharing resources and benefiting native populations. For instance, the World Bank, whose official mission is "to end extreme poverty and promote shared prosperity in a sustainable way" fulfills its two goals through loans to individuals and businesses. However, it does so as bank, not as a charity. While it removes the stigma of the latter it also imposes the duties and constraints of the former, facilitating an intrusion into local affairs that many see as inappropriate.

In some cases, foreign involvement has had an overall positive influence in most aspects of a country's economy, such as Japan immediately after World War II. Japan's situation was dismal and the economic objective was to catch up to the rest of the developed world. Under the guidance of the Allied force (the General Headquarters) all efforts were directed towards democratization on the political and economic fronts. The United States' influence led to the establishment of the Fair Trade Law and the Economic Power Excessive Concentration Elimination Law in 1947, and to American-style market rules such as anti-trust and securities exchange laws. There has naturally been an equally radical evolution on the societal and cultural fronts, and few countries have changed as much as Japan. While the Japanese economic recovery has often been described as miraculous, it is also noteworthy that Japan was a defeated and conquered nation in no position to object.

As the goals of the World Bank demonstrate, the West is ever conscious of its earlier shameful exploitation of underdeveloped countries, and many international organizations have been established to protect them from further economic abuses. Nevertheless, many argue that multinational corporations are also echoing the actions of those who came earlier to acquire land and displace people. Although invited by local governments and usually generating profits at the higher levels of local society, their presence does not always benefit ordinary people. For instance, a timber plantation owned by a British company (The New Forest Company) caused the eviction of 22,000 people in Uganda. In the Philippines, the army is often deployed to protect an increasing number of mining companies from hostile locals. Despite local protests, governments of developing countries usually believe that the benefits of foreign investment more than offset individual inconvenience.

The two main economic powers influencing development in Africa today are Russia and China, both with the advantage of never having colonized it and having in fact supported its emancipation from Western European control. The trade volume between Africa and China, in particular, has grown from $10 billion in 2000 to $75 billion worth of contracts in 2014, with a further pledge for $60 billion for projects in a variety of fields. A Forum of China–Africa Cooperation (FOCAC) is held every three years, but Chinese expansion is severely criticized, notably by the United States. Peter Navarro, Director of Trade and Manufacturing Policy in the Trump government, said in his book, *Death by China*, "[China's] million-man army is moving relentlessly across Africa and Latin America locking down strategic natural resources, locking up emerging markets, and locking out the United States…"

Indeed, China, through its One Belt One Road initiative expects to extend its economic supremacy over ASEAN (ten countries grouped into the Association of Southeast Asian Nations) and impose its economic and potentially cultural influence over parts of Africa.

SLAVERY HAS DISAPPEARED OR, RATHER, IT flourishes in many parts of the world under other names: cheap labour, domestic servitude, sex trafficking, forced and bonded labour, and even child labour. Developed countries mostly stand to benefit from these antiquated practices and are *de facto* complicit with local entrepreneurs and exploiters who organize the workforce. Many Western firms that sign contracts with businesses in developing nations plead ignorance of living and working conditions, but usually vow to improve them when confronted with the reality and the attendant publicity. Notably, when the working conditions imposed on the garment workers of the Rana Plaza disaster were made public, more than two hundred international companies (including American Outfitters, Abercrombie & Fitch, Zara and H&M)

signed the Accord on Fire and Building Safety in Bangladesh in the hope of preventing new tragedies.

A similar commitment occurred earlier in 1995, after two young Canadians exposed the use of child labour in the carpet-weaving industry. Twelve-year old Craig Kielburger and his brother Marc took action following the murder of a child slave who had escaped from a Pakistani carpet factory. There had been reports that some of the main exporters to the US and Europe, notably Germany, were using carpets made mostly through child labour. But the Kielburgers' campaign drew the attention of ordinary consumers to child abuse and slavery. It resulted in the creation of the Indian Rugmark Foundation, which monitors carpet factories to ensure that no children are employed, and the creation of several product consumer labels: Rugmark, STEP, Care & Fair and Kaleen (whose label reads, "A portion of the proceeds of this sale is going to the rehabilitation of children").

In the West, there is a desire among ordinary people, aware of the tremendous disparity between themselves and what was known as the Third World, to do the 'right' thing. For instance, the Fair Trade movement was initiated almost simultaneously in the United States (through Ten Thousand Villages) and Europe (through Oxfam) in concert with local organizations to help local producers achieve optimum trading conditions while improving social and environmental standards in the regions where the goods are manufactured or the produce is grown. The first European Work Shops conference took place in 1984 and today an ever-growing range of handicrafts and commodities from developing countries receive Fair Trade certification. As well as providing northern outlets to over a million southern workers, there is a strong program of raising awareness and advocacy to support trade injustices and serious imbalances of power in the workplace.

However, consumers continue to call for cheaper goods and corporations continue to meet the demand. The manufacturing work, featuring extremely low salaries and less than ideal conditions, takes place at the other end of the world, sight unseen. And, just as slave trading was once in the hands of Africans, so is the supervision of sweat shops left to local businessmen. When events like the collapse of Rana Plaza create waves of support for workers, and potentially serious negative economic consequences to corporations, conditions improve. But another disaster, another mass shooting, another scandal takes our attention away and our sympathy focuses elsewhere, or we become apathetic or distracted. Soon, things are back to normal—we consume more, complain about the prices, and the corporations respond accordingly.

No one is innocent, even if many of us try to ease our conscience by contributing to international health and educational organizations, supporting cooperatives granting small loans to women, or even buying the odd goat for an African family. Yet, even our good intentions can have unintended consequences, as when we tire of barely used clothes and give them to local charities that partly support themselves by selling them in bulk, mainly to sub-Saharan Africa. The enormous influx of used clothing into African market places has meant that local manufacturers can no longer compete. It is both an economic loss whose impact is yet to be fully measured and also an important cultural one as long-established native costumes with their own traditions lose out on the omnipresent T-shirts, blue jeans and ill-fitting coats.

So, are Western consumers the real source of the dreadful working conditions in the developing world? Or are they an essential source of income that, however slowly, lifts the disadvantaged out of poverty? In 1992, while in Bangkok, I succumbed to the lure of the 24-hour suit proposed by my hotel, torn between what I suspected were the working conditions of the tailors and seamstresses (I realize now than my suspicions were actually optimistic) and the thought that my modest contribution would provide an income for them. Today, I would attempt to get closer to the sources and buy some local product that would benefit more directly its actual manufacturer.

Future American president Theodore Roosevelt, then Governor of the State of New York, thought 'The White Man's Burden' was poor poetry but made "good sense from the expansion point of view." It gave colonizers the rationalization they needed to justify their imperial ambitions as a moral duty. While modern exploitation in no way matches the cruelty of previous versions, disasters like the collapse of Rana Plaza remind us that the developing world, as before, can be the source of immense wealth to other countries with little benefit to itself. Morality is not such a hard taskmaster that its voice cannot be muted, at least temporarily.

CHAPTER FOUR

VOX POPULI

IN JULY 2018, A LARGE BALLOON floated above Parliament Square in London. The six-metre tall snarling baby—orange-faced with tiny hands (one holding a smartphone) and wearing a diaper held with a large safety pin—was instantly recognizable. The balloon was the only Trump in attendance among the crowds in London that day, and was greeted with much rejoicing. The organizers of the controversial American president's visit may have been taken by surprise when it became clear that the 'special relationship' between the US and the UK did not extend to the incumbent president. The cheers expected to greet the leader of a friendly nation would have turned into very vocal booing had the real Trump shown himself. Plans for the visit were changed and, in the end, Donald Trump restricted his time in London to the night of his arrival.

PROTEST

Public protests and taking to the streets have long been the most visible expression of *vox populi*, the people's voice, and have been used to address concerns of all kinds, many spawned by poverty and hunger. The Women's March from Paris to Versailles in October 1789, started by a few women calling for a more accessible price for bread, their staple food, quickly gathered some 7,000 people, mostly women, who marched all the way to Versailles in pouring rain, brandishing pitchforks and shouting their demands.

During the early part of the twentieth century and the Great Depression, the Hunger Marches in the United Kingdom drew crowds to Parliament to make their claims heard. In small Canadian towns, people gathered in front of post offices that, as federal buildings, were imbued with a semblance of officialdom. The numbers were greater in the United States and the needs even more difficult to meet, but the same pattern of public demand and demonstrations occurred. In both North American countries, 'riding the rails' gave protesters the mobility to search for work while they carried their message of need across the country.

More recently, and arising from the same sense of powerlessness, the Occupy Wall Street movement spread to several cities around the world with the same righteous claim against greedy bankers, venal politicians, opportunistic or mean-spirited government cuts and the increasing worldwide gap between the rich and the poor.

Vox populi does not always reflect the opinions of the majority, but it draws attention to matters that would otherwise remain hidden. None of its manifestations are discreet and well-behaved affairs—the point being precisely to make noise and draw as much attention as possible to the plights of hunger, poverty and inequality, or any cause it supports. Vox populi is always as loud as it can be and has, on occasion, been accompanied by spectacular gestures.

- The suffragettes demonstrated noisily in the streets of England before World War I, loudly defying all social conventions and putting themselves at risk to obtain the right to vote. Their cause received dramatic public attention when Emily Davison walked out on the track at the 1913 Derby and was killed by the king's racehorse. The suffragettes partially succeeded in achieving their goals in 1918 and more fully in 1928.

- The powerful marches of the Civil Rights movement in the United States during the 1950s and 1960s. The 1965 marches from Selma to the Alabama state capital of Montgomery remain iconic. First repelled with billy clubs and tear gas, accompanied by violence that culminated in the Bloody Sunday of March 7, 1965, they found a focus in several leaders, notably Luther Martin King, Jr. Under President Lyndon Johnson's pressure, these efforts eventually led to the adoption of the Voting Rights Act of 1965.

- In the end of the 1960s, campuses across the United States attacked the same president on another matter as they reverberated with chants of "Hey, hey, LBJ! How many kids did you kill today?" These demonstrations against the Vietnam War, mostly triggered by the success of the 1968 North Vietnamese Tet Offensive against both South Vietnamese and American troops, divided America. The tragic shooting of four protesting students at Kent State University by the Ohio National Guard resulted in a shift of public opinion.

- The early Pride parades were relatively sombre political protests, but over the years have developed into colourful affairs, celebrating lesbian, gay, bisexual, transgender and intersex culture and pride with extravagant costumes, music and dancing. Underlying the annual celebrations, political activism remains, drawing attention to the important message of extending legal rights (such as same-sex marriage) to all.

All of these demonstrations were charged with the same motives and followed the same pattern. First, they drew attention to a situation they believed to be full of disorder and caused by either undefined or specific bad intentions. In reaction, and to increase pressure, protesters created even more disorder through marching crowds, extravagant music or solemn silence, acts of vandalism (breaking store windows, upending or burning cars, looting) and riots when crowds soon became uncontrollable. The ultimate goal is to re-establish order, but in a different form, through friction and conflict, both violent and non-violent, with the hope of achieving a more satisfactory status.

Marches or physical demonstrations are not the only means of applying pressure. Political and social force can be applied through less overt methods, such as petitions, letter-writing campaigns and boycotts. Social media platforms have provided an ever-increasing voice to thousands of organizations who now vent on Facebook and Twitter instead of taking to the streets.

Protest may also take a passive-aggressive form—a refusal to participate or, in the more drastic cases, to eat. This was a strategy employed with some success by English women in the suffragette movement. Mahatma Gandhi's seventeen long solo fasts during the Indian freedom movement, mostly during the 1930s and 1940s, were peaceful but effective. Far more provocative were the hunger strikes in the Maze Prison of 1981, violent events driven by the demands of IRA prisoners to be treated as political prisoners rather than as criminals. Ten protesters, including their leader Bobby Sands, died before the strike was called off.

Prison inmates, estranged from the mainstream, have their own codes, particularly among those in solitary confinement (which pushes imprisonment an ultimate step further) for whom communication and the expression of claims and complaints is usually one-sided. In an earlier study, I examined graffiti written by prisoners in solitary confinement cells in a Canadian penitentiary and discovered several 'conversations' written by successive occupants, ranting against the faceless system that oppressed them:

- Justice is a word not reconiced by the Establishment
- Whoever wrote the Criminal Code should be Procuted & killes
- using an anonom for the word torture we can say the Canadian Penitentiary System!
- Abolish Solitary Confinement
- the whole dam system SUCKS!!!!!! Sign up her if you want to change the system (signed, in succession, by men who would perhaps never see each other: Ziggy, Rick, Moose, Billy, Darren, Steve)

These claims of unfairness and torment (but not of innocence) were an expression of carceral vox populi that, combined with other forms of advocacy, recently led to a successful challenge of the practice of solitary confinement.

CHARIVARI

The protest in London was both a spontaneous reaction against Trump's policies and a well-orchestrated event planned for maximum effect. In addition to flying the Trump baby blimp, organizers of the concurrent Bring the Noise rally encouraged protesters and marchers to create "a wall of sound" by taking "pots and pans out of the kitchen…and onto the streets, banging to show our disapproval and claiming our political voice in public space." In Glasgow and Edinburgh, the press reported that the protest would take the form of a "carnival of resistance," including country fete-style games mocking the president.

On all counts—effigy, noise, protest, intent to shame—the British crowds were part of a long tradition that had ordinary people acting on their opinions and righting what they thought was wrong. They could not do anything to change American politics under Trump, but they intended to show their disapproval by exploiting an old tradition—charivari.

Also known as shivaree or chivaree, this tradition of creating a loud and often mocking din, has a number of alternative names in the British Isles: 'lewbelling' (from 'lewd' and 'belling,' roaring and bellowing), 'tin-panning,' 'skimmington' (named for a large wooden spoon, the weapon of choice for husband-beating wives), and 'stang riding' (referring to the long pole men carried on men's shoulders to transport a heavy burden such as a transgressor). In Spain, it is called *caceralozo*, from the word for saucepans. This noisy custom is hundreds of years old and originally combined self-righteousness with a sense of sanctimonious mischief as the participants derived much enjoyment from inflicting humiliation on others. Prevalent during the Middle Ages in small communities where everyone reputedly knew everyone else's affairs and felt entitled to comment on them, noisy groups intent on preserving community values loudly and crudely serenaded those who were deemed to have violated common standards or sensitivities: unfaithful husbands or wives, widows remarrying too soon, matches between people of unusually disparate ages or stations in life, obvious cases of wife (or husband) beating, or women bearing children out of wedlock. Anything that could make a noise was used with great advantage to accompany the shouting: horns, pots and pans, skillets and spoons, kettles and other kitchen implements, the choice of instrument indicative of a preponderance of women participants, although young men also took a particularly active part in the proceedings.

When signs of weakness were involved, such as a man reputedly not satisfying his wife, mockery was a favourite weapon. In cases of adultery, easily recognizable effigies of the guilty parties were paraded around or exposed for several days before being burned. In other cases, more violent manhandling occurred and those considered guilty of wrongdoing were dragged into the streets by small mobs uttering threats of even greater violence. Public opinion was not forgiving, and the fear of public exposure and humiliation was effective in maintaining 'decent' behaviour, acting as a deterrent where private counselling or unpublicized sanctions might not have succeeded. At its most extreme, charivari led its victims to self-exile or even to suicide.

The power of shunning resides in separating individuals from the groups that have sustained and nurtured them from childhood. Among traditional cultures, it was often tantamount to issuing a death sentence since exiles could not survive in total isolation. Ostracism still exists today as a punishment for deviating from the norm, primarily through religious disaffiliation: excommunication from Christian churches and shunning from a number of religions or sects (Jehovah's Witnesses, the Church of Scientology, even the gentler Amish). Shunned individuals who were brought up in tight communities with little formal education, far away from modern stress and influences, struggle to fit in when forced into the outside world.

In Canada, shunning is formally practised by a fundamentalist church, a local offshoot of the Mormon Church, known as Bountiful (a location in British Columbia where it is practised), and the leading polygamous community in Canada. But informal, secular examples continue to exist as when, for example, many urban communities, annoyed at seeing prostitutes propositioning customers on their streets, started campaigns known as Shame the Johns. These consisted of loudly drawing attention to male customers, and publicly posting their photographs and their cars' licence plates, sometimes with the unobtrusive support of police, media and community leaders. This only stopped when the streetwalkers began operating in more remote areas, where the traffic no longer offended the populated neighbourhoods but where they exposed themselves to greater danger.

BULLYING

Organizers of charivari and their participants thoroughly enjoy their sense of power over their victims, while hiding behind the excuse of promoting morality and the good of the community. Bullies, on the other hand, revel in their power without invoking either. Their only interest is boosting their egos through belittling others.

As social animals, we work at attaining and maintaining a certain position in the social hierarchy. To establish our eligibility and form relationships with others, we stress our credentials, including ancestry, appearance, profession, possessions, beliefs and character traits that make us particularly desirable company. In doing so, we expose ourselves to the possibility of rejection and, perhaps even worse, mockery. We suffer from insults against the integrity of the image we wish to project. This is particularly true of adolescents who have yet to confirm their identity or establish their accomplishments.

There have been tragic cases of young people who committed suicide, unable to bear the violent rejection and the mockery they faced either in person or on social media. In Canada, two suicides at the extreme ends of the country—Amanda Todd in British Columbia (2012) and Rehtaeh Parsons in Nova Scotia (2013) awoke the country to the consequences of online harassment through social media. Their helplessness against a hidden enemy and the relentless humiliation they endured highlighted the loneliness and impotence of victims of cyberbullying. In other cases, bullying manifested in its traditional form. The suicide of 15-year old Jamie Hubley (2011) in Ottawa, a result of sustained torment at school, led to legislated anti-bullying programs and legal protection for gay–straight alliances in Ontario schools.

While legislation and other adult interventions have helped, enlisting children to influence their peers has been more effective. In France, the organisation SOS Racisme created a movement in 1984: *Touche pas à mon pote* (Don't lay a finger on my buddy), whose symbol was a halting hand raised in a stop sign. In 2007, two Nova Scotia boys donned pink T-shirts to confuse bullies harassing other boys for wearing less-than-macho clothing. The initiative spread and Boys and Girls Clubs created pink T-shirts with the motto Bullying Stops Here. As more schools became involved, the United Nations declared May 4 Anti-Bulling Day. Such movements can be seen as an alternate form of charivari, retaining mockery but substituting symbols for cymbals to rectify nefarious behaviour.

Adults are also vulnerable to the devastating effect of malignant and totally unwarranted attacks, the innocent victims of conspiracy theories and 'fake news.' Even President Obama had to show publicly his birth certificate to prove he was born an American citizen. The trend, started on online by ultra-right forums, reached its full power with the site known as Infowars run by Alex Jones. The 'news' it spreads was obviously dubious, but many people caught in the process became targets of its attacks, some even losing their professional and personal reputations.

One case of harassment involved the father of one of the twenty children murdered at Sandy Hook Elementary School in 2012, a mass killing that Infowars called a hoax. As he tried to re-establish the truth, showing proof of his child's death, the father became the target of a campaign run by Infowars followers through hundreds of pages of hateful web content. "I don't think there's any one word that fits the horror of it," he wrote. "It's a phenomenon in the age in which we are, a modern day witch-hunt. It's a form of mass delusion."

Similarly, when Dr. Paul Offitt attempted to highlight the dangers of the anti-vaccine movement by setting up the Vaccine Education Center at the Children's Hospital of Philadelphia, he was vilified, called both Satan and Nazi by anti-vaxxers. Protesters appeared outside his medical practice carrying signs branding him as terrorist. "It was devastating. It hurt, it always hurt, it still hurts," he said.

Others have been victims to the most outrageous 'fake news' accusations—notably James Alefantis, accused in 2016 of running a pedophile ring, masterminded by Hillary Clinton, in the basement of his pizza restaurant (which does not have a basement). He received abusive messages on the internet, urged on by Infowars and Alex Jones who suggested people go and investigate for themselves; one man did, carrying an AK-15 rifle. Alefantis asked his persecutors why they hated him so much. "I realized they live in fear. That there is a sense of abandonment and powerlessness where young people online believe the government is conspiring against them or stealing their children… It feels at times that things are out of control, that hate is on the rise." A 2014 University of Chicago study estimated that half of Americans believe in at least one conspiracy theory; among the most familiar ones is the belief that the 9/11 attack was an American government hit job. By the fall of 2018, the number had risen to 61 percent.

Everyday bullies, who know exactly what they are doing, occasionally attempt to pass off their attacks as mere jokes. There is, for instance, an internet site listing "75 funny insults which are incredibly brutal." Gratuitous brutality is indeed their common characteristic as they belittle the looks, intelligence and ancestry of the people at the receiving end of these attacks.

Once, race was the insult of choice. Michele Mendelssohn's recent book about Oscar Wilde (*Making Oscar Wilde*, 2018) reveals the most extraordinary level of baseness and insult shown by some of his American audience while he was on a speaking tour in 1882. These were educated men at prestigious universities who objected to his accent and manner of dress and deemed his delivery and topic (the English Renaissance) boring, so they mocked him without pity. Wilde also caused offence by his birth: in this society made up of immigrants, the Irish were on the bottom rung of the hierarchal ladder, ranked as low as the despised negroes. His audiences in the Midwest and deep South, in particular, were only too willing to associate the two. Official commentary on his tour showed the same trend and seem incredible today. For instance, a Currier and Ives lithograph entitled 'The Aesthetic Craze' shows two black women and Wilde drawn with an afro hairstyle, thick lips and a brown skin. The caption reads "What's de matter wid de Nigga? Why Oscar you's gone wild." Not satisfied with what was considered the worst possible insult, the comparison then reached into the animal world. A woman in New York told him that she was glad to have finally seen a gorilla and the *Washington Post* described him as "the Wild Man of Borneo," while *Harper's Weekly* published a picture of a monkey drawn to resemble Wilde.

The widespread and gratuitous attacks on Wilde were an early example of celebrity trolling. Those who are seen as successful and who owe their reputation to publicity become targets for mockery. People feel perfectly entitled to underline and criticize what they perceive as shortcomings, covering the gamut of human foibles. Such gratuitous yet punitive actions have become part of everyday life. Magazines and online sites detail every actual or imagined flaw of celebrities' physique or character and, while the racial attacks against Wilde would now be punishable by law, paparazzi photographs taken on private beaches routinely show excessive adipose tissue and cellulite; today's fatso is yesterday's negro, with the same degree of nastiness and gratuity in the attack.

The bias is not an imaginary one. The Rudd Center for Food Policy and Obesity at the University of Connecticut reports that 54 percent of overweight adults feel they are stigmatized by co-workers, while 69 percent believe their doctors attribute all their symptoms to obesity and do not bother investigating their conditions further.

Insults are damaging when they attack people's self-image and reputation. Yet, they have their place in society, and some cultures have created a built-in system of 'joking relationships' that help relieve tension. Insults, meted out with the utmost care, can denote levels of friendship and inclusion within certain groups. While I was researching modes of expression among street women, one inform-ant defined for me their self-imposed limits: "I have this friend that's half-Indian. I call her, 'Hey you, fuckin' waggon burner!' and she calls me 'Puerto Rican cunt!' and people who see us together think we're gonna fight. But we're friends and we know just how far we can go." A well-administered joke, even if crude and insulting, expressed by a person permitted to do so by rank, relationship or cultural agreement may go a long way in maintaining established order, provided everyone recognizes and accepts the process.

CURSES

Bullies and internet trolls seldom use subtle language, since they want their words to insult and hurt their victims. There was a time when those who really intended to shock others did so by attacking the sanctity of God. Profanity, which seems merely rude today, was profoundly offensive, a desecration of what religion held holy and society believed to be fundamental.

In the Middle Ages, swearing threatened a basic social value, and being guilty of it was a serious matter. Henry I, the son of William the Conqueror, ordered the following fines for swearing in proximity of the royal residence: a duke, forty shillings; a lord, twenty shillings; a squire, ten shillings; a yeoman, three shillings and four pence; a page (who likely owned nothing save for his backside), a whipping.

Across the Channel, Louis IX of France (also known as Saint Louis and presumably even less sympathetic to those who used the name of the Lord in vain) decreed that swearers must be "branded upon the face with a hot iron for a perpetual memorial of their crime," while later ordaining that they should be "set in a public place in the high stocks...similar in form and more of punishment to that inflicted upon cutpurses in England."

Over time, conventions and language changed. By the eighteenth century, the choicest expletive in the general population was 'bloody.' Often later misconstrued as a swear word, the term derived from 'blood,' a young aristocratic rowdy, and did not actually refer to the blessed blood of Christ, nor was it an alteration of 'By Our Lady' (as is occasionally asserted). Rather than blasphemy or obscenity, bloody was mostly used for emphasis. 'Bugger' and 'fucking,' with their sexual connotations, had by then also become common curses. Neither were ever printed in full and were mostly represented by asterisks. What passed for profanity and rude language in the eighteenth and nineteenth centuries is still considered as such in the twenty-first.

The accepted characteristic of swearing is the use of taboo words (like fuck, shit or damn), not literally but in formulaic fashion to clearly signal the speaker's state of mind. While there may be enormous variations in the words themselves across languages, these principles remain generally valid. What is taboo in a culture—be it religion, sex, madness, bodily excretions—serves as the source of profanity.

Swearing has other functions than attacking the underpinnings of society: swearing can be abusive, intended to offend or intimidate; it can be cathartic, expressed when banging one's thumb with a hammer, for example; it can be dysphemistic, deliberately using an offensive word instead of a milder one to rally or bond; swearing can be emphatic, merely used to underline the nature of an object or an event; or it can be idiomatic—such as adding 'fucking' to every other word in a sentence. Only the abusive use of swearing intends to do what it does: disconcert and offend; the other usages are simply manners of speech, become ordinary due to the erosion of language.

Speakers sometimes attempt to soften the polluting effect of cursing by sanitizing the profanity: Shit is daintily transformed into sugar or shucks and fuck into fudge or (as former Canadian Prime Minister Pierre Trudeau once suggested) 'fuddle duddle.' This fools no one and the pollution remains by implication. The British navy's Sweet FA refers to Fanny Adams, a murdered girl, who was chosen for her initials, which imply Fuck All.

Any words can be effectively substituted for 'bad language' if pronounced with enough force, such as *Tintin*'s Captain Haddock's "Billions of bilious blue blistering barnacles!!!" Similarly, to avoid the constraints of television's bans on swear words, new words—frak, blurgh, jackweed, shazbot, smurf—are used to the same effect, their offending intention deriving from either the context or the intonation.

In the past, victims of curses and insults might challenge their tormentor to a duel to restore their honour and reputation. The last fatal duel in England (1852) involved two French political exiles, inflamed by passion for their causes. In France, the last officially recorded duel took place in 1897, while 1873 saw the tradition end in Canada. Section 71 of the current Criminal Code of Canada prohibits "challenges or attempts by any means to provoke another person to fight a duel." Its violation incurs a maximum penalty of up to two years in jail. However, in countries with a strong duel-ling tradition, there have been a few modern challenges issued and accepted (in 1949 and 1967 in France and 1994 in Great Britain).

Today, punishment for insults and other attacks to a person's reputation are the responsibility of recognized authorities rather than private individuals. Insults of the nature suffered by Oscar Wilde would now be called hate speech in Canada and prosecuted under the Criminal Code provisions against the spreading of hate propaganda. While the Canadian Charter of Rights and Freedoms guarantees the right to "freedom of thought, belief, opinion, and expression, including freedom of the press and other media of communication," this right is not absolute and it excludes criminal activities such as perjury, the distribution of obscene material and the hate speech of many bullies. Equally illegal is defamation (libel or slander) that leads to harming a person's reputation through false statements to a third party. Finally, to ensure that people are not unnecessarily offended, Section175 of the Criminal Code makes it a criminal offence to "cause a disturbance in or near a public place" by "swearing...or using insulting or obscene language."

HUE AND CRY

Charivari began as an *ad hoc* medieval custom for enforcing social norms. Closely related to it but with more legitimacy, 'hue and cry' was an accepted method for applying the rule of law in the absence of an organized police force. It first appeared in Anglo-Norman documents of the thirteenth century when King Edward's Statute of Winchester (1265) charged people with the duty of shouting and giving the alarm whenever they saw a crime in progress and then chasing the criminal through the streets. The intervention of ordinary people and their apprehension of criminals were usually quite successful.

The statute and its later amendments (1586 and 1735) were repealed in Britain in 1827. However, the concept survives as today's 'citizen's arrest' and through community organizations intended to assist law enforcement. Some, such as Neighbourhood Watch, Block Parents and Canadian Citizens on Patrol, are sanctioned while others border on vigilantism and are generally discouraged. Creep Catchers, for example, pose as minors in chat rooms and on dating sites in order to identify adults looking for sex with minors and then post videos of them. Creep Catchers may feel they are on the side of good and purity fighting corruption and dissonance, and thus having the higher moral ground, but they participate equally in an unsavoury, dangerous and disruptive activity.

Victims themselves, when denied redress through the courts, can raise the alarm by telling their stories. Among them are the former Korean 'comfort women' forced to service Japanese soldiers during World War II. Deeply ashamed and facing an administration that denied the existence of military brothels, only 239 of them made their voices heard. These old women, a handful alive today, still stand in protest outside the Japanese embassy in Seoul every Wednesday.

Among the silent witnesses are also the marching mothers of the Argentinian men and women who 'disappeared' during the Argentina's Dirty War (1976–1983). Suspected dissidents and those deemed subversive—social workers, students, militants, trade unionists, writers, journalists, artists and all left-wing activists— were subjected to gross human rights abuses including kidnapping, torture and murder. It is estimated that as many as 50,000 civilians, known as *Los Desaparecidos*, disappeared during this time. Among those arrested were pregnant women who were kept alive until their babies were born. These children were then illegally adopted by families supporting the regime, mostly in the military. The Grandmothers of the Plaza de Mayo *(Asociación Civil Abuelas de Plaza de Mayo)* is a human rights organization founded in 1977, devoted to identifying these children and attempting to return them to their biological families. So far, they have succeeded in locating some 10 percent of the estimated five hundred children kidnapped and illegally adopted.

In recent years we have witnessed contemporary examples of hue and cry. In 2011, French politician Dominique Strauss-Khan lost any chance he might have had at running for the presidency after being accused of raping a maid at a New York hotel, an early clue that sexual misconduct by powerful men would no longer be tolerated. The public mood was confirmed when similar allegations emerged first again Bill Cosby, an admired comedian, then against movie producer Harvey Weinstein. Dubbed 'Hollywood's biggest scandal,' the Weinstein case sparked a sweeping movement that exploded on the world scene, known in English as #MeToo (showing commonality of purpose through different experiences) and in French as #*Balance-ton-porc* (the far more violent 'Rat out your swine').

Women started loudly denouncing the men who had used their power to sexually abuse and harass them. So powerful was the movement from the start that it soon generated an offshoot, #Time's Up, started in February 2018 by Hollywood celebrities to provide legal assistance to women wishing to attest to their own experience. Within a month, it had raised $20 million and gathered more than two hundred volunteer lawyers.

Faithful to the principles of hue and cry, the main focus of #Me Too and #Time's Up was to denounce sexual exploiters' behaviour, alert others to it, and hold alleged perpetrators accountable. With a speed that the legal process might envy, the negative effects of public opinion quickly resulted in the firing of the accused men from their positions or in their resignations. It was accompanied by much disbelief that these respected and powerful men could be guilty of such despicable behaviour and abuse of power, which they usually denied, although some promptly resigned, not wishing to be exposed further, and a few others acknowledged and apologized. There was also another type of disbelief—that of the accused men themselves, surprised to see that a behaviour they had never questioned, that they thought befitted their status and power, would now be their undoing.

The shift in popular opinion is perhaps best measured by a question: What happened in the interval between the confrontation of Anita Hill and Clarence Thomas in 1991 and that of Christine Blasey Ford and Brett Kavanaugh in 2018? In both cases, a woman of good social and professional standing accused a man seeking appointment to the Supreme Court of the United States of sexual misconduct. The accusations were similar and the animosity against the women by those in power often sounded much the same, but their impacts differed greatly. Anita Hill certainly had her supporters, but her accusation did not fit into current thinking and may have even created some embarrassment among people who did not wish to think or speak of such matters. While Blaisey Ford was no more successful in validating her claim than Hill had been twenty-seven years earlier, the hearings, though partisan, resonated in an environment where sexual misconduct by men in power has become common and acknowledged currency.

The immediate success and following of #MeToo demonstrated how deeply women felt about their state of subservient infantilization and sexual exploitation in the work force. Almost a year after it started, daily articles in the press were still addressing various aspects of the scandal.

Their tone was frequently vindictive, raising complicated questions. Had the movement gone too far? Have innocent men and their families been hurt by false accusations? What are the appropriate consequences for behaviours that are inappropriate but not criminal? The Blaisey Ford–Kavanaugh case raised questions about the burden of proof, particularly when incidents occurred decades earlier. Most notably, should the men be forgiven and, if so, when? In the absence of due process, there is no mechanism for either punishment or formal atonement.

HUMAN NATURE SEEMS TO HAVE CHANGED little when dealing with such basic emotions as anger at (or fear of) the behaviour of others, followed by the urge to 'correct' them so they may act more conventionally and re-establish proper social or moral order, even when the methods of correction can be worse or far more violent than the acts to which the reformers object. In China, for instance, computerized facial recognition has been used to shame jaywalkers, a uniquely modern combination of charivari and hue and cry. Technological control in China now regulates citizen's movements across the country, preventing travel for a substantial number of people unwilling or unable to behave as expected.

While social media, particularly Twitter, has provided a new global platform, the process used to decry the behaviour of others follows a traditional pattern. First, there is identification of dubious behaviour that must be amended (whether truly evil as in the case of the *desaparecidos* of Argentina, or politically motivated in the case of the Trump visit). The next step is the characterization of the misdeed. Whom does it offend? A few? Many? Everyone? Are legal sanctions available or must ordinary citizens take up the cause? Then comes the gathering of like-minded supporters, for these means of social correction are a group manifestation, both to provide protection in numbers and to intensify its impact. Next comes the decision on the manner of protest (silent marches, banging on pans, burning effigies, chasing the culprits through the street, naming names through the media) generally influenced by political and social contexts; and, finally, comes the execution.

Public opinion—whether protest, charivari or hue and cry—is often the weapon of the righteous. Those who exercise it are convinced they are acting for the best, regardless of the cost to their victims. They may suspect that their cause would not qualify for more serious consideration, or they may know, as in the case of bullying or trolling, that their position is indefensible. Ordinary people may resort to it when no other means are available, or if they decide that public demonstrations will be more effective than legal remedy. One way or another, vox populi, whether strident or muted, is always heard.

CHAPTER FIVE

A BODY'S WORTH

IN 2014, A FREEDOM OF INFORMATION request determined that a British hospital, Walsall Manor, had inadvertently stored the fetal remains from eighty-six abortions and miscarriages for up to four years. An independent inquiry determined that a series of administrative oversights led to the remains not being released for cremation; there were no procedures for their proper disposal nor bereavement services available for the parents. The story was fundamentally shocking, because of the disregard for the sanctity of the body and thoughtless treatment of human remains. We believe that treating a human body carelessly, even in its embryonic form, is unacceptable.

Any human body—young and old, attractive or not, hale or puny, a source of pride or misery—is much the same as any other body: 65 percent oxygen, 18.5 percent carbon, 9.5 percent hydrogen, 3.2 percent nitrogen, 1.5 percent calcium, 1 percent phosphorus, 0.4 percent potassium, 0.3 percent sulphur, 0.2 percent each sodium and chlorine, 0.1 percent magnesium, and traces of several other elements. Yet, were we to put all these elements together, would we arrive at a human being? Even though the moment at which a fetus becomes a person is still passionately debated, it is clear that a person is more than the sum of their organic constituents. The presence of an *anima*—a spirit, a soul—is intrinsic to our conception of what constitutes a human being.

Descartes, in particular, influenced western thinking by conceiving this essential dualism as the interplay of our mental and physical substances. Mary Shelley explored similar themes in her 1818 novel

89

Frankenstein. The book's subtitle is *The Modern Prometheus*, refer-ring to the Titan of Greek mythology, who created man from clay and stole the all-powerful fire from the gods to give to mankind. When Victor Frankenstein, a passionate university student studying chemistry and natural philosophy, discovers the ravages of death and sees how "the worm inherited the wonders of the eye and brain," he resolves to create life. Naturally, the outcomes are disastrous, and the reader is left to ponder the nature of humanity, the power of scientific creation and whether humans should be trusted with it.

We cherish our bodies for themselves and as the hosts of our animas. We feed them, tend to their ailments, enjoy whatever plea-sures they give us and usually try to keep them functional and healthy as long as we can. As they age, we dread what may loom ahead since, as well as constituting our physical selves, they contain our dearest attribute—the way we think. But, while body and mind form an indi-visible union, their partnership is not always trouble-free. When, for instance, we feel unable to control our environment, we may instead exert our will over our bodies. This may manifest as various stress-related illnesses, eating disorders or self-harming such as cutting.

Any transaction involving our bodies is loaded with emotional meaning, whether we acknowledge it or not. Advancements in sci-ence have permitted us to transform our bodies into commodities in many ways: we can provide organs for those whose own have failed; we can opt to donate our corpse for scientific research; fertile wombs can grow embryos for those who cannot procreate; blood is easily donated and received by others, as are sperm and eggs. A more ancient trade has been the sale of bodies for transient pleasure, loaning them out to the lonely, the loveless and those who have too much imagination for their partners. Some of these transactions we may find morally repellent, others seduce us into seeing a form of transcendence.

As we consider the potential uses for our flesh and bones, we must confront taboos imposed by tradition, society, religion, philosophy and laws. Intimate or invasive physical exchanges are never inconsequential and, particularly when one of the bodies is dead, the innate or cultural apprehension may be immensely intensified. For each of us, whether giver or taker of body parts, there is always an ethical decision to be made.

CANNIBALISM

Several traditional cultures once consumed the flesh of enemies killed in battle or of members of their own group who had died of natural causes, in order to either defile or incorporate their spirit. It was a troublesome topic for the anthropologists who studied these communities—they often admired the people, even as the cannibalism they practised was so deeply antithetical to their own culture.

Today, we consider cannibalism an inherently abhorrent act associated with mental illness, deep psychological trauma, or extreme emergencies when, faced with no other chance of survival, some may overcome their innate repugnance and eat human flesh. The Donner Party, trapped in snow on their way to California during the harsh winter of 1846–47, resorted to it, as did starving Russians during the siege of Stalingrad (August 1942–February 1943), after all edible animals had been consumed. In past centuries, when the perils of maritime navigation created extreme circumstances, the 'custom of the sea,' as it was known, was accepted as an unavoidable fact of life. While starving may not have been the acknowledged rule, it certainly was not the exception and large numbers of ships were commonly becalmed, lost at sea, or wrecked on shoals, and some owners' misguided sense of economy compounded the dangers of starvation. There are as many as thirty ships on which cannibalism was known to have been practised and the actual list to be much longer.

Going a step further and causing the death of a man (or boy, as was more often the case) to feed on his body was another reality of sea life. In 1759, *Gentleman's Magazine* reported on Captain Baron and his crew in the *Dolphin* sloop:

The captain and people declare that they had not had any ship provisions for upwards of three months; that they had eaten their dog, their cat, and all their shoes, and in short, everything that was eatable on board. Being reduced to the last extremity, they all agreed to cast lots for their lives, which accordingly they did; the shortest lot was to die, the next shortest to be the executioner. The lot fell upon one Antony Galatia, a passenger; they shot him through the head, which they cut off and threw overboard; they then took out his bowels and eat them, and afterwards eat all the remaining part of the body, which lasted but a very little while.

In theory, all being equal in this deadly choice, men were supposed to draw straws, the loser getting the shortest one. In practice, however, there was a hierarchy to the selection, the weakest and most vulnerable dying first. Neil Hanson in *The Custom of the Sea* (1999) lists the ranking as: slaves, then black men before white, women before men, passengers (as with Antony Galatia) before crew, unpopular crew members before the rest. Even within the crew a similar hierarchy prevailed: cabin boys (the most frequent case) and apprentices first, then 'idlers' (carpenters, cooks, and other specialists who did not keep watches and were not really seen as part of the crew).

A few instances of crews feeding on the bodies of their comrades were made public. In 1820, a whaleship found a small boat drifting off the Chilean coast with two men on board. Sitting among the bones of some of their former shipmates were Captain Pollard and a sailor, Charles Ramsdell, of the whaleship *Essex,* which had been rammed by a sperm whale three months earlier. Years later, Captain Pollard, talking about the events that occurred on the *Essex* to a missionary he met in Raiatea, said, "I can tell you no more, my head is on fire at the recollection. I hardly know what to say."

Another famous case was that of the yacht *Mignonette,* bought in England by an Australian who asked to have her delivered to Sydney. She sailed from Southampton in July 1884 with Captain Tom Dudley, mate Edwin Stephens, able seaman and ship's cook

Edmund 'Ned' Brooks, and ordinary seaman Richard Parker. They were beset by monstrous waves off the coast of Africa, and the *Mignonette,* having shown signs of weakness, ageing and lack of proper repairs from the beginning, sank. The four men escaped in a small boat and, without water or provision, eventually resorted to sacrificing the sickest—seventeen-year old Richard, who was already comatose after having drunk sea water. The others were all family men, a status that perhaps also weighed in the decision. When they were rescued, after drifting for twenty-four days, they were warmly welcomed back by the staff of the Sailor's Home. As was customary, they immediately reported the events to the Custom House and to the Board of Trade. The victim's brother publicly shook their hands after they had made their deposition.

To everyone's astonishment, the Home Office, upon receiving its copy of the report, issued an order for the men's arrest. The presiding judge, Baron Huddleston, laid the charge that they "feloniously, wilfully, and of their malice aforethought, did kill and murder one Richard Parker." In a similar case ten years earlier, the Home Office had charged survivors of the *Euxine* with manslaughter but decided to forego prosecution to protect the reputation of the ship's owner, a Member of Parliament. In that case, the charges were dropped and the sailors returned to sea after signing a pledge not to seek redress against the ship owner.

The cook and able seaman, Brooks, struck a deal to act with the prosecution but Captain Dudley and Stephens were tried for murder (instead of manslaughter). Sea people immediately sided with the crew, even hiring a lawyer for the men, while land people initially followed the lead of newspapers that wrote of "revolting actions," "cold-blooded narrative," "callous tragedies," "brutal destruction," "horrible repast" and "diabolical tradition." The accused pleaded not guilty but were sentenced to death (a statutory penalty) with a recommendation for mercy that, owing to strong popular support, was later commuted to six months in jail.

The outcome of the trial had lasting legal and practical consequences. Baron Huddleston had from the start dismissed the possible defences of necessity and self-defence, usually invoked and accepted in such cases, thus outlawing the traditional custom of the sea. Dudley bitterly remarked to his lawyer, "Never again will men return to these shores and freely confess what they have done." Indeed, only two, the crews of *Teckla* (1893) and the *Drot* (1899), ever did again—both times without legal consequences for the survivors.

Many sailors believed that eating human flesh was despicable and reduced them to a state of savagery, and the mere fact of hunger also did away with every sign of humanity they might otherwise have shown. Psychologists believe that in these circumstances (such as in the Nazi concentration camps), men form a feral community, the extreme stress forcing them to an almost animal state, driven by the most basic motivations.

As with other catastrophic events, including the plague and the French Revolution, folklore played a part in normalizing extraordinary circumstances. Cannibalism at sea, perhaps inspired by the dreadful wreck of the French flagship *Médusa* in 1816, filtered into a children's song and circle dance, its violent context obliterated along the way. *Il était un petit navire* (*There was a little ship*) relates how, after several weeks at sea without food, the cabin boy—on the point of drawing the short straw—was rescued through the miraculous intervention of thousands of small fish jumping into the boat.

Similarly, adults use satire to defuse cultural taboos. 'The Yarn of the Nancy Bell,' a poem written by W.S. Gilbert (of Gilbert and Sullivan) was rejected by *Punch* as being in poor taste but was published in *Fun* in March 1866. The humorous verse relates the tale the sole survivor of a shipwreck, whose joke is that he is "a cook and a captain bold, / And the mate of the Nancy brig, / And a bo'sun tight, and a midshipmite, / And the crew of the captain's gig."

Modern ships and their crews are connected through instant communication systems with their shipping companies and with whatever services might provide help, rendering the need for cannibalism at sea highly unlikely. However, the much-publicized crash of the Uruguayan Flight 571 in the Andes in 1972 shows it could still happen today. Of the forty-five people on board, eighteen died in the crash or soon afterwards. Ten days later, hearing on a portable radio that the search had been called off and faced with starvation, survivors agreed that they would eat the bodies of those who had previously died and had been kept frozen by the cold weather. They further agreed that, should they also die, the others would consume their bodies.

Seeing no hope of rescue, two of the twenty-seven survivors decide to attempt hiking out to seek whatever help they might find. After an arduous trek, they reached safety, and the alerted authorities were able to save the others, seventy-two days after the crash. The initial public horror at learning they had eaten their dead companions eventually subsided when it was accepted that they had no other choice. Once again, very special circumstances were deemed sufficient to justify normally aberrant behaviour.

PROSTITUTION

Cannibalism is the rarest and most extreme use of a human body by another. At the other end of the spectrum lies prostitution, "the world's oldest profession." It stands as a parody of a real act of love and, despite its prevalence, we still find the exchange of sex for money troubling. Even though many old-fashioned prostitutes, long in the trade, disclaim any notion of intimacy (for instance, refusing to kiss their clients), we find it difficult to accept sex as a basis for commercial transactions.

In societies where chastity was highly prized, prostitution was usually rife. The dichotomy is a familiar one, as women are sometimes thought to belong to only two groups: virgins (that might include virtuous mothers, for we know motherhood is sacred) or whores. Those words are usually evoked in capital letters since they really belong to archetypes.

In ancient Greece, for instance, the trade was very active and well regulated. In most cities and ports, brothels included both male and female prostitutes, while the clientele was usually male. At the same time, a wife's virtue and fidelity were sacrosanct; adultery was severely punished, and the wronged party could legitimately kill the offender if caught in the act.

Towards the end of the Roman Empire, around 400 CE, there were forty-six brothels in Rome for a population of some 70,000 (far more remarkably, there were also twenty-eight libraries). Men had free and open access to prostitutes but the women themselves (usually slaves or former slaves benefiting from few of the rights and advantages of Roman citizenship) were deemed to be of shameful character. By contrast, the inviolable Vestals Virgins, whose chastity was ensured by the prospect of being immured alive should they falter, were among the most respected members of society.

In straight-laced Victorian England, dominated by the image of a virtuously widowed monarch and *materfamilias*, the number of prostitutes was estimated at around 80,000 in London alone, according to an article of the *Lancet* in 1887. In an era when men in the fast-growing middle-class were expected to marry only when they could support a wife and family, many remained single until their middle years and provided an ample supply of clients. The sanctimonious Victorian age, as well as openly patronizing child labour, was guilty of closing its eyes to child prostitution, since the age of consent was thirteen and some prostitutes were even younger.

Nineteenth-century urbanization brought poverty, disease, over-crowding and a much greater proximity between rich and poor. Women who plied their trade on the street were highly visible and, in a prudish age, highly offensive. In Britain, the 1839 Vagrancy Act first attempted to deal with the problem, with no significant result. The Contagious Diseases Act (1864), introduced to reduce the transmission of venereal diseases, particularly syphilis, was somewhat more successful in curbing the evidence of prostitution when it closed down the public baths. America suffered from the same invasive problem; in New York, for example, Water Street alone boasted thirty-eight houses of prostitution, operating within sight of respectable citizens.

The French recognized that prostitution was as inevitable (and in a sense as necessary) as the equally unsavoury services that provided garbage removal and sewers, and thought it best to regulate it, just like those other services. Streetwalkers had to register at local police stations that kept track of their medical visits and minor criminal activities; those who refused were often the recipients of petty police harassment. Alternatively, prostitutes could live in brothels where a modicum of protection was afforded and medical check-ups were enforced. In theory—and for the time—a solution appeared to have been found. The openness of the brothels seemed to offer advantages to prostitutes (protection from violent men and payment of a part of their earnings), their clients (regular checks of their partners' health, no fear of pimps), and society (safe and unsullied streets, appearance of a controlled situation). To be properly identified, brothels were required to show their street number prominently over their door beside a red light—the origin of the familiar 'red light district' popular in many cities. However, France closed the brothels in 1946 "to cleanse the debauchery," forcing all the women back into the streets.

While attempts at protecting the interests of both society and sex workers have been generally well meant, no legislation has ever been enacted that entirely satisfies the needs of a society that judges prostitutes while using their services. The official position of many countries reflects this ambiguity. The Netherlands has often been receptive to social experimentation and so it was with prostitution, made legal as early as 1830, with brothels legalized in 2000. Other countries (the United States, with the exception of Nevada and Alaska; the former USSR; China; the Scandinavian countries) opted for the prohibitionist route. Others (Portugal, Germany, most South

American and Asian countries) prefer the regulatory model, or the abolitionist one (Canada, Great Britain, France, Japan, Italy).

The goal, whatever the legal format adopted, is to control the physical evidence of prostitution, prevent its unchecked expansion into densely inhabited areas (particularly when drug use and trafficking are also involved), and to make it as difficult as possible for predators and exploiters to operate at the expense of both the community and the prostitutes themselves. A very tall order, particularly considering that it usually operates within a moralistic and censorious context.

Until 1972, the Criminal Code of Canada, section 175 (1c), ruled that everyone committed a vagrancy who "being a common prostitute or nightwalker is found in a public place and does not, when required, give a good account of herself," and that such a person "is guilty of an offence punishable on summary conviction." Two points are worth making: that the prostitute was automatically deemed to be a 'her' and that there was no definition attached to 'common.' On the latter point, some judges decided that proof of previous convictions would suffice.

In 1972, the Code was amended to read that "every person who solicits any person in a public place for the purpose of prostitution is guilty of an offence punishable on summary conviction." The amendment then included male prostitutes and, putting the focus on the word 'soliciting' (also referred to as importuning) without actually defining it, gave rise to some very creative ways of negotiating without stating obvious terms. Prostitution was not a crime in Canada but the various activities surrounding it (importuning, paying for sex, keeping a house of ill repute, profiting from the earnings of a prostitute) were illegal.

After long years of stagnation during which legal prostitution continued to be accompanied by illegal practices that encompassed all aspects of the work, the Supreme Court declared in 2013 that the sections of the Criminal Code related to these practices were in violation of the Canadian Charter of Rights and Freedoms of 1982 because they imposed conditions on prostitutes that made their living unnecessarily dangerous. The following year, the Protection of Communities and Exploited Persons Act shifted focus from the prostitutes to their clients—it became legal to sell sexual services, but illegal to purchase them. This was known as the 'Nordic model' or the 'end demand' approach and was often accompanied by a Shame the Johns campaign, where ordinary people use humiliation in order to change behaviour. Canada and France, who adopted this model, actually found that it made prostitution even more risky by forcing it further into the shadows.

Streetwalkers have long been portrayed as needy creatures and ill-fated victims. Many songs and stories describe streetwalkers' activities in the gloomiest streets of large cities—young women destined to a life of poverty who found that none of the menial tasks and petty thefts to which they could resort were as profitable as prostitution. It is a convenient image that played to some extent into a widespread vision of women as powerless victims. In my experience of interviewing female prostitutes imprisoned for drug trafficking, I found the stereotype to be true up to the point when the women ceased to be merely prostitutes and started trafficking drugs as well, thus regaining some street credibility and a sense of self-worth. The street too has its hierarchy and the cheapest form of prostitution is not highly ranked.

Society has long distinguished between street prostitution, usually fuelled by poverty or drug use (when the cost of a 'trick' is usually related to the price of heroin), and its more elusive form, often practised by independent or part-time women who do not solicit openly and may have a regular clientele. While morality should be above social hierarchies, it is more usual for streetwalkers and their common trade to be the focus of censure than the more discreet call girls and their better class of clients, suggesting that we tend to be far more accommodating when not directly faced with the objects of our contempt.

In Canada, the distinction is well illustrated in British Columbia where, thanks to the early preponderance of male loggers and fishermen and to the clemency of the weather, street prostitution has been flourishing for a century and a half. The Vancouver City Archives and the Police's Rogues Gallery show that the sentence for being an inmate of a bawdy house usually ranged from $15 and costs (or, in default, twenty days in jail) to $50 (or, in default, two months in jail). On the other hand, the offence of street (or night) walking and soliciting carried a higher penalty—six months in jail or three months in jail with hard labour. The nuisance aspect was more severely penalized than the offence itself.

Societies have generally been more forgiving of courtesans. Unlike women who made their living on the street or in brothels under the strict rules of a madam, courtesans ruled their own lives. Some even once ruled empires, such as Theodora whose talents led her from brothel to throne and she ruled, with much intelligence, the Eastern Roman Empire with her husband, Justinian I, in the sixth century. Similarly, the influence of royal mistresses was often felt behind some of the actions of French kings, notably Madame de Maintenon, long-time mistress and eventually morganatic wife of Louis XIV after the queen's death.

With lesser aspirations but still socially ambitious, courtesans flourished in Paris during La Belle Epoque of 1900–1914. Known as *cocottes, demi-mondaines* and *grandes horizontales,* their excesses fitted well in an era when wasteful abundance co-existed with the utmost misery. The three reigning and most sought-after queens of that period were the ethereal and elegant Liane de Pougy (whose real name was the more plebeian Anne-Marie Chassaigne), la Belle Otero (a luscious Spaniard named Augustina Otero Iglesias, reputed to have been indefatigable in the practice of her trade) and la Païva (aka Esther Lachman, a Russian). The men who paid for their rich lifestyles were wealthy industrialists, landed aristocrats and even a few crowned heads of Europe, notably Grand Dukes Peter and

Nicholas of Russia, the Kings of Greece, Serbia and Spain, and England's Edward VII.

There was little doubt in these women's minds that they were in a far better situation than were the wives they supplanted. It has often been the prostitutes' argument that marriage is only a form of legitimized prostitution where women trade financial security for the duties of motherhood and housework, hiding their true venal condition with the hypocrisy of social conventions. By flaunting their own independent status, prostitutes often rationalize they are more honest than wives.

Prostitution involves the performance of a physical act whose moral, social, and medical implications profoundly affect the legal stances taken by countries where it is overtly practised. Some groups advocate for decriminalization or legalization, pointing to prostitutes who exercise a satisfactory control over their practice and assume full responsibility for their choice of occupation. Many have long argued that they should be called 'working girls' or 'sex workers,' and treated as ordinary members of the work force— paying taxes, being insured and having access to appropriate social and medical services. International organizations such as Amnesty International and UNAIDS also endorse the decriminalization of prostitution.

Some involved in the trade are clearly victims, held in a form of servitude, often having been introduced to it under false pretences. Some initially believe that they are in a genuine romantic relationship with their pimp, while others accept bogus job offers in western countries. Situations vary with location. In Western Europe, for instance, after the introduction of women from eastern and central European countries came another wave of prostitutes from Africa. With no other prospects of survival, they face the hatred of the local women with whom they compete by asking for lower payments and accepting any type of services.

While some women are clearly in need of protection, this is

not necessarily the case for all prostitutes. In 1957, the influential Wolfenden Report recognized that prostitution is "a social fact, deplorable in the eyes of moralists, sociologists and...the great majority of ordinary people" and that the law should not be concerned with abolishing it or making it illegal, but "what the law can and should do is to ensure that the streets...be freed from what is offensive or injurious and made tolerable for the ordinary citizen who lives in them or passes through them." The real question remains—whom should the legislation protect? Or is the very notion of specific protection a thing of the past, given that overt cases of abuse are normally covered by existing legislation?

SCIENCE

The long history of using human bodies for scientific purposes or to benefit the life of another offers many examples of exploitation. In the eighteenth century, the teeth of paupers' children were implanted into the mouths of the well-to-do. This was to the children's lasting detriment, since they were unable to chew and draw proper nourishment from the food bought with the money received in exchange for their teeth. This form of self-righteous entitlement was also reflected in the habit of using wet nurses for the newborn of the well-to-do who, plump and rosy, enjoyed the rich milk denied to the women's own children.

Using a body for scientific or altruistic purposes challenges philosophical and religious notions of the sanctity of the whole person, particularly for those who believe it was created in the image of God. There is a universal abhorrence, and in some cases taboo, attached to tampering with the human body or being made unclean through contacts with it (such as the rules about menstrual blood in many traditional cultures or rules of hygiene that exclude contact with saliva among the Brahmin). Our current vision of a body being physically approachable (and, in the extreme, usable) results from a very long evolution. Some medical procedures we take for granted today would once have been inconceivable, partly because of the techniques involved, but mostly because of the infringement on prevalent beliefs.

In antiquity, the examination of entrails, strictly limited to animals, was left to the haruspex and reserved for purposes of divination. Cutting into a human body was another matter entirely and only warranted in exceptional circumstances. For instance, around 300 BCE, the Greek city of Alexandria allowed the public dissection of criminals—the horror and desecration of it being deemed the ultimate deterrent.

The first known forensic autopsy took place in 44 BCE, on the body of Julius Caesar, to determine which of the twenty-three stab wounds he received had been fatal. Even Galen of Pergamon, two centuries later, still had to content himself with dissecting monkeys and pigs (his vivisection of pigs actually earning him much popularity). It is only with Andreas Vesalius and his *Humani Corporis Fabrica* (On the Fabric of the Human Body), published in 1543, that human dissection acquired its full scientific validation and became accepted as a teaching tool.

Earlier, dissections had only been permitted rarely and with limitations. In Salerno, for example, only one was allowed every five years. Venice allowed one a year and, in Lerida, anatomists were allowed to dissect one criminal every three years. Jacalyn Duffin, in her *History of Medicine: A Scandalously Short Introduction* (1999) describes a scene in which the professor sat high above the dissection area, reading from a Latin edition of Galen (the authority on such matters), while mostly illiterate barbers dissected the corpse while listening to the lesson.

In Britain, human dissections were first officially performed in Scotland in 1506 when King James IV allowed the Barber–Surgeons of Edinburgh to dissect the "bodies of certain executed criminals," who, having defiled the expression of God in themselves, had earned this extra punishment, deemed even worse than death. Henry VIII followed suit in England in 1540. Until the eighteenth century, medical students in the United Kingdom studied human anatomy by watching their masters perform dissections on the cadavers of executed criminals.

Resources were scarce. In London, for instance, the numbers were only extended from four in 1540 to ten in 1723. The situation was also bad in Edinburgh, where anatomists had to wait until 1694 for an expanded list of permittable bodies. This included those who died in the correction houses, foundlings (who died before starting school or a trade), still-births and those executed for crimes.

The supply increased when, to intensify the deterrent effect of the death penalty, Parliament passed the Murder Act of 1752, replacing the public display of executed criminals with their dissection—still deemed to be an even worse punishment. A much larger number of bodies were then made legally available to anatomists but, particularly with the greater number of teaching hospitals opening during the eighteenth century, demand still far outstripped supply.

A fierce competition ensued, and riots became commonplace at execution sites, from where anatomists collected legal corpses. In 1741, Samuel Richardson described in a letter to a friend a scene where a "tumult" erupted between "the Friends of the [five] Persons executed" and people "sent by private Surgeons to obtain Bodies for Dissection. The Contests between these were fierce and bloody, and frightful to look at."

The numbers were still too low to satisfy the hospitals' demand, and body-snatchers, also known as resurrection-men, began exhuming freshly buried bodies. While the practice was deemed hateful, it was not illegal since bodies did not legally belong to anyone. Nonetheless, their very profitable trade became risky and body-snatchers were often attacked. Night watches started patrolling graveyards, and burial practices began incorporating more secure coffins, heavy stone slabs and mortsafes to protect the graves.

Demonstrating the extremes to which the resurrectionists would

resort, a contemporary poem by Thomas Hood gives voice to the
ghost of a young wife:

> The body-snatchers they have come.
> And made a snatch at me
> It's very hard them kind of men
> Won't let a body be.
> You thought that I was buried deep,
> Quite decent like and chary,
> But from her grave in Mary-bone,
> They've come and boned your Mary.

Although the number of bodies robbed across the nation every year
was estimated to be several thousand, demand remained strong and
the trade then started extending to live victims. Among several cases
of killing and selling bodies was that of two female body snatchers
in Edinburgh (1752) who murdered a child and sold the remains
for 2s. 6d. The criminal behaviour culminated in 1828, also in
Edinburgh, with the murders of sixteen people, mostly women and
children, whose bodies were sold by two men, William Hare and
William Burke (to whom is owed the coining of a new word, 'burk-
ing,' signifying murdering for dissection). Burke was hanged and,
somewhat ironically, his body was dissected. The anatomist Robert
Knox, to whom he sold the bodies, was not charged but his professional reputation was shattered.

As a result, the House of Commons appointed a committee, whose
report stressed the importance of anatomical science and the scarcity
of available bodies, noting that 592 bodies had been dissected by 701
students in 1826 at a time when the number of death penalty executions had substantially decreased. It recommended that the bodies
of paupers also be made available for dissection. Four year later, the
Anatomy Act led to the issue of licences for the lawful acquisition of
unclaimed cadavers from workhouses for the exclusive purpose of dissection. Even then, numbers may not have satisfied the demand, and
body snatching was reported sporadically until 1844.

The Mother and Baby Homes Commission Investigation, created in 2015 by the Irish Government, revealed another and far more shocking source of bodies suitable for dissection in medical schools: those of children born of single mothers (950 in Dublin alone), a practice that apparently continued until 1977.

In 1798, France became the first country to pass legislation regulating the use of bodies for dissection. Then came the first of the American states, Massachusetts (1831), the United Kingdom (1832), Canada (1843, revised 1859 and 1864) and Prussia (1844). Most American states held ambiguous feelings about dissection and waited till the end of the Civil War to pass legislation (1865). The last state to legislate, Pennsylvania, did not do so until 1883.

In the west, we have evolved from utter repugnance at opening up a cadaver to generously donating our bodies after our demise, a pragmatic approach that would have astounded our ancestors. It is a remarkable shift in our thinking, perhaps indicating greater concern for others and continued belief in the progress of science as much as a loss of power of the Church and its dictates. Public relations techniques have also worked well, with more sensitivity shown by medical practitioners. The original and overt coarseness of medical students in dealing with bodies obtained from jails and pauper houses has been replaced with demonstrations of gratitude and respect, under the guidance of medical schools, some of which even hold annual ceremonies to honour the donors and their families.

Even more common than dissection is the practice of offering our various organs for post-mortem use. The transplantation of body parts from one person to another is a modern technique that has prospered with medical and surgical progress and, with a few exceptions based on religious beliefs, is now widely accepted. Since the first kidney was successfully transplanted in 1954, followed by liver, heart, pancreas and lung through the 1960s, the need for suitable human organs has steadily increased. Scarcity has meant that animals—having already served in the thousands as practice for transplant experiments—have also been pressed into service. Thus, a young baboon's heart beat for twenty-one days in the chest of Baby Rae, a fourteen-day-old premature little girl (1984), and an adult baboon's liver was transplanted into a man who survived seventy-one days (1992). Mechanical hearts still offer only temporary help and human heart transplants are still the best solution.

Parallels have been drawn between the modern international demand for human organs for transplantation and that of human bodies for dissection two centuries ago. Today, extraction of donated organs from dead bodies must be performed with the same unseemly haste as body snatching then was—even leading to extraction from bodies deemed to be 'brain dead' but whose hearts may still be beating. As well, the same pressure exists to increase numbers. In the face of an always growing demand for body parts and human tissues for transplantation, countries such as China also authorize their automatic extraction (also known as harvesting) from executed criminals. In other parts of the world, dire poverty is the cause of voluntary donations of live organs and perhaps even criminally obtained ones.

In cases of both dissection and transplantation, the ultimate goal is the betterment of mankind in general, and individuals in particular. The unfortunate side effect is that the benefits of science can be soiled by the criminality sometimes involved when urgency and expediency, as well as profit, combine to exploit the poor and the helpless. The parallel cannot be ignored—while the intentions can be deemed positive in both cases, the side effects can be cruel and illegitimate for disadvantaged groups.

Many believe that only voluntary live donation and authorized post-mortem donation are legitimate. While this option assuages some of our concerns and satisfies our sense of morality, it does not negate the deep sense of pollution we may experience, one that goes far beyond the legitimate fear of contamination or rejection and renders the procedures unacceptable to some philosophies or religions.

Morality similarly informs our view of donating replaceable parts of our bodies: blood, sperm and eggs. While British obstetrician James Blundell performed the first successful blood transfusion in 1818, organized blood donation systems grew out of twentieth century wars and are inextricably linked to notions of altruism. Blood drives rely on the reward of good citizenship, particularly when the donors' compensation only consists of a soft drink and a cookie (as in Canada). We find the idea of selling parts of ourselves distasteful and worry about the exploitation that cash payments may invite. The counterpart, naturally, is that there is no certainty that voluntary donations will be sufficient.

Considerations of provenance and compensation increase the ambiguity we still feel about the potential usefulness of the human body. We are willing to entertain the thought of using every bit of it for research and transplantation, while at the same time enforcing legislation to punish the desecration of human corpses—including dismemberment, disfigurement, mutilation, or any act that would further damage them. The two concepts are at odds with each other and illustrate our profound confusion when considering the body as a disposable object rather than the corporeal side of a thinking and feeling entity—a person.

SURROGACY

In the past, and if the family could afford it, an unmarried young girl and her mother might go abroad on holidays for two or three months, and on their return, the mother would be holding her newborn child. Propriety was preserved and nobody asked questions, but everyone suspected that the true mother was not the one holding the child. It was, in a sense, an early form of surrogacy. More willingly, a young wife with children of her own might agree, out of the kindness of her heart, to carry the child of a barren close relative.

There are precedents for such actions. In the most ancient form of surrogacy, the husband of an infertile wife would impregnate another woman, usually a servant or a slave, and the child would be brought up in his home. In Genesis 16:3, Sarah, unable to conceive, offered her servant Hagar, who may not have been in a position to object, to her husband Abraham as the mother of his future children. This was reputedly not an uncommon practice among Hebrew tribes, even if personal feelings sometimes interfered (as they did with Sarah) to complicate matters. One of the most ancient codes, the Babylonian Code of Hammurabi, made provisions in the eighteenth century BCE to protect children born from such arrangements. Similarly, in ancient Rome, there were regulations concerning the status of a citizen born of a female slave.

Commercial surrogacy is a recent convenience, first reported in Michigan in 1976, when a woman accepted $10,000 to be impregnated with the sperm of a stranger—and then allegedly changed her mind. Another noteworthy birth was that of the first 'test tube baby' (Louise Brown, 1978, in England) that set a precedent for both gestational surrogacy and modern in-vitro fertilization. A decade later, both Australia and the United States reported births through donated eggs. The ability to transfer embryos, the complication of new family structures, and the globalization of trade (including fertility) have led to the rapid expansion of surrogacy.

Once an act performed out of affection, friendship or duty, carrying a child for another woman has now become a worldwide business that employs medical staff, lawyers, counsellors and agencies in increasing numbers. Women and their husbands unable to conceive naturally, as well as male homosexual couples, frequently seek the services of a surrogate or rely on the generosity of a woman friend. It may be seen as a preferable option to attempting the unpleasant and expensive process of in-vitro fertilization (with its attendant hormone injections, doctors' appointments and outpatient surgery) that so often fails.

Surrogacy has grown so fast and has expanded so widely that the protection of the surrogates, the future parents and the children issued of the transaction have not been thoroughly considered and legislated. A few cases have shown how the rights of surrogate mothers and babies can be threatened by the whims of parents and corrupt agencies, particularly in poor countries where they usually operate. In fact, so many problems have arisen that some countries, notably India and Thailand, have made commercial surrogacy illegal.

Today, much of the discussion around surrogacy is of a practical nature, concerned with the method (either gestational or traditional), the motive (either altruistic or for profit) and the means (where to find women to carry the embryos). In traditional surrogacy, the child is biologically related to both the father and the woman whose egg is artificially inseminated and who gives birth. In gestational surrogacy, a donated egg is fertilized in vitro and the embryo is then transplanted into a surrogate who carries it to term; there is no biological connection between woman and embryo. This is deemed to be the preferred method as it reduces the possibility of the surrogate becoming emotionally attached or challenging the custody of the child. The financial arrangements are different in each case: the altruistic surrogate is only paid the medical costs of the pregnancy, while a substantial amount of money can be exchanged if the surrogacy is for profit. However, as altruistic surrogacy (the only form authorized in some countries) only constitutes two percent of the cases worldwide, much of the discussion focuses on the morality of a controversial commercial arrangement.

In the United States, where surrogacy is at its most expensive and best regulated, feminist groups have denounced the vulnerability of the women and the sordid commercialization of the process, such as that described in a legal contract made in California in 2015. Its relevant points relate to the "compensation [to the surrogate mother] for the loss of an organ as direct consequence of the pregnancy: ... Removal of the Fallopian tubes or of ovaries, $2,500 each... Uterus removal, $5,000." The contract also stipulated that the future parents, not the surrogate mother, were free to decide to terminate the pregnancy in case of problems. Finally, the surrogate mother was forbidden to have sex during the pregnancy, had to remain within state boundaries, could not swim in the sea and was not allowed to eat or drink products containing saccharin.

The European Parliament condemned surrogacy in 2015 because "it undermines the human dignity of the woman, since her body and its reproductive functions are used as a commodity." The Council of Europe also rejected a recommendation to create international guidelines for altruistic cases. As a result, each country within the EU is forced to arrive at its own solution while recognizing that, where surrogate pregnancy is illegal, residents will simply go abroad.

In France, the question emerged in the 1980s and was soon dealt a severe blow. The court declared that surrogacy was contrary to the public good, and legislation confirmed the court's opinion in 1994: surrogacy arrangements, whether commercial or altruistic, are illegal. Most French people are said to support the prohibition of surrogate motherhood due to ethical concerns for the child, the surrogate mother and society as a whole. However, demand is growing from women who seek surrogate mothers abroad. When Judge Claire Legras, a member of the French national committee on bioethics, published an article in 2015 on this topic, she received many letters passionately defending a process that has given couples the children they could not have themselves. One letter is worth citing because its author unintentionally illustrates the concerns and ambivalence many have about surrogacy:

> All over the globe there are many women who work as surrogate mothers. For some of them it's a chance to earn money for their poor families... Now in Europe the leader in this field is the Ukrainian Clinic Biotexcom. It is so popular because in Ukraine many healthy women who are ready to become donors or to bear a child for somebody. And I can say for sure that these people who help us infertile women and men to have healthy children must be blessed but not accused. And I want to note that a surrogate

mother writes a special certificate that [she] has no rights and obli-
gations concerning the child [to whom] she gives birth... From
the first day of the program she understands that it's just a program and the child is not hers.

In Spain, two contradictory movements lead the discussion. *Son
Nuestros Hijos* (They Are Our Children) is a pro-surrogacy parental
association representing some four hundred families that makes the
case for altruism but is not against economic compensation, suggesting a fair price should be set by an international commission. They
ask, "When is a woman exploited? When she is paid or when she
is not?" On the other hand, the position of the feminist movement
No Somos Vasijas (We Are Not Vessels), created in 2015 when the
debate entered the political realm, is that "bodies are the limits of
what can be bought and sold." The Spanish socialist party decided
they could not "embrace any practice that means undermining the
rights of women and young girls or reinforcing the feminization of
poverty" and its secretary general, elected in 2017, openly opposed
surrogacy, "I am not in favour of using the female body for prostitution, for trafficking, or for surrogate motherhood."

Yet, one of the largest European agencies operating surrogacy services, Subrogalia, has its headquarters in Barcelona and deals mostly
with surrogate mothers from Kiev, where there are few, if any, regulations. The agency has offices in several countries and has recently
opened one in Greece that, unlike Ukraine, has the advantage of
being within the European Union and requires the authorization of
a judge, thus inspiring more confidence in the parents. The agency
director sees a great future for Greece in the surrogacy business and
explains, "In Ukraine, you can advertise in the press. Instead of plac-
ing an ad about Coca Cola, you put one in for surrogate mothers.
In Greece there are clinics that bring the women directly to you."
The clientele is mostly Spanish, but also includes Italians, Chinese,
French and Germans.

In Canada, the passing of the Assisted Human Reproduction Act in 2004, made it legal to donate eggs, sperm and surrogacy services. Canadian surrogate mothers (like those in the United Kingdom) can only be reimbursed for the costs associated with their pregnancies; anything else would be punishable by a fine of up to $500,000 or a prison term of up to ten years.

While Canada would seem to have deftly handled the question of morality, reality may be otherwise. In an article for *The Globe and Mail* ('How Canada became an international surrogacy hotspot,' 2018) Alison Motluck argued that the actual situation is at odds with the intention. She bases her interpretation on anecdotal reports (the only kind available), many of which were gathered by former Statistics Canada Director Pamela White of the Kent Law School in Britain. The problem for Canada, if indeed there is one, would stem from several sources: increasing worldwide demand, scarcity of donors as several countries now forbid commercial surrogacy, no Canadian restriction on foreign participation, generous parental rights for the surrogate mother, and excellent gestational and neonatal care funded by Canadian taxpayers.

Since the law that makes commercial surrogacy illegal in Canada does not apply abroad, surrogate Canadian mothers do not incur any penalty if their embryos are transplanted abroad and the transactions are also paid abroad—while still benefiting from generous Canadian pregnancy and neonatal care. Karen Busby, law professor at the University of Manitoba, believes that Canada is becoming an international surrogacy magnet, with residents of China, Japan, several European countries and Muslim states (where surrogacy is not permitted) seeking out Canadian surrogates. As provinces do not keep records on the parents' residency, the claim that many come from other countries cannot be verified.

Even though surrogacy is today an established practice, the basic questions, not likely to be soon resolved, are whether it interferes with the integrity of the human body in ways that are inherently unacceptable, and whether national philosophies and policies can be reconciled with individual desires. As well, since the line between altruism and capitalism remains vague, more practical question are raised: why should donating nine months of one's life, the discomfort of pregnancy and accepting the potential dangers of childbirth not be rewarded? And how can appropriate regulations be administered in an environment of rapid technological advancement, growing demand and globally mobile capital? Alicia Miyares, a philosophy professor and spokesperson for *Non Somos Vasijas,* admits, "We know that countries that allow it for altruistic purposes cannot stop reproductive tourism, and that it's impossible to avoid under-the-table payments." As ever in such cases, the possibility of abuse of the poor by the rich is obvious.

OUR BODIES' USEFULNESS SEEMS BOUNDLESS, DEAD or alive. Some would say they also harbour our souls, and it is indeed the duality of our physical and metaphysical attributes that constitutes our unique identities. Any interference with our bodies, whether permanent or transient, raises fundamental issues of morality, religion, free will and social mores.

Commercial surrogacy and organ transplants are both in their scientific and legal infancy, cannibalism remains acceptable as a last resort, and we seem no closer to coming to terms with the age-old practice of prostitution. While all can be legitimate and freely performed, the possibility of abuse, exploitation and harm remains a *leitmotif* that has shown little improvement over time. Legislation, acting as an agent of the people's will and reflecting general public opinion, attempts to control the worst excesses but runs the risk of forcing controversial practices underground, making them even more dangerous for their victims.

Perhaps the future rests with scientists rather than lawmakers. They have already provided internal and external adjuncts to the body to assist or replace organ function (the iron lungs of the 1940s and 50s, heart bypass machines used during surgery, ongoing dialysis treatments for renal failure, pacemakers), attempted the manufacture of artificial organs, and continue to research the creation of new regenerative cells.

In another field altogether, the manufacture of sex dolls is becoming more sophisticated all the time, and the news media even mention the possibility of setting up 'responsive' sex doll brothels to replace, or at least, supplement human prostitution, with robotics finding new applications in this field.

More seriously, scientists are now investigating the possibility of creating sperm and eggs (the gametes that combine in fertilization) from ordinary or somatic cells from the body. In 2007, two Japanese biologists showed that somatic cells could be turned into stem cells. Since then, further experiments to reproduce the evolution of the cells in a petri dish have been attempted, using mice as cell donors. The same group of Japanese scientists have also experimented with the creation of sperm.

Scientific legal specialist Henry Greely predicted in *The End of Sex and the Future of Human Reproduction* (2016), "I expect that some time in the next twenty to forty years... sex [for reproduction] will largely disappear." Should the experiments ever succeed in creating human embryos, it would definitely alter the current landscape of reproduction through surrogacy. However, it could also introduce a new moral dilemma—bespoke babies, specifically designed to favour certain characteristics over others.

Technology has made our lives more complex, and it could well be that scientists end up creating far more controversy than lawyers ever did, without answering the fundamental question—who are 'we' with regard to our bodies?

CHAPTER SIX

THE HYSTERICAL FEMALE

IN 1992, A MOTHER IN MARTENSVILLE, Saskatchewan, became concerned that her two-year-old daughter might have been molested. A police investigation of the child's daycare quickly mushroomed into widespread accusations of ritualized abuse culminating in rumours of a satanic cult called The Brotherhood of the Ram. Nine people, including five police officers, were arrested. One person was convicted; the remaining charges were ultimately dismissed and several of the accused successfully sued for compensation.

The Martensville case was one of a spate of sensational sexual assault accusations erupting in the 1980s and the 1990s that included vague descriptions of satanic rituals, animal torture and killings, and sexual abuse, in this instance made by children. Similar allegations were once used to describe witches' practices, and we react by using the same vocabulary of fear and disgust. Incidents like these—although each arises from a unique set of circumstances—are nonetheless grouped together under the rubric of 'mass hysteria,' a term that can be used to describe both the escalation of the children's accusations and their parents' reaction to them.

The dictionary definition of hysteria as "an exaggerated or uncontrolled emotion or excitement, especially among a group of people" is a modern one that has lost its original connection to gender. The term derives from the Greek word for uterus, *hysterika,* literally 'womb disease,' probably coined by Hippocrates. It went on to refer to any mental illness related to the mysterious female body functions and the vagaries of the female mind. Equating female sexuality with mental illness also allowed churches, societies and men in particular to rationalize something they did not understand and that caused intense disruption in the good order of male-driven codes of behaviour. Standards of 'common decency' were intended to separate the power of procreation from its embarrassing mechanism—female sexual organs.

As symptoms included fainting, anxiety, sleeplessness, irritability, nervousness, being troublesome, excessive vaginal lubrication and erotic fantasizing, hysteria was a natural diagnosis for ailments that could not be otherwise identified, particularly when the symptoms seemed to be of a sexual nature. Thomas Sydenham, the seventeenth-century 'English Hippocrates,' once declared that female hysteria, which he attributed to "irregular motions of the animal spirits," was the second most common malady of the time.

The treatment for such an elusive condition was unusual—clitoral stimulation. Pieter van Foreest, the sixteenth-century 'Dutch Hippocrates' described the procedure:

> When these symptoms indicate, we think it necessary to ask a midwife to assist, so that she can massage the genitalia with one finger inside, using oil of lilies, musk root, crocus, or [something] similar. And in this way the afflicted woman can be aroused to the paroxysm. This kind of stimulation with the finger is recommended by Galen and Avicenna, among others, most especially for widows, those who live chaste lives, and female religious, as Gradus [Ferrari da Gradi] proposes; it is less often recommended for very young women, public women, or married women, for whom it is a better remedy to engage in intercourse with their spouses.

Doctors would sometimes administer the treatment themselves but there was a certain distaste attached to the procedure and van Foreest suggested that doctors seek "every opportunity to substitute other devices for their fingers, such as the attentions of a husband, the hands of a midwife, or the business end of some tireless and impersonal mechanism." This treatment was administered through-out Europe and in America until the 1880s when the impersonal mechanism became, with the patented invention of Dr. J. Mortimer Granville, the vibrator.

Jewish mythology created a character that embodied many of the least attractive female features and attempted to explain their perversity—Lilith, Eve's counterpart. She was a dangerous figure of darkness, sexually wanton, and a baby thief. In the mysterious ways of myths, Lilith answered the puzzling question of why a woman, created from Adam's rib to be good and to have an essential dependency on men, could stray from the path she was meant to follow. The answer was simple: she had an avatar, whose perversities could be vaguely related to hysteria. Sexual congress with demons, stealthy affairs, stealing babies away through abortion—all could be explained through her erratic womb, hidden in the mysterious recesses of flesh and brain.

In other cultures, the fear men had of the female sex often achieved mythical proportions, as with the fearsome *vagina dentata*, or 'vagina with teeth,' intended to preserve women's virtue by castrating men. *Funk & Wagnalls Standard Dictionary of Folklore and Mythology* shows how widespread the belief was: "The toothed vagina motif, so prominent in North American Indian mythology, is also found in the Chaco and the Guianas. The first men in the world were unable to have sexual relationships with their wives until the culture hero broke the teeth of the women's vaginas. According to the Waspishiana and Taruma Indians the first woman had a carnivorous fish inside her vagina."

Similarly, Shintoists believed that a sharp-toothed demon originally hid inside a woman's vagina, emasculating her husband. To help her, a blacksmith made her an iron phallus to break the creature's teeth and permit normal sexual intercourse. Stories from India also transmit the now familiar notion that young women had ferocious sexual appetites and could only be made safe for sex with men by breaking the teeth inside their vaginas. Within nascent psychoanalysis, Freud believed that the castration anxiety suffered by men was rooted in a fear of female genitalia and ordinary sexual intercourse, echoing an earlier belief that witches could cause men to become impotent.

WITCHCRAFT

A French proverb from the thirteenth century, *Qui veut noyer son chien l'accuse de la rage (Whoever wants to kill his dog will say it has rabies)*, encapsulates much of the past attitude towards women: unless they toed the line and did as they were told, any excuse would do to condemn them. The history of witchcraft is a case in point.

Witchcraft was closely interwoven into the details of daily life over which people had little control. The accusations involved every type of misfortune suffered by man or beast, including impotence, poor crops, unexplained fires, bad weather, diseases and unwanted pregnancies. Moreover, all these could be procured at a distance, without physical contact between the witch and her victims. It was impossible to prove innocence and, as the accused could escape punishment by blaming others (who could then be charged for these crimes), it is only too easy to see how scapegoating, personal jealousies, financial profit and other motives far removed from any genuine notion of witchcraft could actually be passed off as such, particularly when the accused were women deprived of support. Men were also targeted and sentenced to death, but far more women fell victim to imaginary accusations of malevolent actions. Some feminist writers believe that only their sex and the male antagonism it aroused determined the fate of female witches.

A famous outbreak of witchcraft occurred in Salem, Massachusetts, in 1692, where a small, religiously conservative town succumbed to mass hysteria amid stories of satanic sex. The Salem accusations and trials for sorcery were particularly arresting because young girls were the source of it and because of the numbers involved: two hundred formally accused and twenty-seven deaths.

It started in the household of a minister, Samuel Parris, whose daughter and niece, nine and eleven years old, began to have violent fits with uncontrollable outbursts of screaming. When a doctor diagnosed bewitchment, several other young girls began showing similar symptoms. Three women were soon arrested, accused by the girls of having bewitched them: the Parris family's Caribbean slave and two equally powerless women, a homeless beggar and a poor elderly woman. The last two denied their guilt, but the slave, perhaps hoping to save herself by acting as informer, confessed and claimed other witches had acted with her in serving the Devil.

The accusations, first started in Salem Village and nearby Andover, spread rapidly and, within three months, twenty-four townships were involved in a common form of hysteria. The accused, who by then also included some of the women's male relatives, were members of the church and often well regarded in the community. They faced a dreadful dilemma: refuse to confess and be executed, or lie and perjure themselves, admitting to witchcraft. The trials of the accused overwhelmed the justice system but a special court was appointed and soon handed down its first convictions. Nineteen were hanged, seven died in jail, and one, Giles Cory, died by pressing by stones after three days of torture, still denying his crime.

The situation in Salem highlighted the need to apply the same standards of evidence to witchcraft trials as to any other crime, and public hostility soon started to wane. By 1693, all those still in jail for crimes of witchcraft were released and the madness died as mysteriously as it had started. Eventually, the Massachusetts Colony passed legislation in 1711 to restore the good names of the condemned and even provided restitution to their heirs. In the witches' village, since renamed Danvers, the foundations of the Parrish house can still be seen, a strikingly small and innocuous site to have led to so much suffering.

Many theories have been built about what really happened in Salem Village during that fatal year, some focusing on the involvement of clergymen in local affairs, isolation from a central government and the justice system, and constant insecurity deriving from the recent conflicts with Indians, whose pagan beliefs were deemed to be also inspired by the Devil. As well, rivalry with nearby Salem Town, more prosperous and worldly than the strict conservative Village, would have created in the latter an atmosphere where strangers or outsiders within the community (such as the first three women accused) were viewed with suspicion. Historian Malcolm Gaskill posits that the claim of devilish possession was a scam to grab land from wealthy owners by accusing them of witchcraft, or to collective hysteria within a climate of religious extremism, false accusations, and lapses in due process.

Particularly prevalent from the twelfth to the fifteenth century in Europe and again during the sixteenth and seventeenth centuries, the persecution of witches was caused by hysteria and paranoia, greed and envy, often in a context of social chaos and religious upheaval. The definition and parameters of witchcraft evolved from Church teachings, incorporating a variety of heresies and inexplicable phenomena deemed hostile to the true faith. These religious propositions developed into a conspiracy against God, requiring systematic repression with all the trappings of legality but none of justice. According to Exodus (20:13 and 22:18), witches had a different place within the human race. Moses was told "Thou shalt not kill" and "Thou shalt not suffer a witch to live." No message could be clearer: killing was a sin but killing witches was an obligation.

Papal bulls against witchcraft resembled bulls against heresy. In 1209, the Church launched a violent crusade against the followers of Catharism, a heretical Christian belief in the dualism of good and evil. The accusations against the Cathars, or Albigensians as they were also known, were very similar to those laid against witches—flying into the air, having congress with the Devil, child murder—both being seen as servants of Satan. Given mankind's almost infinite capacity to delude itself, the substantial financial benefits to the Church from its actions against heretics and witches could be rationalized as mere deeds of religious faith.

By the end of the fourteenth century, the reality and power of demons and witches were common belief. In 1484, two Dominican priests outlined the position of the Church in the *Malleus Maleficarum* (The Hammer of the Witches). It maintained that "the belief that there are such beings as witches is so essential a part of witchcraft of the Catholic Church that obstinacy to maintain the opposite opinion manifestly savours of heresy." Specifically, "the world now suffers through the malice of women…All witchcraft comes from carnal lust, which is in women insatiable. They consort even with devils."

Women's sexual surrender to the Devil was believed to be part of their impure and depraved nature. Indeed, while early accusations of witchcraft had been made against both men and women, after the publication of the *Malleus Maleficarum*, the immense majority of accusations were aimed at women who, because of their insatiable carnal lust, were more easily "found infected with the heresy of witchcraft." The lore of copulating with the Devil in the shape of a goat with an enormous phallus, diabolic rites and flying through the night developed in the minds of prosecutors, no doubt aided by the confessions of some women, extracted under torture. Single women, both spinsters and widows, were particularly vulnerable, since they were deprived of proper and regular sexual activity and existed without the social validation and legitimacy of having a man at their side. For every Joan of Arc, sinfully and proudly dressed as a man, assuming the unfeminine stance of military command and defending herself against accusations of heresy and witchcraft, there were millions who perished, without recourse against their accusers, and often unaware of the nature of their crimes.

During the seventeenth century, a time of political and social turmoil, European countries were particularly given to attributing anything outside the ordinary to witchcraft. Witch-hunts may also have occasionally been ploys to deflect attention from other concerns, such as the aggressive restoration of Catholicism in Germany, the high price of grain in Denmark, treason in Scotland, or other events in France and Italy. In Bavaria, for instance, 1,200 people were killed between 1626 and 1631, and many others of were suspected of witchcraft. Their guilt was often tested by a water ordeal, and in France the Bishop of Rheims in 1644 bemoaned the fate of innocent people "maltreated, driven out, or physically attacked; they are burned while it has become customary to take the suspects and throw them into water, then if they float it is enough to make them witches. This is such a great abuse that up to thirty or forty are found in a single parish."[1] No firm figures can be obtained on the actual number of women who, between the thirteenth and the eighteenth centuries, were executed for witchcraft—drowned, hanged, beheaded or burned at the stake (as they were in France and Germany so that their bodies could not be resurrected)—but the estimates range from several hundred thousand to nine million.

By the end of the seventeenth century, the madness was waning. In 1682, a French royal ordinance referred to "alleged witches" as mere blasphemers or charlatans, eventually leading to the decriminalization of witchcraft. The last execution of a witch in France took place in 1718, while in Britain witchcraft was decriminalized in 1736.

ADULTERY

A cuckold husband made to wear horns may be the butt of jokes and the topic of farces, but female infidelity was traditionally no laughing matter. While promiscuity was tolerated in men, women's fidelity was of paramount importance. Both the Old Testament and the Quran favoured death by stoning as punishment for the adulterous wife. Today, in some parts of the world, she might still be stoned and killed in other ways. A lesser consequence would be repudiation and the irreversible shame brought to her whole family.

---

1. Malcolm Gaskill, *Witchcraft. A Very Short Introduction* (Oxford, New York: Oxford University Press, 2010), 79.

The penalty inflicted on wayward wives was severe because of the serious social consequences associated with a woman's infidelity: before DNA testing became available, there could be no certainty about the identity of a child's father. Among those who owned property, marriages were based on political alliances and economic factors, and the introduction of a potential bastard, particularly a son who would inherit the estate, carry the name and continue the bloodline, was seen as catastrophic. When husbands were away, inviolable chastity belts were sometimes thought to be the solution, reassuring the wellborn that their offspring would be legitimate.

Emotional diversion, on the other hand, was permissible among those who could afford it, and wellborn wives could legitimately have young male companions. In the Middle Ages, the courtly love tradition permitted troubadours and young male attendants to attend to ladies and entertain them in an atmosphere of devoted platonic love. European society historically distinguished between love, of negligible economic or social value, and sex, with its attendant procreation.

The nature of women's infidelity, and the discrepancies between marriage conventions and inner emotional demands, are personified by the two most notorious fictional adulteresses of the nineteenth century, Anna Karenina and Emma Bovary. The women evolved in two distinct societies—the sophisticated Russian aristocracy and the confining atmosphere of small-town French bourgeoisie—but both died for breaking the rules.

When Emma, married to a dull, well-meaning country doctor, is invited to a ball in a château she discovers a world of charm, elegance and carefree sensuality she did not know existed outside the romantic novels of her youth. She becomes obsessed and seeks love elsewhere: first with young Léon, a notary's clerk who is initially flattered then overwhelmed, then Léopold, owner of an estate and a man of the world. When she goes too far and implores Léopold to flee with her, he heartlessly ends the relationship through a letter and reflects, "What an imbecile I am!...No matter. She was a pretty mistress." Jilted, Emma falls prey to the moneylender who had funded the elegant lifestyle suited to her aspirations and her life becomes a nightmare: "The lusts of the flesh, the longing for money, and the melancholy of passion all blended themselves into one suffering." She takes arsenic and dies, deeply mourned by her uncomprehending and ruined husband, who eventually dies of grief.

Unlike Emma, whose affair is the only adultery related in the book, Anna Karenina lives in a milieu where affairs are common but remain contained within certain acceptable parameters. Marriage is a social convention and the Karenins have done what was expected of them. The first inkling of Anna's dissatisfaction comes as an inner surge. "It was as if an excess of vitality so filled her whole being that it betrayed itself against her will now in her smile, now in the light of her eyes." Her falling for Vronsky seems inevitable although she feels intense shame and guilt when she first succumbs. She gives birth to his child and soon becomes ill.

Karenin forgives her but social pressure intensifies and challenges him—"that coarse and mighty power which overruled his life and to which he would have to submit." Anna's position is similarly challenged. Were she to leave Karenin for Vronsky, she would also abandon her social position. "She felt...that the position she held in society was dear to her, and that she would not have the strength to change it for the degrading position of a woman who had forsaken her husband and child and formed a union with her lover."

Yet she goes to Italy with Vronsky and their child, avoiding people she knows, as their position is socially unacceptable. Vronsky, forced to abandon his military career, becomes increasingly detached, adding to Anna's insecurity. "She was jealous not of any woman, but of the diminishing of his love." Unable to sleep, she takes opium and feels increasingly desperate, caught in a tight circle of social structure, moral code and restrictive divorce laws, from which she sees no escape, save death.

For both Anna and Emma, tragedy lies in the intensity of their characters, as they both lose control of their emotions. Both see things as they are not—a tragic flaw that leads to their self-destruction when they finally face reality and understand there is no place for them in such a world. Both pay with their lives for betraying their marriage vows, defying social conventions and belying the orderly governance of their respective societies—a fate their lovers are spared.

Female infidelity is still seen as a dissident act. When women seek excuses for it they usually fall back on emotions that society deems understandable and in accordance with the conventional female character. Based on 155 interviews in 1992, psychologist Shirley Glass concluded that love was the overwhelming reason given for female infidelity, followed by the need for emotional intimacy. A desire for more intense sexual pleasure was relatively rare and may have carried more feelings of guilt, shame, and unworthiness. Men, on the other hand, appear to require less self-justification and often cite a search for new sexual experiences as the reason for infidelity. It is likely that, given the stronger female self-assertion in many other domains, the need for rationalizing extramarital affairs is today less urgent than a few decades ago. Yet, the flavour of dissidence still taints it. Psychiatrist and addiction specialist Kenneth Paul Rosenberg characterizes infidelity as "the end product of our normal impulses for love and lust gone haywire."

ABORTION

Abortion, with its impact on the family and its massive derogation of societal and moral imperatives, has given rise to more hatred and misunderstanding than almost any other action taken by women, save witchcraft. Until effective methods of contraception became available, otherwise powerless women, victimized by uncontrolled fertility, poverty or the fear of public opinion, have made difficult decisions, often infringing the laws of the land. It seemed to them they had no option than to rebel against the rules of an orderly society and, when married, to undermine the stated purpose of matrimony.

The termination of pregnancy was forbidden by the Hippocratic Oath but was not uncommon in the Greco-Roman world. While Christianity disapproved of infanticide, abortion and contraception, the only certain ways of preventing unwanted pregnancy were abstention and *coitus interruptus*, such as practiced by Onan when ordered by his father to impregnate the wife of his dead brother Er (a wicked man slain by God) so she could have a child. At the last minute, it came to pass that Onan "when he went unto his brother's wife, that he spilled it on the ground, lest that he should give his seed to his brother." (Exodus 38). This so displeased the Lord that He slew him also.

The Lord was easily displeased and apt to slay at will when opposed, but a layman may wonder what was so abhorrent in Onan's behaviour. Biblical scholars provide several interpretations, but an interesting one seems to be simply based on greed: Had Er's wife had a male issue, his property would have gone to his son. Otherwise, it would be added to Onan's own inheritance. Other interpretations are more generous, but the fact remains that the spilling of seeds—each seen as a potential human being—was not to be pardoned.

The biblical ban on *coitus interruptus* may not have been entirely effective as one Sébastien Mercier wrote in 1771, "The husbands themselves take care in their raptures to keep from adding a child to the household." It was one of the very few options for families where women were kept in an almost constant stage of gestation. While sheaths, made of linen impregnated with chemicals or the intestine or bladder of animals, were used from the middle of the sixteenth century, they were mostly intended to prevent the spread of syphilis. The eighteenth-century adventurer Casanova was the exception, using condoms (the name first appeared in the mid-seventeenth century, probably originating from the Italian for 'little gloves') for birth control.

The church, already peeved that sexual congress should occur for pleasure as much as for procreation, was opposed to any contraceptive method, except the highly ineffective one (recommended since 1873) of observing a woman's ovulation cycle and abstaining when she was fertile. Called sterile-cycle sex or the rhythm method, it became the standard practice for observant Catholics.

The state had as much to say as the church about what happened in the bedrooms of the nation: in Canada, all methods of contraception other than observing a woman's 'rhythm' were illegal until the 1960s. That included douching, sponges, condoms, caps, diaphragms and abortions. Even the mere dissemination of information about contraception was declared obscene and liable to a prison term of up to two years. Lest we think Canada backward in her thinking, such were also the laws in Europe and America.

Before women went to work outside the home, their environment and support were usually limited to the women of their immediate and extended families, under the dominance and protection of titular males. Historian Judith Leavitt, working from women's diaries, shows that a woman could spend more than twenty years of her life either pregnant or nursing, on top of all her other duties. Until sympathetic legislation allowed abortions to be performed in a secure environment, desperate women were reduced to seeking illegal back-alley abortions at the hand of what the French called *faiseuses d'anges* (angel-makers) without any medical follow-up, or to inducing it themselves at great risk of complications and death.

Whenever botched abortions led to the women's deaths, their surviving children were also victims and the whole family suffered, often in shame and silence. My cousin's wife, a woman exhausted and unable to face yet another child while already coping with the demands of a large family, died following an illegal abortion in 1952—or so I gathered from overheard snippets of mournful conversation, since the matter was never discussed openly, my mother's family being intensely respectable.

The dilemma faced by many married women was even worse for girls. The English author Penelope Lively, who was born in the 1930s, observed that "Abortion was the awful spectre for girls. Each of us knew someone to whom the worst had happened with accompanying whispered horror stories about backstreet addresses and £100 in a brown envelope."[1] Jennifer Worth, a nurse and author of the bestselling memoir, *Call the Midwife*, underlined the lack of knowledge shown by abortionists. "It is not their fault that they were medically untrained; the legislation was to blame. Fatalities among women undergoing an abortion were high, but they were far higher among women who tried to do it themselves, unaided." It is then quite remarkable (and particularly indicative of the shame involved in giving birth to an illegitimate child) that some 12,000 abortions a year were performed legally in Britain in the 1950s on the ground that terminating the pregnancy would save the woman from the terrible stress of giving birth in adverse conditions.

In the west, a combination of medical advances and social changes led to a more liberal approach beginning in the 1960s. The birth control pill gave women a greater feeling of freedom and the sense they could at long last effectively control reproduction. Inextricably linked to a dynamic women's liberation movement, birth control also facilitated the practice of 'free love' without constraints and responsibilities.

The mood also corresponded to an easing of the law regulating abortion which led to a backlash from those who described themselves as pro-life. An American film, *The Silent Scream* (1984), purported to show the anguished reaction of a fetus at being terminated, utilizing the conventions of a horror film. Critics of the film described it as deeply manipulative, pointing to significant scientific inaccuracies concerning the actual stages of embryonic development.

1. David Kynaston, *Family Britain, 1951-57* (London: Bloomsbury Publishing, 2009), 564.

The issue of abortion and a woman's right to choose split most western societies. Several physicians who practised abortion were killed, injured or harassed in Canada and the United States as the direct targets of extremist pro-life proponents. Among those attacked, Henry Morgentaler was repeatedly prosecuted for setting up abortion clinics in Canada—and always acquitted. Vancouver doctor Garson Romalis survived two attempts on his life, one as recent as 2000.

Opinions on abortion continue to vary and so do national policies, from countries where it is offered freely to those where it is repressed and penalized. In Canada, the Criminal Law Amendment Act legalized abortion in 1969, provided that doctors certified it was required for the physical or mental health of the mother. In a later ruling (1988), the Supreme Court ruled that proviso unconstitutional, making abortion legal at any medically safe stage of the pregnancy. Under eight weeks, a medical miscarriage can often be triggered with pills, while surgical abortions, administered with local anaesthetic, pain killers and anti-anxiety drugs are a better choice for a more advanced stage. While officially and freely available, many women complain that obtaining an abortion in Canada is not easy for everyone as facilities are not available everywhere.

In 1971, 343 French women, in an act of public disobedience, confessed in *Le Nouvel Observateur* to having had illegal abortions. Abortion being a crime, they were not entirely protected by their status—most were women who had achieved a significant position in society, such as writer Françoise Sagan, philosopher Simone de Beauvoir and famous film actresses Catherine Deneuve and Jeanne Moreau—but none were prosecuted. France legalized abortion until the tenth week of pregnancy on a trial basis in 1975 and permanently in 1979. In the United Kingdom, the Abortion Law Act of 1967, a European first, continues to provide a wide number of grounds for seeking abortion.

In the United States, the matter still remains very controversial, reawakening the fear that women may once more have to resort to illegal means—in spite of landmark Roe v. Wade (1973) and the Supreme Court rule that recognized the right of women to abortion. Since then, various states have adopted either emphatic pro-choice or pro-life positions, and legislation varies accordingly.

As legislative, technological, and cultural changes have allowed women to take control of their reproductive lives, the associated stigma of abortion has diminished or, in some cases, even entirely disappeared. Ironically, there can now be new victims—female embryos. As a side effect of progress, when medical science supplanted folklore in guessing the sex of an unborn child, it gave sounder grounds for aborting healthy but undesirable foetuses in cultures when sons are deemed highly preferable to daughters.

FEMALE GENITAL MUTILATION

One manifestation of the obsessive concern with female genitalia is far more serious: female genital mutilation or FGM. A World Health Organization report (2018) indicates it has been performed on two hundred million girls and women alive today in thirty countries in Africa, the Middle East, and Asia. Others believe the number to be around one hundred million, but obviously exact figures cannot be confirmed.

There are four types of genital mutilation: clitoridectomy (removal of the clitoris), excision (removal of the clitoris and labia minora), infibulation (narrowing of the vaginal opening by cutting and repositioning the labia minora or majora to create a seal over the vagina), and other interventions that involve a variety of procedures such as pricking, piercing, incising, scraping, and cauterizing women's genital area. None carry any medical validation, all interfere with the woman's natural functions, all cause severe pain and can even lead to death. Equally troubling is the fact that FGM is most frequently performed by women, often related to the young victim of the practice, and themselves having been similarly mutilated in their youth.

Social acceptability is among the greatest motivators, and the elderly female relatives performing the mutilation believe they would be remiss in taking away such an asset, since it signifies virginity upon marriage (the morning-after waving of a bloodstained cloth as a proof of virginity is not a thing of the past) and greater desirability as a bride. The girls' families are eager to ensure their acceptability, and these mutilations are deemed a necessary part of preparing them for marriage. Moreover, the practice is deemed to render women cleaner and more beautiful after 'unclean' body parts have been removed, particularly when some of these parts seem outrageously to mimic maleness in appearance. Men naturally benefit from these mutilations: the girls are likely to be virgins, and the wives will be unlikely to engage in sex outside marriage if extra pain is incurred.

FGM is also said to repress the greatest *bête noire* of all: female libido, the much-feared insatiable carnal lust considered one of the manifestations of witchcraft in the *Malleus Maleficarum*. The dark mystery of female genitalia and sexuality—the original hysteria—has long confused, fascinated and frightened men. Modern man may not remember the old myths, but he still considers rape a weapon of war and desperately seeks to finally hit on the elusive G-spot.

NATURE ITSELF HAS CONTRIBUTED TO MAKING the female sex a mystery by keeping most of its organs hidden inside women's bodies. While we accept the display of penises in classical sculpture, we balk at the representation of the female sex as shown, for instance, in the realistic depiction of a woman's wide open thighs painted by Courbet in 1866. It may no longer scandalize us, but it may still make us uncomfortable. Courbet, by titling his work '*L'origine du monde*' (The Origin of the World) adds the mysterious power of creation and procreation to an organ that remains unrevealed and, most often, taboo. St. Peter Damian, an eleventh-century Benedictine, articulated the pathogenic misogyny characteristic of many sectarians:

You bitches, sows, screech-owl, night owls, she-wolves, blood suckers, [who] cry "Give, give! without ceasing" (Prov. 30:15-16). Come now, hear me, harlots, prostitutes, with your lascivious kisses, you wallowing places for fat pigs, couches for the unclean spirits, demi-goddesses, sirens, witches, devotees of Diana, if any portents, if any omens are found thus far, they should be judged sufficient to your name. For you are the victims of demons, destined to be cut off by eternal death. From you the devil is fattened by the abundance of your lust, is fed by your alluring feasts.

Rather than wonder whether women are basically prone to hysterics, a better question might be whether the ignorant fuss and misery created around female sexuality is not itself far more hysterical.

Historically, women who were unfaithful to their wedding vows, underwent abortions, or exhibited some characteristic of vulnerability or non-conformity were easy victims in various ways. They were accused of satanic possession, humiliated in charivaris, forced into uncontrolled fertility, deprived of individual freedom, repudiated and dispossessed. At the heart of their difference was often what men least understood about them—their forbidding and mysterious sexual identity and what was deemed to be their hysterical behaviour. In one way or another, they all embodied the evil spirit of Lilith.

Cultural mores have changed over time, but the underlying distrust of the hysterical female has not necessarily disappeared. In professional fields or the business world, behaviour that might be praised in men is decried in women: male assertiveness is female bossiness while strong emotion is described as passion in men and hysteria in women. Women's very voices, lighter and higher than men's, displease when raised (called 'strident') and do not convey authority. Any change in mood, acceptable in men and rationalized under the general label of stress, becomes—depending on age—a sign of either premenstrual syndrome or menopausal woes. Sometimes women themselves become convinced of their own estrogen-induced irrationality.

CHAPTER SEVEN

TESTOSTERONE AND TOGETHERNESS

IN THE CANADA OF 2018, ST. Michael's College School, a small Catholic private school for boys, was much in the news due to allegations of brutal hazing incidents, the latest in a series of abusive initiations into sports teams and other elite groups to find its way into the press. With each instance, the public was appalled, families were mortified, sanctions meted out, supervising adults reprimanded or fired, promises for more sensitive training made. Soon enough, the storm abates and everything falls back into place, even though the psychological damage may be long-lasting or permanent. It is perhaps ironic that religious schools, under stress for past abuses by teachers and caretakers, tend to focus on potential misdeeds by staff, all the while unaware that the students themselves could be abusers, and that the abuse could so often be of a sexual nature.

Rites of passage—the very word 'rite' implies a ritualized, codified, cultural approach to the process—exist in every society to signify elevation to a worthier status, another step in life's progress to higher levels of adulthood and valued tribal responsibility. In the past, they were often fearsome and dangerous, sometimes imbued with an almost supernatural nature during which the initiates' true identities were revealed and they acquired their mystical or totemic names.

When officially abandoned or debased, as in our modern society, ad hoc derivative improvisations occur and the so-called rites of passage can become both incoherent and aberrant. The ordeals imposed on the boys at St. Michael's and elsewhere are far more about displaying the personal power held by a few than the true desire to accompany initiates on their quest for acceptance into a special group of equals. From being a recognized and onerous process sought by individuals ready for different phases in life, they have become coarse and immature instances of abuse. Instead of being proud of having overcome rightful and sanctioned hardships to mark a new level of integration, boys facing this modern indoctrination can only feel resentment and diminution at experiencing a viciously perverted process. Similarly, the silence that used to be part of a higher mystery becomes a fear of seeming disloyal and a shameful acceptance of a status quo against which the victims see no recourse.

Private schools, whose pricey existence reveals much about our hierarchical thinking, are often organized according to a model that evolved in Great Britain for transforming turbulent youths into worthy leaders—the motto of St. Michael's is *Doce me bonitatem et disciplinam et scientiam* ("Teach me goodness, discipline, and knowledge" Psalm 118). Particularly in residential institutions (which does not include St. Michael's), small numbers of older men were invested with quasi-parental rights to dispense what discipline they thought appropriate, sometimes using corporeal punishment such as flogging (naturally not to the extent prevalent in the navy and the military, but both painful and humiliating), birching and caning. In Canada, corporeal punishment in schools was officially banned in 2004 but had in fact already been suppressed since 1973 (in British Columbia) and 1998 (in Quebec). Traditionally strictly segregated, with separate boys and girls' school, in recent decades modern private schools have been forced to become coeducational in order to survive, only slightly adjusting the original model.

Underlying this model is a long-standing belief that the essence of manhood is moral strength combined with the ability to sustain physical effort and to endure pain stoically. One of its rewards is a strong sense of solidarity derived from belonging to an elite group, a common factor displayed among many cohesive male assemblies. Throughout history, military organizations have relied on *esprit de corps* to strengthen their ranks. Guilds of artisans were organized in confraternities to control their trades, sometimes with secret undertones—the Freemasons, who still exist today, were once such a fraternal group that regulated the work of stonemasons. But the nature of masculinity and the power of cohesion are perhaps best exemplified by seafarers during the Age of Sail, when voyages were long, conditions harsh and communication with the outside world limited.

SEAFARERS

Faced with isolation for many months and assigned specific tasks on which their collective welfare depended, their very survival often at stake, seafarers inhabited a separate universe, sometimes known as the 'wooden world,' with its own hierarchical rules and element-driven logic. More than most, the wooden world met the conditions of maleness, isolation and interdependence conducive to the creation of strong bonds. In spite of their often disparate origins, cultures and languages, seafarers would accept the established customs and its vocabulary became the onboard *lingua franca*.

During the eighteenth and nineteenth centuries, men at sea all endured intense hardships while performing work that required strength, endurance and precise coordination. Moreover, poverty meant they had otherwise little or no control over their lives, and human connections were all the more valuable to them, especially in times of great uncertainty (mutinies, dangerous fishing expeditions, long voyages, pursuits and battles) when common effort could make the difference between success, escape or death.

There are touching reports of men joining spontaneously in song to celebrate or give thanks for successful crossings. The nineteenth-century naval officer-turned-journalist Gabriel de La Landelle wrote:

> We were returning from Brazil and approached the coast of France in the middle of winter. The sailors were shivering; they had got together in a tight bundle walking along the gangway between the fore-mast and main-mast: they were stamping in time, and in this way, close together, they were singing.

What they sang to accompany their rough stamping dance was a simple folksong about being close to home. Similarly, the men on the *Pinta*, upon sighting the islands of the New World, sang and danced around the mainmast to the accompaniment of pipes and a tambourine. They may have sung a hymn, perhaps the 'Salve Regina,' sometimes mistakenly thought to be an old Spanish sea shanty because it was so often sung on board those ships.

On board, no task was done in isolation and all seafarers needed to know they could rely on one another, whether sailing under their country's flag, on merchant ships, hunting whales or as pirates pursued for their crimes. Symbolic events sometimes evolved from these conditions, such as the ritual developed to mark the crossing of the equator. Initially, it took the form of perilous and unpleasant triple ceremonial dunking into the sea but was later softened to a mere dunking into a large pool of seawater contained in a sail. This line-crossing ritual was considered a form of baptism, acknowledging the sailor's passage from green 'pollywog' to seasoned 'shellback,' and celebrating his becoming a real seaman. Some could buy their way out through a contribution of alcohol, yet, however unpleasant the experience, very few did. All those who attended had themselves gone through the same initiation and custom had become its binding element. It made them all equal in the face of the sea and the new initiates could look forward to witnessing another group of pollywogs having to go through the same process on future crossings before being rightfully integrated into the sailing fraternity.

Another universal custom was their behaviour on shore leave, where seafarers found their release—drinking, whoring and having a good time—ignoring warnings such as those found in the traditional sea shanty 'New York Girls': "Your hard-earned cash will disappear, your rig and boots as well, For Yankee gals are tougher than the other side of Hell." Having landed in Sailortown (there was one district so called in almost every port) seamen, used to violence and always ready for a fight, were indistinguishable from land-based rowdies. William Bolton, born in 1840 and gone to sea at the age of twelve, reminisced on his younger days, "It was a favourite diversion among sailors ashore to take a walk down the Highway, and if their hearts were not cheered by the sight of some fight of disturbance already going on, to set about creating one without delay."[2]

While the wrath of the sea and the vagaries of the winds were the same for all—as was the often fierce discipline—each type of maritime occupation (naval, merchant, whaling or pirate) had its own culture. Men might move from the merchant service to the navy and back, or even end up briefly joining a pirate crew after experiencing the privateers' life, but the conditions on board these vessels were very different. What remained constant was the need to rely on one another.

The Navy

The very hierarchical British Navy, often victim of patronage at the highest level, knew how to put every man in his place, making brotherhood and mutual trust below deck a system of defence and self-protection—particularly since many of these sailors arrived on board through impressment and under initial duress or deception.

Unlike other European nations, Britain did not rely on conscription and, when there were not enough volunteers to man her ships, she resorted instead to impressment, a military custom dating from Saxon times. At the beginning of the war with France in 1793, a decree of Parliament raised the Royal Navy numbers to 45,000. The demand grew to 85,000 the next year and to 120,000 by 1799—an enormous burden for a population estimated at 8.6 million. Forcibly pressing men into wartime service was a fact of English life that gave rise to widespread frustration and misery and to several cases of violent resistance. A great many folk songs and sea shanties (often our main sources for understanding the

2. Roy Palmer, *The Oxford Book of Sea Songs* (Oxford, New York: Oxford University Press, 1986), 198.

common man's experience) describe young men innocently on their way to town, or finely dressed for a wedding, walking alone or in groups, being seized by pressgangs and taken to sea, many never to be seen again.

Whether as pressed men or volunteers, life was extraordinarily harsh in the British Navy. Most historians, but none more than John Masefield in his book *Sea Life in Nelson's Time* (1984), have commented in the strongest terms on the conditions endured by the men:

> Our naval glory was built up by the blood and agony of thousands of barbarously maltreated men. It cannot be too strongly insisted that sea life, in the late eighteenth century, in our navy, was brutalizing, cruel and horrible... There was the barbarous discipline, bad pay, bad food, bad hours of work, bad company, bad prospects.

Yet these men were proud of being at sea and felt superior to the landlubbers they despised. They felt pride at being part of the most powerful navy in the world and almost every naval victory was celebrated with its own song, each one ending with a toast to the successful commander and, always, to the 'brave tars,' the 'valiant men' who fought the battle for him, for they knew well enough their worth. Downtrodden, grossly underpaid, often flogged, dying young, these men proudly sang, "And may we always prove that in fighting and in love the true British sailor is the dandy, O."

The tars built the nation, made it rich and successful, yet were punished without mercy for the slightest infraction. Crews were controlled through fear and violence, and flogging was the preferred method of discipline. The Navy Articles of War, first issued by the Lords Commissioners of the Admiralty in 1653, recommended flogging "For the good of all, and to prevent unrest and confusion," but definitions were vague and a great deal of discretion was given to captains. A handful of captains known for their foul tempers and sadistic dispositions (Captains Lake and Pigot, notably) went to unbearable extremes, while others only used it to prevent what all sea captains feared most—mutiny of the crew. Other common but irritating behaviours such as malingering, gambling, stealing and an attitude known as 'silent insubordination' could also be punished by the lash.

Flogging was a measure of the fear groups of potentially unruly men inspired in those charged with controlling them. Yet, discipline was usually applied according to rules. A flogging of three dozen lashings normally required a court-martial, while a lesser sentence could be imposed at the captain's discretion. By the mid-eighteenth century, twelve lashes were the maximum authorized, although more were sometimes still handed out. They were publicly administered at the gangway by the boatswain and his mate, using a cat-o'-nine-tails (nine waxed cords each one ending with a small knot; actual cats being said to hold fire in their tails, this name gives an idea of the severity of the punishment). Floggings often took place on a Saturday to allow a period of recovery over Sunday. After the man was cut down from the mast to which he had been strapped, he would be taken to the sick berth by his mates to have salt rubbed into the wounds on his back to prevent infection.

Until the late 1700s, thieving sailors could be punished by 'running the gauntlet'—two lines of the ship's crew, each armed with a short length of rope to beat him further—after receiving the usual twelve lashes, followed at the end by another dozen lashes for good measure. Another sentence, 'flogging around the fleet,' required the offender to receive a number of lashes from the boatswain of each ship in turn, a punishment so harsh that the man sentenced to it was often offered the gallows as an alternative. When he did not survive, as sometimes happened, his mangled body was rowed ashore and buried in the mud below the tidemark, without religious rites. The men who did survive was usually reputed to be broken ever after. John Nicol, a seaman below deck, described what he personally witnessed while serving in the navy:

It was a dreadful sight; the unfortunate sufferer tied down on the boat and rowed from ship to ship, getting an equal number of lashes at the side of the vessel from a fresh man. The poor wretch, to deaden his suffering, had drunk a whole bottle of rum a little before the time of punishment. When he had only two portions to go to his punishment the captain of the ship perceived he was tipsy and immediately ordered the rest of the punishment to be delayed until he was sober. He was rowed back to the *Surprise,* his back swelled like a pillow, black and blue; some sheets of thick blue paper were steeped in vinegar and laid to his back. Before he seemed insensible, now his shrieks rent the air. When better he was sent to the ship where his tortures were stopped, and again renewed.

In 1797, mutiny —the very type of event severe disciplinary measures were intended to prevent—exploded in the Royal Navy, first at Spithead, then at Nore. Crews, already united by successful naval battles, banded even closer together in the uncertainty of their rebellion. Their songs elevated the previous 'brave tars' to 'brother seamen' as they urged others to add strength to their numbers, hopeful their demands would be accepted and they would escape punishment.

The mutineers created a 'parliament' to orchestrate their demands and named delegates to represent them. Their demands were not outlandish: more shore leave, better food, better treatment for the wounded, the removal of specific officers and a small increase in pay (which had remained the same for 144 years despite inflation and was moreover significantly below salaries in the merchant navy, particularly in peacetime when it was also frequently withheld). Although the negotiations with the Spithead delegates broke down, the Admiralty acceded to some of the mutineers' demands, particularly a small pay raise, and the men were pardoned. Their actions had been peaceful, even if their spirit had appeared rebellious.

The mutineers at Nore were not as lucky. Their demands exceeded those at Spithead and their location made it possible to block access to the Thames, something the Admiralty could not allow. A bill was immediately passed to outlaw the mutineers, who were court-martialled and flogged, hanged or transported to Australia.

Today, we consider flogging an aberrant disciplinary measure. Yet it was common in the militaries of most western countries. Soldiers were flogged for desertion and other serious offences, but some-times also for actions that modern sensitivity might see as morally praiseworthy. For instance, when refusing to fire on his compatriots to quell a small local rebellion at the Cartwright Mills in the West Riding of Yorkshire in 1812, a British soldier was sentenced to three hundred lashes—a sentence later reduced to twenty-five lashes at the request of the mill owner himself. In separate incidents in 1846 and 1867, two privates died from the consequences of flogging, and public protest eventually led the army to join the navy in abandon-ing the lash in 1881.

Flogging naturally also existed on American ships. In 1850, Senator John P Hale urged the American Congress to ban flogging, even when 234 of the 241 officers consulted advised against ban-ning it. Hale's inspiration came from Herman Melville's description of a brutal flogging in *White Jacket*, published the same year and evi-dence of the power of literature. Flogging was eventually abolished in the American Navy in 1861, almost twenty years before the Royal Navy followed suit (except in naval prisons).

In France, flogging as a means of maintaining military discipline was abandoned during the Revolution. While otherwise a bloody affair, the French Revolution resulted in the creation and main-tenance of a series of rights that respected the dignity of citizens, including the right not to be flogged.

Merchant Seamen
Much less is known about the merchant service at sea, as official records were neither as thorough nor as consistent as those of the navy, but it has routinely been seen as a training ground for the

latter. Indeed, impressment looked first for men with sea experience, and pressgangs often visited merchant ships for that purpose. The merchant service had its own methods of recruiting, some even more extreme than the Navy's pressgangs, and quite a few sailors were made to enlist when dead drunk or utterly broke—shanghaied (referring to the destination of many impressed crews) by men known as 'crimps,' acting in concert with naval captains. Desertion in ports was frequent, usually followed by re-enlistment on another ship, often with someone the deserter already knew and could vouch for him. In a world filled with violence and insecurity, trust in the man at their side could make all the difference.

Conditions on board merchant ships had much to do with the captain's behaviour. They could be even harsher than in the navy, particularly when captains or ship owners operated under the misplaced desire to save on provisions. Greed was often the only motive and profit the ultimate goal, and unfit ships, fully manned, were sometimes sent to sea, meant to sink for their insurance value. The situation was so scandalous that a series of protective steps were eventually legislated, thanks to the efforts of a British politician, Samuel Plimsoll, dubbed "the seamen's friend" by the press.

When violence occurred among the crew, the merchant marine hierarchy of captains and officers, while different from that of the Royal Navy, had the same powers to subdue the men—without many of the controls exercised in the king's service. Whereas the navy provided a chain of command with responsible officers along the way and recourse to courts-martial, sailors in the merchant service were left at the mercy of individual captains and ship owners. If a crew refused to sail on obviously unsafe ships, they were usually imprisoned as another, more desperate one could soon be found to sail in its place.

On American merchant ships, corporeal punishment routinely occurred right up to the introduction of 1915 Seamen's Act. Until then, merchant crews would be punished with whatever was to hand, including belaying pins and marlin spikes.

Whalers

Whalers were a group apart, highly specialized and only sailing during the period of the hunt. They often came from the same region, the same port, and even from the same close group.

Whaling crews were often hired according to their competence—a man went by his reputation as an effective whaler or, alternatively, as someone who could not be trusted or had run out of luck—the latter sometimes known as a 'Jonah.' In addition to the common seafaring problems, they were exposed to the extreme danger of the whaleboats, often capsizing in the hunt or being smashed to pieces. They could be at sea for long periods, scouring the Pacific Ocean from north to south for the elusive whales needed to fill their quotas.

The tight collaboration required on any ship was particularly critical for whalers at the time of the hunt, when the slightest false move could have catastrophic consequences. The traditional song, 'The Greenland Voyage' also known as 'The Whale Fisher's Delight,' already deemed to be old when it was published in 1725, describes in detail—almost blow by blow—the preparations for a voyage, the excitement and disappointments of the chase, the success and effort, and the team work involved, including each man's name and his unique position in the boat according to his function.

Shanties record the prolonged and repeated efforts of whalers and acknowledge the power of the formidable animals they hunted, exalting the whaling experience as unique among the various reasons for going to sea.

> We stuck the whale the line paid out,
> But she gave a flourish with her tail,
> The boat capsized and four men were drowned,
> And we never caught that whale, brave boys,
> And we never caught that whale.
> To lose the whale, our captain said,
> It grieves my heart full sore,
> But oh! to lose (those) four gallant men

It grieves me ten times more, brave boys
It grieves me ten times more. ('Greenland Whale Fisheries')

While Navy captains may well have been distressed to lose the valuable resource an able seaman represented, another soon took his place up the mast or at the guns; their primary emotion was likely pride in the battles fought and in the men who won them. Whaling captains, by contrast, grieved losing individual men, with whom they likely shared close ties even on land.

Pirates and Buccaneers

Disenfranchised men, mostly British sailors, who found themselves ill-suited to more conventional forms of maritime life sometimes became pirates, sailing under the white skull and crossbones. They are thought to have started as a group of white sailors and perhaps escaped slaves who, in the late seventeenth century, gathered around an idealistic Captain Mission, who may have founded a society they called Libertalia (or Libertatia) in Madagascar.

These highwaymen of the sea attempted to build a model society of outlaws ruled by consensus. Their regulations appeared in *A General History of the Robberies and Murders of the Most Notorious Pyrates* (1724), attributed to a fictitious Captain G. Johnson. Many believed it was written by Daniel Defoe, but some scholars suspect that its real author had personal experience of a pirate's life. Regardless of its provenance, this work covered all aspects of life on board a pirate ship, which offered much better conditions than those men had previously experienced. In fact, several measures were taken precisely to avoid the pitfalls of sailing with merchantmen or national navies:

> They chose a captain from among themselves, who in effect held little more than that title, excepting in an engagement, when he commanded absolutely and without control. Most of them, having suffered formerly from the ill-treatment of their officers, provided carefully against such evil, now they had the choice

in themselves. By their orders they provided especially against quarrels which might happen among themselves, and appointed certain punishment for anything that tended that way; for the due execution thereof they constituted other officers beside the captain, so very industrious were they to avoid putting too much power into the hands of one man.

Their democratic aspirations—the very antithesis of usual sea life as they had experienced it—included giving every man a vote in the affairs of the group and equal title to provisions. Among the most revolutionary aspects of their government was the way they took care of their own, ensured fairness in their conduct with each other, and compensated their wounded according to a regulated scale. The latter in particular offered a drastic contrast with the lack of care provided by the navy, whose shame it was to see its wounded and maimed seamen, no longer employable, relying on public charity in the streets of London and other ports. With their missing limbs and begging bowls, they were a sad and common sight.

An earlier maritime republic, the buccaneers, had also ruled themselves consensually, all the while plundering Spanish galleons in the Caribbean. Settling in Tortuga around 1640 and calling themselves The Brethren of the Coast, they were originally French hunters attracted to Haiti by the cattle brought from Spain, living in the bush and learning from the native Arawaks how to smoke meat on a grill (*boucane*). They were joined by derelicts from many countries (primarily England, Ireland, France, Holland and Belgium) including convicted felons, religious or political dissidents and prisoners of war. Like pirate society, they ensured fair distribution of the proceeds of their attacks and tended to their wounded, with no allegiance other than to themselves.

Pirates and buccaneers were brutal men made even more brutal by circumstance. Their lives were predicated on terror, which they evoked as a tool to avoid confrontation, elicit information about booty, or punish sea captains. They usually acted atrociously toward their victims, with the odd exception of magnanimity. Unlike the fictional Jack Sparrow's insouciant countenance and devil-may-care attitude, actual pirates were dark and ill-fated men who survived from day to day, and whose career was usually brief. All knew they were doomed, and they often justified their crimes as fair retribution for the way they themselves had been treated.

In 1720, pirate Calico Jack's vessels and crews were captured, and the Colonial Admiralty Courts were established. The Piracy Act of 1721 enabled the Royal Navy to destroy the pirates' strongholds on Mauritius and Reunion, and 1722 was disastrous for pirates operating in Africa, with the largest trial ever held (264 pirates) at Cape Town Castle. At the same time, French vessels patrolled the Persian Gulf and Dutch vessels safeguarded the Red Sea. The era of the pirates came to an end. In spite of—or perhaps because of—the consequences of their rebellious ways, the everyday harshness of their lives and the constant perils to which they were exposed, seafarers of all stripes relished most of all the privileged status that set them apart from everyone else. They saw it as the unique mark of a proud manhood, for these very conditions made them the outstanding cluster of brave ruffians they were, who only had one another to rely on. Each man could have adopted for his own the pirates' motto, "a Pyrate's life is the only Life for a Man of any Spirit."

HOOLIGANS
Definitions of masculinity started to change with the Industrial Revolution. Physical attributes, the purview of youth, became less important and were gradually supplanted by education or skills that took time to acquire, leaving by the wayside frustrated young men who once had their place in an orderly world. Youthful criminals formed urban gangs and one such, based in Lambeth in London, was labelled the Hooligan Boys by police and the press. As early as the 1880s, hooliganism became associated with the sport of soccer,

when aggressive supporters began intimidating neighbourhoods and attacking referees, players and even spectators. Instances of violence increased over the years until, by the 1960s, about twenty-five violent incidents were reported every year and the term 'football hooliganism' was coined.

Its frequency and severity may have been new, but disruptive behaviour associated with sport had long been an English tradition. As early as 1314, Edward II banned football (then a sort of free-for-all that involved tossing a pig's bladder across the local green) for fear that village violence might lead to social unrest. More generally, rowdy behaviour once accompanied almost every form of sport and game and was an intrinsic part of English fairs. Dickens, for instance, described the atmosphere of the Greenwich fair as "a periodical breaking out…a sort of spring-rash: a three days' fever, which cools the blood for six months afterwards, and at the expiration of which London is restored to its old habits of plodding industry." (*Sketches by Boz*, 1836)

Not surprisingly, these outbreaks were often accompanied by another traditional pastime on these occasions—drinking. Fairs were intense moments when many of the usual rules were overlooked if not entirely broken; in addition to drinking and rowdiness, robbery and sexual licence were common practices. The brash success of fairs and the accompanying noisy confrontations led to their eventual closure, leaving a gap in the built-in safety valves society provides to its young men. Modern interpretations of the causes for hooliganism still revolve around excessive drinking in combination with violence in sports, ritualized male violence, unemployment and the consequences of permissiveness in a society unable to control its youth.

Generally associated with the working class, hooliganism was mainly a young man's preoccupation, although women introduced their own brand of misbehaviour after the end of World War I. An article in the *Daily Express* reported in November 1920: "Women have now begun to take a hand in the scenes of misbehaviour by spectators that occur at football matches when the play or the control of the game is not according to their taste."

Also known as 'the English disease,' hooliganism consists of taunting the supporters of opposing teams, fighting with them, and generally causing mayhem before, during, or after a match, a behaviour known as aggro (for aggravation) or bovver (the Cockney pronunciation of bother). Hooligans exhibit a strong pack mentality that includes obscene songs and chants, specific manners of dress and ultra-partisanship. A sense of allegiance to a specific territory is another hallmark—in France, for example, violent fights and post-game riots, complete with car burning and shop window smashing, is almost *de rigueur* whenever the northern Paris Saint-Germain plays the southern Olympique de Marseilles. When black players were hired in national clubs, racial slurs found their way into the usual panoply of insults, prompting French teams to launch a counter-initiative under the united and alliterative banner of *"Black, blanc, beur"* (black, white, French from North Africa).

Hooliganism transcends borders, and rowdy fans often follow their teams abroad, where they delight in fighting their counterparts, often involving the general public in the disorder they cause. During the 1985 European Cup final, a riot involving supporters of England's Liverpool and Italy's Juventus led to the collapse of a wall in Belgium's Eysel Stadium, causing the death of thirty-nine people and injuries to 600 others. Thirty-four people were arrested, and fourteen Liverpool fans were convicted of manslaughter. Furthermore, English clubs were banned from European competition for five years, Liverpool for six.

While hooliganism is now a world-wide phenomenon, with particularly strong roots in South America and Eastern Europe, Great Britain is its apotheosis. Most of its clubs have been involved in one form or another, but the most notorious are Chelsea (where an electric fence was built to keep hooligans at bay, but not used), Leeds (banned from European competitions after rioting in the

1975 European Cup final in Germany, also involved in riots in Birmingham in 1985), Manchester United (first booted out of the 1975 European Cup in France after their fans rioted, then reinstated), Millwall (also famous rioters during a 1985 game at Luton), Tottenham Hotspur (rioting at the 1974 UEFA Cup final and again in Rotterdam in 1983, and known for their racial and homophobic taunts), Wolverhampton (with dozens of fans convicted of hooliganism in the late 1980s) and, of course, Liverpool.

After the deaths in Belgium, the Thatcher government stepped in to curb violence in football, with the support of club owners alarmed by declining attendance and revenue. Among the new measures were banning alcohol and racist chanting, compiling registers of known hooligans, barring misbehaving fans, banning potential weapons, searching suspected hooligans, checking their vehicles on international routes, dispersing suspicious groups, segregating opposing fans behind fences, increasing police presence and creating safer all-seated stadia to reduce crowd movement. The police also use preventative powers to disperse groups, authorized by the Anti-Social Behaviour Act (2003). As hooliganism and violence decreased, nonviolent fans no longer feared for their security. The fan base broadened and gentrified, and more women started attending matches, contributing to a gentler atmosphere. On the whole, crowd self-regulation, better stadium organization and stricter police control have succeeded in obtaining some relief for a sport that, at its best, has been called 'the beautiful game.'

The trends that accompanied the decline in hooliganism continue, making the professional sports industry one of the largest and fastest growing in the world. Regional allegiances remain strong and sports fans continue to paint symbolic marks on their faces, wear the colours of their clubs, and place brightly frizzy wings askew on their heads. They still chant and sing team songs (hymns are favoured in Wales, beer mugs in hands). While many women are among them, males still dominate. Physical prowess is celebrated, traditions are revered and camaraderie is valued. Fans have a strong sense of belonging and, for short periods, are content to allow the rules of the pack to control their actions.

YOUTH GANGS

The word gang originally referred to people similarly engaged, often going on a journey, and to groups of men operating in close proximity with common interests requiring mutual trust and reliance. By the early seventeenth century, the term had taken on nautical connotations, becoming the root of such terms as gangway, gang-plank and pressgang ('prest' referred to the small amount of money given to seamen upon being recruited). The modern use of the term, with its criminal overtones, dates to the middle of the nineteenth century. After studying 1,313 cases in the 1920s, American sociologist Frederic Thrasher arrived at the following specific definition that is still valid today:

> The gang is an interstitial group originally formed spontaneously, and then integrated through conflict. It is characterized by the following types of behavior: meeting face to face, milling, movement through space as a unit, conflict, and planning. The result of this collective behavior is the development of tradition, unreflective internal structure, *esprit de corps,* solidarity, morale, group awareness, and attachment to a local territory.

Young men come together to attain a status otherwise denied to them. Charged with inquiring into the nature and causes of juvenile delinquency in the 1960s, journalist Roul Tunley exposed the difficulties experienced by one ordinary male teenager deprived of the functions previously assumed by youths working on the family farm or contributing to the family's income with odd jobs after school. The young man was further confronted with today's array of expensive goods and the promotion of sex through television and other media, and was frustrated by his lack of access to these rewards through a form of prolonged infantilization.

Paradoxically living in the most privileged nation in history, he finds that for him the most important privilege of all—proving that he is a man—is denied him. Registering his importance to his family and to the community, and thereby taking his place in adult society, is indefinitely and dangerously postponed.[1]

Gangs provide a home of sorts to disaffected youths who find in them the validation and inclusion society at large is not able to provide. Much like hooligans (indeed, English hooligans have sometimes been associated with skinheads and German ones with neo-Nazis), gang members are typically teenagers and young men, defiant of any type of control save their chosen gang's strict code of conduct. It is true today that girls (once the mere appendages of 'bad boys') can now be full-fledged members of their own gangs, but it is the aura of testosterone that continues to permeate violent rebellious behaviour. Their names may evoke specific affinities (with motorcycles, for instance) or neighbourhood or ethnic groupings (most prone to turf wars); they may also reveal a strong sense of brotherhood (such as Brothers Keepers and Wolf Pack, the names of two Vancouver gangs).

In fact, gangs share many characteristics with the pirate societies of a previous era: self-government, strict observance of rules, the belief that respect from their peers is their greatest reward, an outlaw mentality based on an antisocial morality, the conscious use of terror tactics to intimidate others and a propensity for dying young. Like the pirates of old, many also observe brutal and secret rites of passage and, like hooligans, most gang members announce their allegiance through prescribed clothing, gang colours and tattoos.

Gangs are attracting younger and younger members, drawn by a taste for violence and a sense of discipline and commitment. The involvement of children in criminal activities is not new, but these used to consist mainly of trafficking contraband cigarettes, particularly in Western Europe after the war, often their only

---

1. Roul Tunley, *Kids, Crime and Chaos. A World Report on Juvenile Delinquency* (New York: Dell Publishing, 1964), 119.

means of survival. Unlike Fagin's young thieves-in-training in *Oliver Twist,* today's young gangsters do not report to an older adult who gives them protection; they are characterized by a new and gratuitous addiction to violence that some blame on television and social media. In Italy, for example, infamous 'baby gangs,' at one point rode scooters through the streets of Naples, armed with Kalashnikovs, creating havoc and terrorizing people, filling a power vacuum created by the arrest of several bosses of the Camorra, the powerful local crime syndicate that dates back to the seventeenth century. In an article on Italian gang violence in *The Independent* newspaper, Robert Saviano (author of *Gomorrah*) is quoted as saying that "organized crime remains among the few areas of economic growth that the city has to offer." The causes of this violence seem self-evident to many: "70,000 people living in five square kilometres, without a single nursery or junior school and there's a secondary school ranked the second worst in the country. Where are the young going to end up, apart from the clutches of the Camorra?"

HISTORIAN CLIVE GAMBLER HAS CALLED MAN'S innate desire to push the limits of his world a "heroic tradition." Some were successful and sailed off to discover other shores. Others remained, stirred by the same impulse to push their personal frontiers but unable to fulfill it. And yet others could only do what overwhelmed men do, work to merely survive, their unrealized ambitions creating the potential for violence.

Western society seems to both revere and fear the power of its young men. The most violent forms of discipline and control have typically been used where they are found in the greatest concentrations, usually set apart from society: in the navy, in the army, in the prisons, even in the schools. It is as though young men in groups would otherwise be uncontrollable and hold the constant threat of turning against authority—as though, in fact, they were the enemy within.

What characterizes the actions of many of these men, past and present—sailors, pirates, hooligans, gang members—is a sense of danger, potentially unchannelled violence and the rupture with established rules of conduct. Most thrive on disorder, whether fighting among themselves or banding together against others. The sailors and pirates of the eighteenth century might have been the hooligans or gang members in ours. Some were misfits, others were merely victims of their social environment. Restless and frustrated, they resented the antagonistic pressure of the higher born, the wealthier, who held power over them. A few lucky ones were acknowledged as leaders and were rewarded for their daring thoughts and deeds, others attempted to redress their circumstances, the majority were reduced to banging their heads against fate, carried along by an urgent restlessness, and always finding strength in the company of their mates.

CHAPTER EIGHT

THE KILLING PLAGUE

STANLEY KUBRICK'S 1968 FILM, *2001: A Space Odyssey (The Dawn of Man)*, begins with a scene depicting two groups of hominids, each using threatening gestures and violent inarticulate shouting to intimidate the other. When one among them discovers, almost accidentally, that a long bone can be used as a club, the next confrontation results in a deliberate act of killing.

The music then explodes. It is an adaptation of the1896 composition by Richard Strauss, 'Thus Spoke Zarathustra,' named after Nietzsche's book about the fundamental tension between good and evil. Zarathustra explains man's position as "a rope, tied between beast and overman—a rope over an abyss. A dangerous across, a dangerous on-the-way, a dangerous looking back, a dangerous shuddering and stopping." In *Ecce Homo: How One Becomes What One Is,* Nietzsche considers that "Zarathustra created this most calamitous error, morality; consequently, he must also be the first to recognize it."

Today, fifty years after the film was first shown, the raised arm brandishing the first homicidal weapon still has the same chilling effect. The music overpowers, underlining the danger without words; we all recognize the raised weapon and the feeling behind it. As we watch the Dawn of Man, we see the foreshadowing of our species' destiny, where evil and dissonance so easily play a dominant part.

Humans killing humans is reputed to have started with Cain and Abel. The crime was accompanied by the devastating notion of guilt, the consequence of the knowledge acquired by Adam and Eve. Only knowledge can inspire guilt and, if we believe Victor Hugo in the poem 'Cain,' (or *'La Conscience*') in *La Légende des siècles,* no man suffered more from knowing the extent of his sin than Cain. Hiding in the darkness of a tomb to escape the omnipresent accusing eye of God, he comes to realize the futility of flight, for "the eye was in the tomb and was looking at Cain."

From gods and kings to bugs and babes, anything or anyone can be killed. Killing is so common that language simply describes the crime by attaching the suffix -cide (from the Latin *cidium* and the verb *caedare,* to kill) to the Latin word for any potential victim: uxoricide (wife), suicide (self), infanticide (baby), matricide (mother), patricide (father), fratricide (brother), sororicide (sister), regicide (king), genocide (species), deicide (god), and so on.

Raskolnikov, the nihilist in Dostoevsky's novel *Crime and Punishment,* had a nightmarish vision of a "killing plague":

> Those infected were seized immediately and went mad... Whole settlements, whole cities and nations were infected and ... people killed each other with senseless rage and went mad. Whole armies were mustered against each other, but as soon as the armies were on the march they began suddenly to tear themselves apart. The ranks dispersed; the soldiers flung themselves upon each other, slashed and stabbed, ate and devoured each other...They started accusing each other, fighting each other, and stabbing away. Fires blazed; hunger set in, everything and everybody went to wrack and ruin.

The same image of an omnipresent, all-pervasive, and inescapable plague spreading hate, evil, and death, contaminating everyone, is taken up by Albert Camus in *La Peste* (*The Plague*):

> The plague bacillus never dies or disappears for good...it can lie dormant for years and years in furniture and linen chest...it bides its time in bedrooms, cellars, trunks, and bookshelves...and perhaps the day would come when, for the bane...of men, it would rouse up its rats again and send them forth to die in a happy city.

The morality of killing other humans is largely determined by motive. When killers are seen to be acting for purely personal reasons (greed, anger, jealousy, perverted love, indifference, fanaticism), their actions are disavowed and punished. Other killers, seen to be acting for the greater good, enjoy widespread support and approval: stopping a criminal endangering others (the police), assassinating a tyrant (such as the attempts on Hitler's life by some German officers) or someone symbolizing a specific political position (assassination of Archduke Franz Ferdinand in Sarajevo), resistance to an occupying enemy force (the French *Maquis,* among many other resistance movements). Other factors that diminish or prevent the exercise of free will, such as mental impairment, also provide arguments for freeing the killers from legal and moral responsibility for their crimes.

When killing moves from the individual to the collective, the moral equation changes. Wars, massacres and genocides rely on the surrendering of individual free will in order to achieve a presumed greater good. Going one step further, wars offer the best possible defence for killing without responsibility—soldiers are trained to obey orders and wars are all about killing the enemy, so refusal to kill constitutes a form of treason. 'Thou shalt not kill' becomes 'you must kill to protect your country and defeat its enemy.' Wars strike the imagination because of this subversion. Even though at least twice as many people died during the Spanish influenza outbreak of 1918 (some estimates are as high as one hundred million) compared to the war that concluded the same year, it is the war that is commemorated, not the epidemic—'lest we forget' the awesome power and consequences of killing, rather than merely dying.

The causes of war are many, from geopolitical to economic, and presuppose an expensively equipped military force. Indeed, mankind may have spent as many resources achieving cheaper and more efficient ways of killing one another as it has on improving health and welfare. Beginning with the long bone depicted in Kubrik's film, how to kill ever greater numbers more efficiently has proved a feast of the imagination for the inventive mind. From catapults to longbows to tanks to Agent Orange, from shaping an arrowhead to splitting the atom, from horses and chariots to fifth-generation jet fighters, the evolution of weaponry has reflected the technological advancements of civilization. Whether this capacity illustrates our evil-mindedness and murderous compulsions, or whether it speaks to our ability to abstract ourselves from the consequences of our actions by reducing the perfecting of weaponry to a mere technical problem to be solved, is a matter for debate. The complexity of our motives seems to accommodate both.

The strong and powerful seeking to destroy the weak or 'inferior' is the age-old foundation for many group-orchestrated killings. But the attendant methods and motives have evolved–Kubrick's hominids have become individuals who, when under attack in situations over which they have no control (such as wars), can become both perpetrators and victims. Both are abhorrent to the sense of equilibrium needed for a mentally healthy life and a dear price is paid by those who fail to reconcile their orders, their deeds, and their conscience and relinquish responsibility to a group. It has been estimated that 20 percent of German soldiers ordered to kill civilians later suffered psychiatric problems such as recurring nightmares, depression, irritability or even criminality. Sometimes the malaise translates into the helplessness and fear that lead to Post-Traumatic Stress Disorder (PTSD, the 'shell shock' of old). Sometimes, as well, individual responsibility dissolves into the irresponsible fear, anger and insecurity of massacres perpetrated by a group.

DEMOCIDE AND GENOCIDE

Not all mass killings are committed by combatants. Some result from systematic government policies instigated against specific groups within its population. After World War II, two new words appeared in the lexicon to describe this phenomenon. *Democide* refers to the routine killing of specific groups as punishment for not obeying policies or failing to meet production quotas. Targeting identifiable groups with the specific desire to exterminate them, is the purpose of *genocide*.

The words may have been newly coined but the actions, particularly genocide, did not originate in the twentieth century. Long before, the Israelites eliminated the Philistines, the Romans utterly destroyed Carthage and its inhabitants *(Cartago delenda est*—Carthage *must* be destroyed—being the constant exhortation of the Punic Wars), the Crusades hounded the Infidels, and the timid Beothuks of Newfoundland were hunted down for sport before eventually dying out from the new diseases brought in by Europeans. Other examples abound.

The archetypical government-led slaughter is the Massacre of the Innocents described in the Gospel of Matthew 2 and depicted in Rubens' 1612 painting of the same name. King Herod of Judea, upon hearing from the Magi that a 'king of the Jews' had been born and could potentially threaten his position, "was exceeding wroth, sent forth, and slew all the children that were in Bethlehem, and in all the coast thereof, from two years old and under." Slaughter has since taken many other forms.

In the Congo Free State (allocated by the 1885 Berlin Conference as the private property of King Leopold II of Belgium before becoming a colony in 1908), democide involved the routine and punitive killing of native workers who failed to achieve their production quotas in the rubber plantations——whose profits helped build many of the magnificent buildings in Brussels. Barbara Emerson, Leopold II's biographer, declares, "Leopold… was greedy for money and chose not to interest himself when things got out of control." Discipline was administered by mercenaries, charged with cutting off hands, noses and ears of terrified workers and required to bring in evidence of their mutilations to be paid. The following statement given by a witness at the time and substantiated by contemporary photographic evidence, describes the methods of one Belgian official known as The Devil of the Equator:

From all the bodies killed in the field, you had to cut off the hands. He wanted to see the number of hands cut off by each soldier, who had to bring them in baskets…As a young man, I saw [his] soldier…take a big net, put the arrested natives in it, attach big stones to the net, and make it tumble into the river… Rubber caused these torments; that's why we no longer want to hear its name spoken. Soldiers made young men kill or rape their own mothers or sisters.

In Cambodia, under Pol Pot and the Khmer Rouge regime (1975–79), massive slaughters were organized against the population, not based on economic considerations but on cultural ones. Buddhists killed Buddhists and every educated Cambodian (the definition being the equivalent of a grade eight education in North America) was deemed potentially antagonistic to the regime. Reports made by refugees to the American embassy in Thailand reported "mass executions of people killed mechanically by a blow of the back of the head with a garden hoe…by teenage boys. Children had been starved, and Buddhist monks asphyxiated." Altogether, upwards of 2.5 million people were buried in 'the killing fields.' Until his death in 1988, Pol Pot was still denying the events.

While the Cambodian government targeted a potentially dissident political group, most institutionalized government killings are based on race or religion. The best known example of this type of genocide is The Holocaust or Shoah, from the pogrom of Kristallnacht (1938) to the Nuremberg Trials (1945–46). It continues to raise questions of responsibility and invokes fear of extremist political regimes to this day:

The Holocaust disturbs us so deeply because it demonstrates that none of the things we associate with the advancement of civilization—peace, prosperity, industrialization, education, technological achievement—free us from the dark side of the human soul. Just as there is evil in the heart of every man, there is evil at the heart of even the most "civilized" society. It

162

is a humbling recognition. Man and society are both capable of the most appallingly depraved behavior. Only in the case of society, it occurs on an industrial scale. (Mark Bowden, *New York Times*, October 4, 2006)

Unfortunately, the Holocaust is neither the sole nor the most murderous example of genocide, even within the twentieth century. Far more people (anything from seven to ten million) died during the Holomodor, the Ukrainian terror starvation of 1932–33. It arose when mainly urban Marxists attempted to collectivize Ukrainian farmers, who had largely voted against the Bolsheviks; the farmers responded by killing their livestock rather than turn them over to the state. Stalin, supported by armed fanatics, retaliated by ordering the seizure of the harvest and preventing the importation of food. To safeguard the 1932 crop against the starving farmers, watchtowers, similar to those seen in prisons, were erected around the fields and manned by guards armed with shotguns. Twenty percent of the Ukrainian population perished; most of their allied Cossacks were either killed or deported to Siberia. A survivor, Miron Dolot, recounted what he witnessed in his 1985 book, *Execution by Hunger: The Hidden Holocaust*:

> The first deaths from hunger began to occur…One could see strange funeral processions: children pulling homemade hand-wagons with the bodies of their dead parents in them or the parents carting the bodies of their children. There were no coffins; no burial ceremonies performed by priests. The bodies of the starved were just deposited in a large common grave, one upon the other; that was all there was to it. Individual graves were not allowed…All [these] events…seem unreal to me because of their cruelty and unspeakable horror.

The term 'ethnic cleansing' was coined during the Bosnian war (1992–94) to describe Serbian president Slobodan Milosevic's campaign to partition and control Bosnia without any concession to the 40 percent of the population who were Muslim. Initially, the 'cleansing' only meant limiting jobs and curtailing freedoms to non-Serb Bosnians, but it soon led to deportation on forced marches and then to elimination. Within the first year, 100,000 Bosnians were killed; many were decapitated or starved to death, but the total number of victims is not known. Systematic rapes were reported to have reached up to 50,000, the women being later killed. The United Nations forces sent to protect non-Serbian Bosnians were soon overrun and 7,000 Muslims were slaughtered at Srebrenica in 1995.

Each of these events was reported and public opinion harshly condemned them. However, people's attention is fleeting, in spite of the pious words always expressed. Events take place far away, good intentions tire of seeing little result or solution, and other distractions soon occur elsewhere, permitting dreadful actions to go almost unnoticed. Such was the case of the slaughter of 1.5 million Armenians by the Turks of the Ottoman Empire, an atrocity eclipsed by the simultaneous events of World War I.

The problem there was not new. Christians in Armenia had been in conflict with their Muslim rulers since being absorbed into the Ottoman Empire in the fifteenth century. Nevertheless, they were often more successful and better educated than their Muslim neighbours and came to be resented for it. Sultan Abdul Hamid II told a reporter in 1890, "I will soon settle those Armenians... I will give them a box on the ear which will make them relinquish their revolutionary ambitions." The box on the ear actually took the form of pogroms over two years (1894–96), sanctioned by the state, and resumed in earnest on April 24, 1915 when the government started arresting Armenian intellectuals, fearful that they (and other Christian minorities) might side with the enemy, Russia.

Although the majority of Armenians expressed their loyalty, they could not escape persecution. Mehmed Talaat, the leader of the ruling Young Turks, explained to the American ambassador why they made no distinction between innocent and guilty Armenians:

"It was utterly impossible, in view of the fact that those who were innocent today might be guilty tomorrow." As Armenians protested, the familiar pattern of deportation and usurpation was repeated. Civilian killing squads (often made of ex-convicts) were organized, killing men, kidnapping children (to be brought up as Muslim Turks) and raping women. Many others were sent on death marches through the Mesopotamian desert.

It is believed that about two million Armenians lived in the Ottoman Empire at the beginning of the campaign to annihilate them; when the killing was officially over in 1922, only 388,000 still remained. It wasn't until 2010 that a US Congressional panel voted to recognize these events as the first genocide of the twentieth century. Turkey continues to deny many of the facts.

MASSACRES

The side effects of war include suspicion of occupied populations and a general deterioration of moral standards. When combined with stress and opportunity, they may lead some small groups to succumb to a momentary and almost psychotic lapse of control, even when there is no evidence that their actions are warranted. They seem carried away by the general madness and confusion of war and, ruled by the urge to destroy, massacre unarmed civilian populations. What renders these actions particularly heinous is the physical proximity between unarmed victims and out-of-control men bearing weapons. Unlike pilots, who indiscriminately killed far more civilians, including young children, in bombing raids, men involved in massacres physically aim at the weakest among them. While war itself is chaos, the massacres within seem to be issued from an even darker and more evil source.

Some massacres are better remembered than others; among those of the twentieth century, Nanking, Oradour-sur-Glane and Monte Sole, My Lai and Rwanda are well documented and illustrate the killing plague at its most frightening. Their common characteristic is the rejection of individual responsibility for crimes committed as a group. It is quite remarkable how few of their most active participants were punished to the extent of the law, as if the deviance from norms and the lack of control they displayed were seen as analogous to temporary madness.

The Rape of Nanking (1937)

The events in Nanking, lasting over six weeks during the 1937 Sino-Japanese War, were exceptional by the cruelty shown and the numbers killed (some 250,000 are estimated). The systematic massacre, apparently started by a forged order, may have begun as a way of dealing with the nightmarish problem of attempting to feed the 500,000 civilians and 90,000 Chinese troops who surrendered to 50,000 Japanese soldiers. Moreover, the Chinese soldiers, executed in groups of fifty, were despised by the Japanese, whose code of conduct and sense of honour did not allow surrender. As one Japanese soldier later wrote, "If my life was not important, an enemies's life [sic] became inevitably less important."

The Japanese seemed to have suffered from an extreme case of ethnocentricity, where outsiders were deemed to be subhuman (a view supported in some of the Japanese soldiers' diaries). Standards of morality reverted to being mandated primarily at the local, tribal level and did not necessarily apply when confronting out-group members, particularly on foreign soil, away from anything familiar. Even so, the Japanese, in the middle of general bloodlust, retained enough self-control not to hurt the non-Chinese living in an International Safety Zone. Race was the determining factor in who was a legitimate target and who was not.

Although the Japanese government officially declared the massacre never occurred, foreigners living in Nanking attested to it, as did some Japanese journalists. War crimes trials were eventually held in Tokyo and Nanking, where some Japanese officers were convicted and hanged.

Oradour-sur-Glane and Monte Sole (1944)

Today, the small French village of Oradour-sur-Glane still bears witness to the unexplained massacre of 642 people, including 247 children, by the German *Waffen-Schutzstaffel* (SS), a combat unit within Nazi Germany's military forces responsible for most of the atrocities committed by the regime. The village may have been falsely accused of harbouring civilian *Maquis* fighters and of holding two SS soldiers prisoner.

On June 10, during their retreat to the north of France, the Germans ordered the men to assemble in the village square and started shooting them, while the women and children were locked in the church. Marguerite Rouffranche, the only survivor of the massacre in the church, testified in front of the 1953 military tribunal at Bordeaux, as quoted in the Official Publication:

> Shoved together in the holy place, we became more and more worried as we awaited the end of the preparations being made for us. At about 4 p.m. some soldiers, about twenty years old placed a sort of bulky box in the nave, near the choir, from which strings were lit and the flames passed to the apparatus which suddenly produced a strong explosion with dense, black, suffocating smoke billowing out. The women and children, half choked and screaming with fright rushed towards the parts of the church where the air was still breathable. The door of the sacristy was then broken in by the violent thrust of one horrified group. I followed in after but gave up and sat on a stair. My daughter came and sat down with me. When the Germans noticed that this room had been broken into they savagely shot down those who had tried to find shelter there. My daughter was killed near me by a bullet fired from outside. I owe my life to the idea I had to shut my eyes and pretend to be dead.

Shortly after the events in Oradour-sur-Glane, in the fall of 1944 residents of the mountainous Monte Sole region of Italy (the villages of Marzabotto, Grizzana Morandi and Monzuno) were punished for partisan attacks on German troops. Historians have struggled to document the number of victims—some sources report up to 1,830 victims; others estimate 955 people killed. Today, the Peace School Foundation of Monte Sole reports 770 victims. This number is closer to the official report by *Sturmbannführer* Reder, who reported the "execution of 728 bandits." Among the victims, 155 were less than ten years old, 95 were aged ten to sixteen, 142 were over sixty years old; 454 were male and 316 were female. Notable among them was Giovanni Fornasini, a parish priest and member of the Resistance, who was accused of crimes committed against the Nazis in the Marzabotto area. He confessed to having helped the villagers avoid execution and was shot to death.

The civilian populations of Oradour and Mazobotto were not killed in the heat of battle by ordinary soldiers, but coldly and systematically by the Waffen SS. In both places, the German troops felt disoriented in the face of impending defeat after years of seeing themselves as the Master Race, victorious on almost every front. Like seafarers set adrift, they had lost their bearings, and, for the first time, were fleeing from the enemy. Many seem to have relied only on the SS motto 'My honour is called loyalty,' subordinating personal responsibility to the higher power of blind and faithful obedience.

The Massacre of My Lai (1968)

On March 16, 1968, more than 500 people were slaughtered in My Lai, a village of some 700 inhabitants in the Vietnamese province of Quang Ngai. Among the victims were 182 women—seventeen of them pregnant—and 173 children, including 56 infants. The attackers were American soldiers from Charlie Company, 1st Battalion, 20th Infantry of the 11th Brigade, Americal Division, led by Lieutenant William Calley. Morale was low (they had already lost twenty-eight members of their group) and they suspected that the villagers were enemy sympathizers hoarding weapons.

Charlie Company arrived at dawn for a search-and-destroy mission to find a quiet village just waking up. The soldiers rounded up the villagers, mostly old men, women and children, before searching their huts. They found no weapons and no one fired at them. Yet, inexplicably (save perhaps for the effect of a long and exhausting war), Calley ordered his men to shoot the villagers. The massacre followed wartime traditions familiar since antiquity—burning huts, slaughtering livestock and raping girls and women. Those trying to escape, even children, were gunned down. Calley himself actively participated in the killing.

An army helicopter pilot witnessed the scene and landed immediately. He was unable to stop the killing, although he succeeded in flying some survivors out to receive medical treatment. The pilot, Warrant Officer Hugh Thompson, later recalled:

> We kept flying back and forth, reconning in front and in the rear, and it didn't take very long until we started noticing the large number of bodies everywhere. Everywhere we'd look, we'd see bodies. These were infants, two-, three-, four-, five-year-olds, women, very old men, no draft-age people whatsoever.

Thompson reported the incident to his superior officer, but it was not followed up. In fact, the events were successfully downplayed until they were fully reported to several congressmen a year later. Investigative journalist Seymour Hersh broke the story in November 1969, resulting in an international uproar and a special investigation.

The court-martial revealed than the killing took a long time and by 11 am, "when [Captain] Medina called for a lunch break," the killing was nearly (but apparently not quite) over. By noon, My Lai was no more: its buildings were destroyed and its people dead or dying. Soldiers later said they did not remember seeing "one military-age male in the entire place." That night, the Viet Cong returned to bury the dead. Twenty months later, army investigators discovered mass graves containing the bodies of about 500 villagers.

"Medina called for a lunch break." If this is true (and why should we doubt such an anodyne detail in the middle of slaughter) it confirms once more that evil can be reduced to an everyday occurrence—you kill hundreds of innocent people, and then you stop for lunch before completing your task.

Of those men of Charlie Company who participated in the My Lai massacre, fourteen were eventually charged, including Lieutenant Calley, Captain Medina and Colonel Oran Henderson. All were acquitted, except Calley, who was given a life sentence, reduced upon appeal to twenty years, then to ten; he was eventually paroled in 1974. None of those involved in the cover-up were ever charged.

Rwanda (1994)

The events in Nanking, France, Italy and My Lai are seen as war massacres, even if they concerned mostly unarmed civilians—they were performed by soldiers, duty-bound to obey their instructions, each level taking its cues from the echelon above. In Oradour, Monte Sole and My Lai, soldiers were given what they took as a licence to kill because of the villagers' supposed actions as enemy combatants, even when it was usually shown, just *before* the killing started, that such was not the case. It seems as if the killing, once set to happen, could not be stopped by reasonable evidence. In each case, the victimized populations were also seen as racially inferior or worthy of contempt, gradually becoming mere fodder for the killing machine that had been deployed.

The situation in Rwanda was different, as the killing occurred within the context of a civil war involving military and civilian forces, along with many private individuals. Since the withdrawal of the Belgian colonizers, tensions had grown between two indigenous groups, the Hutus and the Tutsis. Resented for their accomplishments (as were German Jews and Armenians before them), the Tutsis became targets of active government propaganda, especially after 1990, when their privileges were deemed to render them 'enemies of the people.' The sentiment escalated even further when the Hutu president was assassinated in 1994, and both Tutsis and moderate Hutus became the targets of hardline Hutus and their followers. Over the course of three months in 1994, 800,000 Tutsi and moderate Hutus were mutilated, raped and murdered by their neighbours. Simultaneously, the Rwandese Patriotic Front (RPF), largely composed of Tutsi refugees living in neighbouring Uganda, intensified their attack on the Hutus. General Roméo Dallaire was the commander of UNAMIR, the small United Nations peace-keeping force, and reported on the Hutus' slaughter and rape. He regularly reported the dreadful fate suffered by the Hutus with requests to intervene; his appeals remained unanswered. The killing came to an end when, after three months of fighting, the RPF gained control of most of the country, including the capital, Kigali.

Events in Rwanda remind us that anyone can fall prey to cruelty and even sadism, a uniquely human pleasure enhanced by committing or witnessing the deliberate infliction of pain on others. This infliction is not gratuitous but deliberate, and the pleasure it causes derives, in the words of Erich Fromm, from "the absolute and unrestricted control over a living being…It transforms impotence into omnipotence."

Scott Peck, a psychiatrist charged with analyzing the psychological sources of the My Lai massacre, uses the term 'group evil' to explain the actions of men who do not appear to have been otherwise evil and who, individually, would not have acted as they did. He argues that group behaviour is more primitive and immature than individual actions. He also contends that the overspecialization that enables groups to be more efficient is accompanied by a fragmentation of conscience. None of the individuals within the group are individually responsible for what the group does collectively:

> In this way, not only does the individual forsake his conscience but the conscience of the group as a whole can become so fragmented and diluted as to become inexistent… The plain fact of the matter is that any group will remain inevitably potentially conscienceless and evil until such time as each and every individual holds himself or herself directly responsible for the

behaviour of the whole group—the organism—of which he or she is a part.[2]

It is thought that perhaps fifty soldiers pulled their triggers at My Lai, that perhaps two hundred directly witnessed the killing, and that perhaps five hundred knew of it within a week. Yet, whatever those substantial numbers may have been, no one reported it—not even the soldiers who refused to participate in the massacre—no one, except the helicopter pilot Hugh Thompson, who reported it to his direct superior. "We were all under orders," Private First Class Paul Meadlo said later. "We all thought we were doing the right thing." Similarly, historians argue that Japanese military training contributed to the Nanking nightmare. At first appalled at being taught how to decapitate or bayonet living prisoners, recruits soon became inured to it, numbed against the instinct not to kill men who were not attacking them.

Another common theme of these massacres, as old and dread as war itself, is rape. Prominent in Nanking and Armenia, it was also used systematically against Muslim girls and women in Bosnia–Herzegovina and Croatia as part of ethnic cleansing. In Rwanda, all adolescent girls who survived some raids were subsequently raped. A UNICEF report of 1996, *The State of the World's Children*, addresses the topic of sexual violence as a weapon of war, documenting its use in conflicts from Bangladesh, Cambodia, and Cyprus to Haiti, Liberia, Somalia and Uganda. A land may be seen as being only truly conquered when all its men have been killed and all its women have been raped—and presumably impregnated by the conquerors.

The psychological immaturity of groups, the dehumanization of military training and racial execration may provide an escape from the responsibility that free will demands when determining our good or evil actions. Anonymity within a group further facilitates the abandonment of normality. A nineteenth-century psychologist, Gustave Le Bon, had already noted the renunciation: "By the

2. Scott M. Peck, *People of the Lie. The Hope for Healing Human Evil* (New York: Simon and Schuster, 1983), 218.

very fact that he forms part of an organized group, a man descends several rungs down the ladder of civilization. Isolated, he may be a cultivated individual, in a crowd, he is a barbarian—that is, a creature acting by instinct." A Japanese soldier, while still denying responsibility, wrote about some of the appalling crimes he had committed in Nanking. "It is terrible that I could turn into an animal and do these things. There are really no words to explain what I was doing. I was truly a devil." This is perhaps the truth— that no words can be found to explain the sadistic violence we can sometimes exhibit against fellow human beings.

SHELL SHOCK

Two twentieth-century conflicts have earned the distinction of being called world wars. Both were well documented and remain present in our minds. World War I—the war that was to end all others—was notable for its trenches, where both sides continuously faced each other, waiting for attacks. Inside the trenches, conditions included extreme fatigue, hellish mud and lice; infectious diseases, particularly dysentery, were common. One of the consequences of the constant exposure to wetness was trench foot, both painful and potentially leading to amputation, and trench mouth, a gum infection thought to be associated with the stress of being under constant bombardment.

The use of poison gas (although banned by two conventions prior to World War I) only added to the men's ordeal. It was intended to demoralize as much as kill and ranged from tear gas (disabling but not lethal) to chlorine and mustard gas. The most feared, yperite or mustard gas (dichlorethyl sulphide), was deployed as a liquid that gave off a lethal vapour. It formed a fine spray that, once inhaled, caused swelling of the throat and lungs, resulting in suffocation. Indiscriminate in its effect (for the wind could turn), its damage could only be allayed by gas masks and capes for men and horses. It caused fewer than a hundred thousand immediate fatalities but led to an estimated one million over time.

Wilfred Owen, a young war poet who died in 1918, bore testimony to the terror it inspired, the cruelty of its symptoms and the obscenity of war itself:

> Gas! GAS! Quick boys!...
> If you could hear, at every jolt, the blood
> Come gargling from the froth-corrupted lungs,
> Obscene as cancer, butter as cud
> Of vile, incurable sores on innocent tongues,—
> My friend, you would not tell with such high zest
> To children ardent for some desperate glory,
> The old Lie: Dulce et decorum est
> Pro patria mori. ('Dulce et Decorum Est,' 1920)

For soldiers in the trenches, gas was an ever-present threat that demanded constant vigilance. The attendant anxiety was exacerbated when ordered go 'over the top' by climbing out of the trenches into 'no man's land' and running in a single line under a barrage of gunfire, potentially over unseen mines. But hardest to bear appears to have been the constant bombardment from shells, bombs and grenades that brought with it the possibility of being buried alive under the fallout of explosions.

Soldiers on both sides of the conflict succumbed to the unprecedented psychological stress. The renowned poet Siegfried Sassoon gives voice to a traumatized British soldier in 'Repression of War Experience' (1918):

> Hark! Thud, thud, thud —quite soft…they never cease—
> Those whispering guns—O Christ, I want to go out
> And screech at them to stop—I'm going crazy;
> I'm going stark, staring mad because of the guns.

Decorated German soldier and author Ernst Jünger, known for his extraordinary bravery, once broke down in tears when the 150 men he led were hit directly by a shell, killing sixty-three. In his memoir, *Storm of Steel* (1920), he wrote of the German front in 1916:

> It is as if one were tied to a post and threatened by a fellow

swinging a sledgehammer. Now the hammer is swung back for the blow, now it whirls forward, till, just missing your skull, it sends the splinters flying from the post once more... the brain links every separate sound of whirring metal with the idea of death and so the nerves are exposed without protection and without pause to the sense of absolute menace... hours such as these were without doubt the most awful of the whole war.

While the war was still raging, military doctors began seeing patients suffering from a previously unknown condition, dubbed 'shell shock' by British physician and psychologist Charles Myers in 1915.

The symptoms of shell shock were varied. Soldiers, who often appeared to be mute or deaf, were found in squatting position or folded in two, unresponsive. Some appeared to be afflicted with a form of paralysis that could not be attributed to physical impairment. Other symptoms included vomiting, wringing hands or twisting feet, facial distortions and staring blindly into the distance.

Physicians, particularly in France and Germany, debated whether the war was actually responsible for these disorders or whether soldiers afraid to fight had developed a form of hysteria. Many doctors used aggressive treatments, such as shock therapy. When soldiers refused these painful treatments, considering them a form of torture, they were brought before courts-martial.

Among those who adopted a more humane approach were Charles Myers and William McDougall, who argued that these patients could be cured through cognitive and affective reintegration—because victims were managing their traumatic experiences by repressing or splitting off any memory of them, the treatment should be to revive their memory and integrate it within their consciousness. Following the thinking of French military neuro-psychiatrists, Myers identified the essential aspects of the soldiers' treatment as promptness of action, suitable environment and psychotherapeutic measures though, in truth, all that could often be provided was encouragement and reassurance. Myers argued that the military should provide specialist units "as remote from the sounds of warfare as is compatible with the preservation of the 'atmosphere' of the front." Four units were created in December 1916, soon to be overwhelmed after the battles of Arras, Messines, and Passchendaele in 1917.

The symptoms exhibited by many shell shock victims were so varied that sufferers were sometimes accused of simulating them in order to get out of fighting. Military commanders feared that, unless what they called cowardice was harshly punished, these 'deserters' would encourage others to flee and discipline would collapse. Courts-martial were carried out speedily and execution, by openly reluctant firing squads, followed soon afterwards. As a result, 306 soldiers from Britain and the Commonwealth and 563 from France were executed for desertion, mutiny or cowardice, many actually suffering from shell shock.

Some of these soldiers, such as James Crozier and Abe Bevistein, were as young as sixteen. Crozier was given so much rum that he passed out and had to be carried, semi-conscious, to the firing squad who, officers feared, might refuse to fire. Before his court-martial, Bevistein wrote his mother, "We were in the trenches. I was so cold I went out [and took shelter in a farm house]. They took me to prison so I will have to go in front of the court. I will try my best to get out of it, so don't worry." Because of their so-called crime, their relatives were usually not told how they had died, nor were their names ever put on war memorials—as if, not content to punish young men for the terror and fatigue they suffered, their families should be punished as well.

The symptoms did not disappear after the shelling stopped—in fact, the effects of shell shock continued to afflict many men long after the war. When it ended in 1918, 65,000 ex-British soldiers were drawing disability pensions for neurasthenia, 9,000 of whom were in hospital, asylums, or rehabilitation centres. A later study showed that only about 39 percent of those ever returned to a semblance of normalcy. When, in 1922, the War Office appointed a Committee of Inquiry into Shell Shock, Myers was so disillusioned by his wartime experience that he refused to give evidence. It was only in 1940, when Britain was at war again, that Myers published his memoirs and explained his theories of treatment—prompt treatment as close to the fighting as is safe, with an expectation of recovery and return to unit. These were widely adopted during World War II. Modern psychiatry, identifying a new condition known as Post-Traumatic Stress Disorder (PTSD), remains in general agreement with the principles Myers identified.

In Britain, the Armed Forces Act of November 2006 pardoned men in the British and Commonwealth armies who were executed during World War I, removing the stain of dishonour without cancelling sentences. Defence Secretary Des Browne said:

> I believe it is better to acknowledge that injustices were clearly done in some cases—even if we cannot say which—and to acknowledge that all these men were victims of war. I hope that pardoning these men will finally remove the stigma with which their families have live for years.

In France, forty of the 'disobedient' soldiers shot 'to set an example' have been pardoned to date. Since some of the men executed during World War I had actually been convicted of murder or rape, the French government does not believe that, for the time being, a blanket pardon for all would be appropriate.

In Canada, as elsewhere, veterans of later wars have suffered from PTSD and its aftermath. In 2018, the Royal Canadian Legion, that each year selects a National Silver Cross Mother honouring women who have lost a child serving in the military, named for the first time the mother of an infantryman who had served in Afghanistan, suffered from PTSD and committed suicide. No better symbolic rehabilitation could have been found for those who had suffered from shell shock.

THERE IS NO WAY OF CONCLUDING on what motivates the killing plague, unless we argue that it is intrinsic to our nature. Many psychologists and sociologists have sought to define its constituent factors in highly technical terms, leading to hypotheses rather than real answers—notably that holding the power to cause death shows that we can control it (and surmount our fear of it). More simply, we might assume that anger and aggression are part of our make-up and ensured our survival in dangerous and competitive times. For evolutionary reasons, males are more likely to engage in violent behaviour, and there is also more traditional acceptance of it, even though women have had their share of murderous deeds. At the individual level, it could simply be a case of arrested development, a painful and cruel mismatch between our reptilian brain and our humanistic aspirations.

A man who probably knew a good deal about good and evil, as well as heroic deeds, was Stan Lee, the creator of Marvel Comics' superheroes such as Spiderman and the Fantastic Four. Describing "the unreasoning hater," he observed that:

> If his hang-up is black men, he hates ALL black men. If a redhead once offended him, he hates ALL redheads. If some foreigner beat him to a job, he's down on ALL foreigners. He hates people he's never seen, people he's never known—with equal intensity, with equal venom. ('Stan's Soapbox,' *Marvel Comics,* 1968).

Simple statements, certainly, but Lee articulates a phenomenon easily recognizable in the world around us.

Indeed, so common is killing and so varied its forms that, in the time it took to write this chapter in October 2018, eleven elderly Jews randomly shot down for their religion and race in Pittsburgh were buried, another mass shooting (defined as at least four persons being killed or injured) took place in Thousand Oaks (the 307th in the United States in about as many days), the investigation continued into the political assassination of a Saudi journalist in Turkey (the forty-seventh journalist to be murdered worldwide so far that year), Toronto had reached its eighty-ninth murder victim (the second highest number ever), and several terrorist attempts had been waged in various parts of the world with the usual results. Migrants continued to perish at sea on unsafe and overcrowded crafts criminally launched, and Yemeni children continued to die of hunger because of a senseless war. Killing—whatever its nature, cause, or rationalization—is like a virus that permeates our world, each eruption with its own specificity.

Conflicts, often motivated by fear, continue to rage or simmer throughout the world, their attempted justification involving complicated political, economic or ideological rationalization, and we have seen that when a government fears its people, systematic killing can be used both as punishment and deterrent. Technology, from the mustard gas of World War I to the gas chambers of World War II to the drones of today, has contributed both to the efficiency and coldbloodedness of these endeavours. Furthermore, killing that was once hand-to-hand and face-to-face can now be performed sight unseen and at great distance, while mass murderers have become anonymous, adding to the depersonalization of the victims and the perpetrators.

As social animals, we rely on interconnectedness and respond to perceived threats in one of three ways: by freezing, fleeing or fighting. When none of these options appear to deal adequately with the threat, we experience intolerable and prolonged stress. In response, we may lash out at groups demonized by propaganda, who often turn out to be defenceless victims. If we are part of a group, it is only one step to go from exercising free will to hiding being the familiar excuse, 'I was only obeying orders.' However, while the instinct to kill to protect oneself or the group may be innate and is often sanctioned by the state, it does not mean that individual humans can absolve themselves from infringing on the respect owed human life.

The excesses of the two world wars gave rise to a re-evaluation of these notions when applied to newly-defined war crimes and crimes against humanity. Tribunals were created to examine them through special trials: Leipzig and Nuremberg. The war crimes trial at Leipzig (May–July 1921) were held before the German Supreme Court, as part of the penalties imposed on Germany by the Treaty of Versailles (1920). Only twelve people were brought to trial, with unconvincing results. By the time of Nuremberg (1945–46), it had been recognized that the examination of such crimes, especially given their unprecedented magnitude, could not be left to the country involved but had to be tried in front of judges representing the Allied powers. Twenty major Nazi members were tried for war crimes and twelve were sentenced to death. A few, notably Hermann Göring and Rudolf Hess, chose to commit suicide in jail either before or after their sentencing.

When the conditions of war are particularly prolonged and onerous, soldiers may end up dissociating from their environment, becoming its psychological victims. PTSD was once rejected as cowardice and simulation. It took time to recognize the trauma suffered by soldiers (and others) as a medical condition. We now know it for what it really is—a consequence of the pity of war, to borrow the title of Niall Ferguson's 1998 book.

Greek mythology knew well enough the conditions of war. Reasonable Athena, clad in her armour, was in charge of military intelligence and strategy, while her brother Ares, rough and untamed, symbolized violence. He was not alone. Riding with him in his chariot were his sons Phobos (Fear, the motive behind so many unreasoned acts) and Deimos (Terror, the source of panic and aggression), as well as his lover Enyo (Discord, the purveyor of fatal propaganda). Such, indeed, are the eternal characteristics of war. Often the outcome of failed diplomacy and the defeat of reason, all greet its arrival with dread—save innocent young men intent on proving themselves and corrupt profiteers anxious to make their fortune. Inevitably, a balanced way of life will soon be destroyed, excessive violence will prevail and the aftermath will lead to permanent changes.

CHAPTER NINE

GAIA ANTHROPOCENE

IN 2018 THE FRENCH GOVERNMENT PROPOSED a new tax to control gas emissions as part of its plan to meet the objectives of the 2015 Paris Agreement on the environment. This led to months of weekend uprisings by the *gilets jaunes* (so named for French motorists' regulation safety vests) that resulted in severely wounded men and women on both the insurgent and police sides. The rioting showed that the precarious financial situation of many French people (made worse by the tax, particularly in rural areas where driving is necessary) was more real to them and seemed more important than an undefined future potentially improved by reduced gas emissions. They weighed their priorities and overwhelmingly decided that the end of the month was more pressing than the end of the world. Their reaction illustrated the most urgent issue of our time—how to reconcile individual prosperity with environmental imperatives.

Our relationship with Gaia, the Greek goddess of the earth, also known as Earth Mother or Mother Nature, seems clear—she nurtures us, we respect her. It is the nature and extent of that respect that we are considering in the Anthropocene, the term currently proposed for our period on earth. We made our appearance some 200,000 years ago and have since affected the land we stand on, the air we breathe and the water we drink. Barely noticeable at first—our numbers few, our industry primitive, our footprint still faint—we succeeded in changing in a few millennia the physical appearance of the world and multiple ecosystems. Finally made aware of the shortcomings of our wanton use and abuse of our planet, we are urgently reconsidering today mankind's physical and metaphorical co-existence with the natural world.

It is not a new notion. The intuition of this interdependence had already informed the work of Aristotle (harmony between man and nature), Nicolas Copernicus (positioning man's place in the universe), Isaac Newton (the laws of nature), James Hutton (interconnection of geological and biological processes), Alexander von Humboldt (co-evolution of living organisms seen as a unified whole animated by interactive forces), Charles Darwin (common origin for all species), Vladimir Vernadsky (the effect of biological processes on oxygen, nitrogen, and carbon dioxide) and, among today's writers, Peter Wohlleben (the "extraordinary balance of all living things").

In the seventeenth century, Francis Bacon worried that the human race had lost dominion over the creation because of the loss of innocence resulting from Adam and Eve's fall from grace. His response was to promote an "inquisition of nature" in the search for truth, whose goal was the knowledge of "causes and secret motions of things, and the enlarging of the bounds of human empire, to the effecting of all things possible." Such thinking would eventually lead to the Scientific Revolution.

So far, science and technology had been concerned with tunnelling into the earth for coal and metals, constructing mills to use wind and water power, deforesting enormous tracts of land for shipbuilding. Some initiatives had meddled with animal species, turning wolves into chihuahuas, hunting others to extinction; others would eventually contribute to desertification and to water and air pollution. More recent interventions are now tampering with genetic engineering and, not satisfied with the limits of our own planet, we even went on to explore others. From being weak and helpless, devoid of natural weapons but blessed with the power of speech, a talent for cooperation, limitless imagination, together with the ability to write our own narratives and justify ourselves, we humans surpassed all other creatures and went on to dominate the earth, our concept of progress generally allied to a patriarchal structure of family and state.

THE DOMINION OF MAN

Our relationship with other animals has been characterized not by peaceful cohabitation but by our continual infringement on their habitat and ensuring their servitude. The Old Testament records God's decree upon creating mankind: "Let them have dominion over the fish of the sea, and over the fowl of the air and over the cattle, and over all the earth, and over every creeping thing that creepeth upon the earth." We were only too pleased to comply.

Dominion implies ownership, leading to the notion that mankind is entitled to use for its own comfort and pleasure the toil, flesh, blood, fur, plumage, skin, milk, eggs, oil, excreta, ivory, companionship, suffering and grossly fattened-up livers of the creatures entrusted to its care, hunted in the wild or bred in unsuitable conditions. The animal–human relationship was unilaterally confirmed as one of inferior to dominant, servant to master, prey to hunter, meat to consumer (we are omnivorous by nature but meat-eaters by taste). Dominion has also led to custom-tailored breeds with specific characteristics useful to man but often detrimental to their own species. Poultry, for instance, whose sole function is to be eaten, is carefully bred according to customers' preference. The US poultry industry has responded by breeding birds to have more breast meat and to put on weight faster than nature intended.

One aspect of man's genius was to see an animal in the wild and imagine how it could be transformed into a machine to serve him. As soon they could be tamed, animals were set to work, to be replaced only much later by more effective mechanical devices. The first ones willingly tamed were the canids (dog family), used for protection, hunting, herding, carrying burdens and pulling carts. The next were aurochs—the ancestors of today's cows—domesticated around 10,000 years ago. They became farm animals bred to enhance the use of the land and to provide sustenance. Some of their qualities, such as the production of milk, were developed and enhanced to suit man's needs.

Beasts of burden helped with the settlement of whole nations. South America was colonized in the eighteenth and nineteenth centuries with mules from the pampas of Argentina—some 500,000 in 1776 in Peru alone—more prized than horses or oxen yet brutally broken in. Without horses and oxen, the American West would not have been settled. Other animals, uniquely adapted to the terrain and climate, have contributed significantly to man's ability to survive in uninviting environments. The dromedary camel, for instance, met the nomads' every need (transportation, food, clothing, fuel, shelter, entertainment and general prosperity) in the desert areas of North Africa, while the llama has provided food and clothing and carted loads for native Andean peoples since the pre-Columbian era.

In a pre-industrial world, the relationship between man and beast was characterized by a semblance of equilibrium. There was little notion of kind treatment, but hunters and fishermen respected nature and only took what they needed to provide sustenance for the group. Deuteronomy instructed that working animals be treated with moderation: they were to be granted a day of rest alongside humans; it was also forbidden to pair together an ox and an ass for plowing, thus sparing the ass from the extra stress of having to keep up with the much stronger ox and, finally, the ox was not to be muzzled while threshing, so that it could feed as it worked for long hours.

The mechanization of the Industrial Revolution and migration to urban areas irrevocably upset this balance. Traditional hunting and farming practices made way for the commercial breeding of animals for meat, milk and eggs. We evolved from picking the eggs of hens living freely in the family compound to an egg production industry and its concomitant abuse. Left to nature, hens seldom produce more than fifteen eggs a year; factory hens have been bred and genetically manipulated to produce almost twenty times that amount.

Milk production was similarly increased. Since the 1800s, the average annual production for a cow has grown from 1,000 litres of milk to ten times that amount through commercial farming. Because lactation can only occur through calving, cows are kept constantly pregnant, with a period of two months' rest between each pregnancy; the calves are taken away within the first few days to reserve the milk for human consumption. While cows' natural lifespan is about twenty years, it is not uncommon for commercial farmers to slaughter them at around five or six years, after four lactations. Single farming operations of 10,000 cows in Europe (or 100,000 in the case of China) preclude any hope of providing decent accommodation and treatment to the animals, and also pose a serious threat to groundwater systems.

With affluence, tastes in foods also changed, particularly in Europe. Margaret Visser, in *Much Depends on Dinner* (1991) described how large sturgeons, a nuisance fish in the North American Great Lakes, only fetched ten cents each at Canadian fish markets in the 1850s and were mostly used as pig feed, two of their unpleasant features being spiny and bony plates on the outside of their bodies and the large amount of roe (up to twenty-five pounds each) carried by gravid females. Although long appreciated in Rome and in Russia, the same caviar was largely unknown elsewhere until the 1920 Paris Gastronomic Exhibition when it was introduced by two exiled Russian brothers and became the rage in Europe. "Caviar is expensive, fabled, exotic, difficult to prepare, to keep, to transport, and to eat. It is also increasingly rare. The combination is irresistible." Roman tables once offered flamingo tongues in a similar spirit of elegant exclusivity.

The same complacent sense of entitlement that characterized man's relationship with animals applied to nature. In the seventeenth century, vast forests still covered most of Europe and North

America, until navies (the pride of many nations) and other industries began harvesting timber at an unsustainable rate. The perils of deforestation were among the first ecological concerns to be brought to public attention. As early as 1664, Englishman John Evelyn wrote in a discourse on forests, "we had better be without gold as without timber," as trees meant the proper running of iron and glass industries, blazing fires in cold winter hearths, and navies to safeguard the country. In France, Colbert, the Minister of Finance under Louis XIV, outlawed the communal use of forests in villages to the benefit of the anticipated needs of the navy, explaining, "France will perish for the want of wood." Two centuries ago, the Prussian explorer Alexander von Humboldt visited Lake Valencia in Venezuela and looked beyond the economic imperative, emphasizing the forests' role in biodiversity and what happened when they disappeared:

> …the springs are entirely dried up, or become less abundant. The beds of the rivers, remaining dry during a part of the year, are converted into torrents, whenever great rains fall on the heights. The sward and moss disappearing with the brush-wood from the sides of the mountains, the waters falling in rain are no longer impeded in their course: and instead of slowly augmenting the level of the rivers by progressive filtrations, they furrow during heavy showers the sides of the hills, bear down the loosened soil, and form those sudden inundations, that devastate the country.

He further noted, "The wooded region acts in a threefold manner in diminishing the temperature; by cooling shade, by evaporation, and by radiation." Unfortunately, his warnings were largely ignored.

THE PETROLEUM AGE

In *The Graduate,* a popular 1967 film, Mr. McGuire observed that "there's a great future in plastics." A mere half century later, in the fall of 2018, a whale washed ashore in Indonesia with some 1,000 pieces of plastic weighing 132 pounds in its stomach, including 115 cups, four bottles and two flip-flops. Evidently, Mr. McGuire was not the only one interested in plastics.

Plastics represent the culmination of a love affair with petroleum that began in the 1840s, when kerosene began replacing whale oil as the fuel of choice. First produced from coal tar and shale oils, then from petroleum (the first modern oil wells were drilled in Pennsylvania in 1859), kerosene was rapidly adopted worldwide, both as home fuel and for the illumination of whole cities. Produced from the distillation of crude oil, it is mostly a mixture of paraffins and naphthenes and includes such toxic compounds as benzene. In Europe and North America, kerosene was largely replaced by natural gas piped from the gas fields and, eventually, by electricity; today its primary use is as jet fuel. However, it is still commonly used in developing countries for cooking, lighting and heating, with its attendant problems (carcinogenic gases and risks of explosion on the home front, and harmful emissions of black carbon into the atmosphere).

Experimentation to power machines using liquid fuel began in the eighteenth century. By the end of the nineteenth, the petroleum-powered internal combustion engine (ICE) was a reality. This godsend brought personal mobility to everyone in developed countries—the initial luxury now accessible almost globally—and transported the goods and chattel on which our wellbeing depends. We appreciated its convenience, easy access and reasonable cost, unconcerned with its reliance of fossil fuel and the carbon dioxide it emitted into the atmosphere. A century ago, the damage was minimal—the few cars scaring horses and pedestrians had not yet morphed into the more than one billion engines spewing gases today. We were unaware of the ecological and climatic consequences of this wonderful addition to our comfort and could only rejoice at the advent of Henry Ford's Model T.

Today, we understand the effects of an ICE and its use of gasoline and diesel, and there is no way to unlearn what we know. We face the conundrum at every turn—our convenience and comfort are tied to the earth's resources, and our health and survival to their good management. We have enjoyed the former without preparing for the latter. Only now have we come to realize that our natural resources will eventually come to an end and we must substantially reduce or eliminate the disastrous consequences of greenhouse gasses and fracking.

Mass production of plastics began in the 1940s, and continued the trend of making our lives easier, but also gave rise to an era of 'throwaway living,' where short-lived accessories to our life seduced us into an over-consumption of easily discarded items. A new term, 'built-in obsolescence,' soon became part of our vocabulary as fashion-conscious consumers discarded still functional furniture and appliances in favour of newer shapes or colours. Women were particularly delighted with the convenience plastic brought to their daily routine—easy-to-clean toys, utensils, and equipment (oblivious to the microfibers being released into wastewater systems). Wildlife supporters approved of it as they saw it replacing ivory and tortoiseshell from endangered species. It is no wonder that these polymers, durable, practical, economical and versatile (transformable into anything from clothes to bottles) found favour with all of us—until we realized, years later, that we could not get rid of them.

Plastic production has more than doubled in the last two decades, rising to just under 400 million tons per year. Unique among pollutants, plastics have their own system of classification by size, origin and dispersion into micro-, meso- and macro-debris. Some forms take up to half a millennium to disintegrate, and earlier efforts to reuse and recycle have also dwindled miserably—prior to 1950, reusable packaging had almost a 96 percent return rate in the US, falling to below 5 percent by the 1970s. Today only between 5 and 20 percent of various types of plastic are recyclable, and developing countries have become the repositories of the greatest piles of garbage the world has ever known. Some are even returning it to us, its original source.

Clogging up the developing world's marketplaces and its garbage dumps are clothes made of synthetic materials—nylon, acrylic, pol-yester, rayon, spandex. Easy to wash and needing no ironing, they provided the carefree life our grandmothers would have so enjoyed. The fabrics are cheap yet generally looked good, and many of us fell into the ease of owning and casually discarding these cheap clothes. Disposable diapers followed suit, and the descendants of those who filled them will be trying, with little success, to dispose of them for many decades to come. Fabulists Aesop and La Fontaine, who had a lesson and moral for every inane behaviour, never envisaged that we could one day choose to drape ourselves in clothes made out of petrochemicals rather than wool and cotton.

If plastic is a bane on land, it is even worse in the sea. In 1997, Captain Charles Moore, while sailing from Hawaii to southern California, saw pieces of plastic regularly floating by in the middle of the Pacific Ocean. He returned later to examine more thoroughly what he had first witnessed—large numbers of plastic items, not merely floating but trapped in water gyres, huge vortexes of rotat-ing ocean currents. Two very large garbage patches have since been identified in the northern parts of the Atlantic and Pacific oceans. The latter extends over 1.6 million square kilometres, mainly between Hawaii and California, according to claims made by Ocean Cleanup, an environmental organization founded in the Netherlands in 2013.

Based on the Ocean Conservancy's annual coastal cleanup, 90 percent of recovered plastic items come from packaging and fast food supplies, supplemented by the usual rubbish we throw away and other types of plastic that eventually break down into smaller pieces under the effects of weather, sunlight and waves. No water on earth, from the Arctic to Indonesia to America's shores, seems to be safe from plastic contamination, however invisible. *The Arctic Report Card: Update for 2018,* issued by the National Oceanic and Atmospheric Administration, indicates that microplastic contamina-tion, posing a threat to seabirds and marine life, may be in higher concentrations in the Arctic Ocean, however remote and far from its source, than all other ocean basins in the world.

Ocean plastic has a significant impact on both animal and human life. Fish, turtles, seabirds, sea lions and whales can either become entangled in it or can swallow tiny degraded particles. A recent study tested seafood in Indonesia and California and discovered that shellfish sold for human consumption contained a measurable proportion of anthropogenic debris. In Indonesia, all the debris was plastic; in the US, debris recovered from fish was mostly microfibers.

While these findings cause much concern, the impact of oil spills on marine life is more immediate and seems even more catastrophic. When the tanker *Exxon Valdez* ran aground along the Canadian northwest coast on March 24, 1989, it spilled eleven million gallons of oil. This relatively modest spill (ranked thirty-sixth in the world) devastated the local environment. The tally was estimated at 250,000 sea birds, 2,800 sea otters, 300 harbour seals, 250 bald eagles and 22 orcas. The direct effect on living fish is unknown, but it is safe to assume that billions of salmon and herring eggs were lost. As a direct consequence of the *Exxon Valdez* spill, the US Congress passed an Oil Pollution Act (1990) instituting a gradual implementation of a double hull design for oil tankers by 2015.

The toll was still mounting one year after British Petroleum's Deepwater Horizon spilled 206 million gallons of crude oil (only a quarter of which could be recovered) and 225,000 gallons of methane into the Gulf of Mexico in 2010. The government's official count included more than 82,000 birds collected at the scene, but bodies kept washing ashore long afterwards and biologists believed the numbers may have been ten times higher. The marine mammals harmed, notably bottlenose and spinner dolphins and melon-headed and sperm whales, amounted to 25,000. Approximately 6,000 sea turtles were also found dead. The effects on fish were devastating, particularly on those already endangered, such as the Atlantic bluefin tuna, the Gulf sturgeon, the small tooth sawfish and the dwarf seahorse. The spill contaminated more than 1,000 linear miles of shoreline, as well as mangrove and marshes habitat.

The 2011 Center for Biological Diversity Report noted that the effects of oil spills are long-lasting. That year, fiddler crabs in Massachusetts were still showing the effects of a 1969 spill, beaches of Alaska had not recovered from the 1989 *Exxon Valdez* spill, and oysters and mangroves in the Gulf of Mexico (a particularly vulnerable site that has experienced some 320 known spills of various sizes between 1964 and 2011) still bore the scars of the 1979 *Ixtoc I* spill.

The oceans constitute almost three-quarters of the earth's surface, are our primary oxygen suppliers and serve to feed about half the world's population. They are also particularly susceptible to pollution. For each oil spill and for each piece of plastic, there is a body count, but the latter is only a small visible sign of the deeper damage, whose actual cost remains largely unknown.

THE GAIA HYPOTHESIS
Humanity took advantage of the earth's bounty virtually unchecked for about three hundred years, exploiting nature in an unfettered quest for progress and prosperity, bearing the responsibility for a massive loss of animal populations through hunting, overfishing and the destruction of habitat. European newcomers to the coast of Newfoundland in the sixteenth century were said to have marvelled at the sight of the cod, stretching as far as the eye could see. But, with cod a staple food in many countries (the ubiquitous *bacalao* of the Iberian Peninsula), the fishing banks were eventually depleted; stocks are only now slowly recovering thanks to a 1992 fishing ban.

Other species completely disappeared: the moa of New Zealand and the poor clumsy dodo of Mauritius, perhaps the most famous symbol of man's taste for casual killing. Vast tracts of land were deforested, especially in the Americas, to meet the needs of growing populations, as slash-and-burn agriculture provided new lands for planting crops and grazing livestock. Forests today constitute about only 30 percent of the planet's land area and are still diminishing rapidly. Waste products ranging from household garbage to toxic chemicals to sulphur dioxide were casually discarded, polluting land, sea and air indiscriminately.

It was not until the second half of the twentieth century that alarm bells began to ring. The World Wildlife Fund was founded in 1961, Rachel Carson's *Silent Spring* (1962) documented the devastating effects of pesticides, Greenpeace began protesting nuclear testing and protecting whales in 1971 and many countries created environmental protection agencies (1970 in the US, 1971 in Canada).

Also in the 1970s, James Lovelock, a British scientist and futurist, together with American microbiologist Lynn Margulis, formulated the Gaia hypothesis, postulating that the earth functions as a synergetic system. The Gaia hypothesis considers the interaction between living organisms and their inorganic surroundings and posits that it constitutes a complex and self-regulating physical and chemical system involving all the elements: atmosphere (air), hydrosphere (water) and pedosphere (soil). It continues to inspire today's ecologists as they monitor the influence of the biosphere's ecosystems and the evolution of organisms on the stability of the earth's global temperature, the salinity of the seas and oceans, and the level of oxygen in the atmosphere that all maintain conditions suitable for life.

Between 1985 and 2006, several Gaia symposia and conferences were held, showing the growing acceptance of the hypothesis within scientific circles. The first, sponsored by the National Audubon Society, asked 'Is The Earth A Living Organism?' The second, in 1988, organized by the American Geophysical Union, examined the Gaia hypothesis in both metaphorical and literal contexts. The 2000 conference focused on the actual mechanisms at work maintaining the stability of ecosystems in a context of long-term changes. In 2006, the keynote speaker was Lynn Margulis, one of the original Gaia hypothesis proponents; other speakers represented various scientific and environmental interests. By then, the Gaia hypothesis/ theory had been accepted as having both scientific and metaphorical value, and symbolically served to focus attempts to address this century's pressing climactic and environmental issues.

The ethos of the Gaia hypothesis has led to gradual but significant changes in our consideration of the planet and a new interest in inter-species relationships. In ancient Greece, the debate focused on the level of consciousness experienced by animals, with Pythagoras and his followers believing in the commonality and reincarnation of human and animal souls and practising a form of animism. A few centuries later, Aristotle declared the absolute supremacy of man over animals, even as he recognized some similarity between the two. Philosophers of the seventeenth and eighteenth centuries debated animal sensibilities, from Descartes and Malesherbes, who believed animals to be without feelings (Descartes actually saw them as *machina animata*, little more than machines), to Voltaire who believed them to have feelings similar to our own. The eighteenth-century philosopher Jeremy Bentham famously argued that the question was not whether animals could reason and communicate but whether they could suffer.

Today, leading French philosopher Alain Finkielkraut argues that God's mandate was misread—man is not the owner but only the caretaker of the planet and will one day be held accountable for his actions. He raises the dangers of 'speciesism' (that human animals have greater moral rights over non-human animals) and wonders whether a new sensitivity to the animals' plight will be able to change the status quo. Like many others who see the world divided between the 'specists' (who argue that man alone is in charge) and 'antispecists' (who urge man to identify with all creatures), Finkielkraut supports the latter. Other antispecists are going as far as advocating that the status of personhood be attributed to animals closest to man, such as the great apes: gorillas, orangutans, chimpanzees and bonobos.

Improvements sometimes comes from unexpected sources. Temple Grandin, a writer and lecturer since the 1980s, used her autism to help translate animals' sensory-based thinking and perception of the world (such as a dog's 'fire-hydrant' information system, where detailed complex information is provided by multiple sources at one location), leading to safer and less stressful animal-centred management of slaughterhouses.

In the West, the growing fashion is towards limited meat consumption, as well as vegetarianism and veganism. Ethical farming is valued and several organizations are attempting to regulate and humanize the industry through proper housing and nutrition, disease prevention and treatment, responsible care and humane handling. Free range eggs and organic produce are now widely available to consumers able to pay the increased cost. Wearing fur is frowned upon, as synthetic furs provide equal warmth and greater variety, and public opinion has turned sharply against circuses, rodeos and other forms of entertainment featuring animals. Using animals for scientific and medical research continues to be controversial and is increasingly restricted to life-saving circumstances.

Biodiversity is becoming valued in its own right, independent of direct economic benefit. Zoological parks or gardens, the earliest established in 1752, originally featured exotic animals in cages or enclosures for public display. The modern focus is on the long-term conservation of endangered species and includes recreating the animals' natural habitat in a cage-free environment. Zoos have started captive breeding programs and reintroduced animals to the wild, collaborating to prevent in-breeding among their animal populations, and aspiring to become centres of education and research. Natural wildlife parks, notably in Africa, have impressive programs of animal protection, breeding, orphan rescue, reintroduction into the wild and education to secure local support. They are also actively engaged in anti-poaching measures, going as far as dehorning African rhinoceroses to foil poachers and save the animals' lives. The World

Association of Zoos and Aquariums (WAZA) is collaborating with UN Environment to control the enormous illegal traffic in wildlife.

The whale trade is an example of speciesism in action. The French Basques were among the first organized hunters in the Atlantic during the sixteen and seventeenth centuries, but it was in New England that whaling flourished two centuries later, driven by the twenty-five to forty barrels of fuel that could be extracted from blubber (particularly from sperm whales that provided the preferred oil, odourless and bright-burning).

By 1790, right whales—so called because they were 'the right whale to kill,' slow-moving, surface-dwelling, travelling close to the coast and floating after they were killed—had been practically wiped in the locals seas, and whalers had to set their sights further afield. There were more than 700 whaling ships operating in the Atlantic in 1840, 400 from New Bedford alone. By the time the Civil War and other circumstances brought the New England whaling fleet to a halt, the bowhead whale and the North Atlantic right whale populations had been decimated. Nonetheless, whale hunting eventually resumed and, as late as the 1930s, whaling nations were still killing some 50,000 animals annually.

Thanks to a 1986 ban imposed by the International Whaling Commission, commercial whale hunting has been much reduced— although three countries (Japan, Norway and Iceland), all with extensive coastlines and a cultural predisposition towards the sea, have refused to end their whaling operations. According to the International Fund for Animal Welfare, the Japanese, under the guise of conducting scientific research, hunt minke whales, Bryde's whales, sei whales and sperm whales beyond acceptable numbers; the International Court of Justice ruled their hunting of minke and fin whales in the Southern Ocean Sanctuary illegal. Norway, who respected the IWC's whaling ban until 1993, has now resumed commercial hunting for minke whales and has increased its quotas from 671 in 2002 to 1,000 today. Iceland, sometimes at odds with the

IWC, has resumed commercial whaling of minke and fin whales, although in smaller numbers than Japan and Norway.

In addition to being hunted, today's whales can be inadvertent victims of man's industrious entrepreneurship, competing for declining food stocks, colliding with ships in narrow sea passages and becoming entangled in fishing nets. In addition, their echolocation and communication systems, as well as their ability to feed and mate, are seriously affected by engine noise from marine traffic, and even more by sonic blasts from commercial airguns searching for oil and gas deposits along the American coast.

While animal abuse of this sort is incidental, deliberately abusing animals for entertainment, particularly baiting or fights, has enjoyed a long history of popular support in Europe and, most notably, in England. A book written in 1583 (*Anatomie of Abuses* by Philip Stubbes) castigated those who attended cock fights, described as "solemn feasts of mischief." Cock fights drew in gamblers are well as spectators, adding to the excitement of the game. Much in favour as well were bull- and bear-baiting, where the animals were chained up and dogs set upon them to everyone's amusement. Special dogs (bulldogs and Staffordshire bull terriers) were even bred for the sport. Not everyone approved and in 1801 Joseph Strutt denounced this "cruel pastime... universally practised on various occasions, in almost every town and village through the kingdom, and especially in market towns."

Eventually, bull-baiting, deemed too rough and disturbingly noisy for the neighbourhood, was replaced by bull-running, where men pitted their speed and agility against animals forced to run through public spaces. Mostly practised by "blackguards, thieves and miscreants of all kinds together," this is how Francis Place, the nineteenth-century English social reformer, described it:

> Its cruelty was atrocious, it led to every species of vice and crime, and proved how very low were peoples notions of morality, and how barbarous their dispositions since they could permit such a vile and mischievous pastime to be pursued without interruption for a long series of years.

By the first half of the nineteenth century, discussions about this very topic—the casual use of animals as entertainment in fox-hunting, bull-baiting, and cock-fighting—as well as about vivisection for scientific research performed on animals without anesthetic and the obvious maltreatment of working animals, resulted in the founding of the Royal Society for the Prevention of Cruelty to Animals (1824). The law followed suit. In reaction to earlier displays of savagery, an Act of the British Parliament of September 9, 1835 started with these words:

> Whereas cruelties are greatly promoted and encouraged by Persons keeping Houses, Rooms, Pits, Grounds, or other Places for the fighting or baiting of Dogs, Bulls, Bears, and other Animals—and the fighting of Cocks—and by Persons aiding or assisting therein; and the same are great Nuisances and Annoyances to the Neighbourhood in which they are situated, and tend to demoralize those who frequent such Place.

Not only were nuisance and cruel behaviour the reasons given for passing the act, but the brutalizing effect of such games on those who attended them was also specified—a significant step towards modern thinking about abuse and cruelty in general, and responsibility towards animals in particular. The two concepts are today linked in the belief that many psychopathic or sadistic adult behaviours make their first appearance in childhood as cruelty to animals.

The abuse of animals for sport continues to exist. The running of the bulls, banned in its coarsest form in the nineteenth century, is still practised in a more lighthearted and regulated fashion in Spain (where the Pamplona bull run is a favourite tourist attraction) and in the south of France (where bullfighting does not lead to the animals' death). In these two tauromachic countries, as well as Mexico, the age-old tradition of bullfighting is viewed as a traditional art form, deserving of preservation, despite protests from animal lovers. In other parts of the world, whether openly or covertly held, cockfights and dogfights, backed by gambling, still have their hard-core aficionados; in England and Wales, cockfighting has been reported as late as 1985.

Our inconsistent relationship with animals is perhaps best illustrated through our treatment of dogs. Still used extensively for rough labour and even for food in some parts of the world, their finer sense of smell has given them a privileged new role detecting forbidden substances or special diseases. But their main contribution in western society has increasingly become to provide unquestioning companionship to stressed-out humans, many as pampered 'fur-babies' with wardrobes of their own. Animals suffer both from the harsh treatment some endure and from the cloying infantilism handed out to others, and the aim of organizations devoted to animal welfare is to see them treated as animals, neither more nor less. The Mahatma Gandhi addressed the importance of this relationship when he wrote, "The greatness of a nation can be judged by the way its animals are treated."

The Gaia hypothesis is also beginning to inform our appreciation of trees. We have acquired a new understanding of them as interdependent, interconnected social beings, communicating in self-protection and communal self-defence through scent, secreting compounds specifically formulated to fight some types of attack. They also signal one another through fungi, forming a 'wood wide web' of interconnection. However, trees' natural defences only help against natural threats and offer no protection against axes, saws or bulldozers. So humans continued to hew trees, seemingly unconcerned by the consequences, save at the local level, responding only to the needs of the present. Among the most dramatic impacts of deforestation has been the loss of habitat for rare animal species (notably the orangutan in Sumatra) and still unrecorded vegetal ones, about 80 percent of which grow in forests. The Pachamama Alliance, was founded in 1997 to work with indigenous organizations in the Amazon basin to defend their interests and support their rights to self-determination, suffered a heart-breaking defeat in 2013 when rainforest lands were auctioned off to oil companies.

In our drive for subsistence, and even prosperity, we are altering the natural world in new ways—inventing, experimenting, moderating, compensating, correcting, fine-tuning, forever adjusting. In the 1960s and 1970s, the need to address the threat of global hunger increased the already extensive reliance on pesticides, fertilizers and irrigation methods. The use of fertilizers surged by 360 percent over the next twenty years and the use of pesticides increased significantly, resulting in the pollution of land, water and air, as well as creating new resistant strains of pests. Beginning in the early 1990s, scientists began introducing genetically modified organisms (GMOs) to remedy a worsening situation. The United Nations Food and Agriculture Organization uses the following definition: "Genetically engineered/modified organisms, and products thereof, are produced through techniques in which the genetic material has been altered in a way that does not occur naturally by mating and/ or natural recombination." In other words, genes are extracted from bacterial, viral, animal or even human sources and injected into totally different organisms.

Proponents of GM technology argue that they are only applying known modern scientific resources to traditional breeding and farming practices, yet their patents would suggest that the process is entirely new. They also maintain that GMOs have not shown negative results in human health in twenty years of use. Their opponents argue that testing is inadequate and too short to be conclusive, pointing out that rats fed modified corn and soy developed liver and kidney problems.

GMOs provide the super crops—herbicide tolerant and insect resistant—that our ancestral farmers could only dream of, and are particularly applied to maize, canola and soybean (about 50 percent of the world's soybean production is now genetically modified). They are almost entirely located in the United States, Brazil,

Argentina, Canada and India and have increased from 1.7 million to 182 million hectares between 1996 and 2014. Yet, less than four percent of agricultural lands grow genetically modified crops and only about one percent of farmers worldwide are involved. GMO proponents, who believe their challenging mission is to feed the world, see their use getting more urgent all the time; the world population exceeds seven billion and is expected to continue growing. Others are pessimistically suspicious and fear that, like the Sorcerer's Apprentice, we may have unleashed something that will soon become too difficult to control.

Generally speaking, the positive aspects of GMOs are found to be in the production of faster growing 'designer' crops with more nutrient value and (particularly with cotton) far more yield. The reduction of tillage practices has also led to decline in soil erosion, particularly with soybean production in the US and Argentina. Less use of pesticide has reduced farmers' exposure to chemicals but has also caused some insect and weeds to become more resistant. Where they are grown, GM crops have increased farmers' income but have also increased their dependency on multinational seed companies.

Opposition to GMOs is particularly strong in Europe, where many feel that the science is still in its infancy. They worry that transgenic modification produces unnatural organisms whose nature is unpredictable and may cause allergic reactions in humans. Some are concerned that the specific resistance of crops to pesticides gives farmers a free hand to poison all weeds. Finally, crosspollination between GMOs and non-GMOs is a constant risk and there is little consistency and obligation to report GMO products, raising consumers' suspicions about the nature of the products they buy.

Biofuels represent another technological innovation intended to return to more natural sources—replacing polluting and constantly depleting fossil fuels with a renewable alternative (corn, soy, switchgrass, palm oil) that produces fewer emissions. Unfortunately, biofuels compete for land with food crops, rely heavily on fertilizers and consume enormous amounts of water (particularly corn, competing with local needs for drinking water in sunny climates where it grows best). There are also significant distribution and pollution issues involved in transporting biofuels from the areas where they grow to those where they will be used. Furthermore, biofuel may require several times more energy to produce and be much less efficient than petroleum-based fuel.

Another serious concern is the extension of monocultures at the expense of a variety of rotating crops—they affect farmers' subsistence and lead to the proliferation of specialized plant pests. Since soybean and corn grown as biofuels are also sources of food, monocultures affect people's alimentation. In addition, much of the cultivation of biofuel crops relies on genetic engineering—with the potential problems and dangers related to it. These were illustrated, with potentially catastrophic consequences, in the early 2000s, when a corn crop (treated to resist a particular moth) was shown to affect the larvae of the monarch butterfly as it migrated through the vast fields of the American Midwest.

The production of palm oil as biofuel to allay the problem of greenhouse gas emissions was a particular *bête noire* of scientists and environmentalists. In Indonesia, the damage done during the 1990s (through deforestation to make way for plantations, draining and burning peat bogs, pollution from heavy truck traffic and tractors tending the fields) made the country one of the world's worst greenhouse gas emitters.

THE 2018 LIVING PLANET REPORT ISSUED by the World Wildlife Fund recognized that "our health, food, and security depend on biodiversity," and reminds us that "all our economic activity ultimately depends on nature." It is unclear whether further development will be possible without healthy natural systems. The message from scientists is almost unanimous—we have brought devastation upon our world and must change our ways. "We are running out of time... Only by addressing both ecosystems and climate do we stand a chance of safeguarding a stable planet for humanity's future on Earth," said Prof. Johan Rockström, a global sustainability expert at the Potsdam Institute for Climate Impact Research.

Our actions, reflecting an attitude of dominance rather than stewardship, are estimated to have led to some species' extinction a hundred times faster than might have happened naturally. The imbalance grows as human population has nearly doubled since 1970 while wild animals' numbers may have been reduced by half. As a result, many scientists speak of our having entered the 'sixth mass extinction' of species and biodiversity—the last mass extinction period corresponding to the disappearance of the dinosaurs. From a practical point of view, what it means is that some of the frogs, butterflies, birds, bees and other familiar creatures we always took for granted may have already gone.

The environmentalists' vision of the future is dark. Yet nature is unpredictable and sometimes self-regulates in ways we had not anticipated, reversing our direst predictions. One such incident of 'invasion biology,' often a major cause of the loss of biodiversity, bore unexpected fruit in the Great Lakes. In 1988, a Russian vessel dumping bilge water into Lake St. Claire also released some zebra mussels, whose normal habitat is the Caspian Sea. These mussels produced eggs, creating an ever-increasing number of zebra mussels that negatively impacted the native aquatic eco-system. They also obstructed pipes and other equipment and were a terrible nuisance, notably to fishermen. Eventually, they moved to Lake Erie, a lake by then declared biologically dead, having suffered since the 1960s from the effects of lakeside industries and agricultural runoff. Such pollution was nothing to zebra mussels, which can filter organic material out of the water. They fed on what they could find and turned the rest into biologically inert 'pseudo-feces' that dropped to the bottom of the lake as sediment. Gradually, the process clarified the water in Lake Erie, allowing light into it—and the fish came back. First the smallmouth bass, then the walleye pike and finally the Atlantic salmon. The zebra mussels remain, however, a costly nuisance requiring constant clean-up. Fishermen and scientists have not reconciled themselves to their presence, and probably never will, but Lake Erie (the eleventh largest lake in the world) is once more alive with fish.

Another unexpected example of natural reversion to the original order is that of the wolves of Yellowstone National Park. The eradication of the wolves started in the nineteenth century at the request of farmers, and were gone by 1930. The elk population then surged and large areas of the park, particularly the riverbanks, were stripped bare. Grass and saplings disappeared, leaving no food and shelter for water birds whose numbers declined rapidly. Beavers, similarly affected by the disappearance of trees, also left the area. The riverbanks became wastelands and, unprotected by vegetation, the land washed away in seasonal flooding, speeding up erosion. Soon the rivers began to meander more. The situation, and the changing landscape, continued until 1995, when wolves from Canada were released in Yellowstone to restore the park's ecological balance.

Changes in the food chain rapidly led to changes in the ecosystem. As the wolves ate the elks, the latter's declining numbers allowed little shoots of trees to start growing again along the riverbanks. The elks felt hunted, became more fearful and no longer lived close to the riverbanks, where fast-growing willows and poplars were given a chance to grow back. Within a few years, the banks became stable again and the river's meandering process stopped as erosion decreased and less soil was washed away. The beavers returned with the trees and contributed in turn to their growth, amphibians found small ponds to thrive in, and the number of bird species increased noticeably. The grizzlies, whose berry-bearing shrubs had been eaten by the elks, and whose numbers had also declined, were happy to see them grow again and they too benefited from the return of the wolves.

The number of wolves initially remained stable because it was controlled by the availability of elks, but ranchers have not accepted their presence. While livestock constitutes only 0.75 percent of the wolves' diet, and farmers can easily and effectively protect their animals against them, they instead refuse to accept the wolves' presence, tracking them down through the radio collars animals wear and shooting them as soon as they leave the park. The wolves' numbers have gone from a high of 174 in 2003 to about one hundred in 2016.

ALTHOUGH OFTEN MISTAKEN AND EVEN MORE often misguided, man generally strives to reach a more sustainable equilibrium. Much of our straying from the path of moderation seems carelessly erratic, yet we recognize that the traditional values at the core of many cultures might propel us to a more sober re-evaluation of our condition. Indigenous people of Australia and the Americas have met to reaffirm their trust in a common holistic worldview, in which respect for the environment, the community, and future generations (sometimes up to the seventh, as with the Mi'kmaq Nation) predominates.

These values, particularly held by the elders and now adopted by the young of many nations, are inherent to the environmental stewardship to which government and non-government agencies must aspire. Many international organizations are proposing programs in the hope of slowing the process of deterioration, moving from the notion of dominion to that of partnership. They propose practical projects of conservation, reduction of waste, and clean-up to involve ordinary individuals at the local level. They hope that concerned citizens and school children, with the backing of scientists, will pressure legislators to act in the interest of the planet.

In the past, public opinion and legislative action successfully banned toxic products (such as asbestos) or reduced their use (tobacco); now the goal is to reduce substantially (rather than recycle, as was once urged) the use of plastics and fossil fuels. The public demand for change has already met with some positive responses and, notably, plastic bags have been banned from many large cities worldwide. The European Union voted to ban the use of throwaway plastic items such as straws and polystyrene cups by 2021. Procter & Gamble and Coca-Cola, among others, were targeted at the World Economic Forum in January 2019 and urged to reduce their use of plastic packaging. Various large companies, notably in Britain, have pledged to eliminate unnecessary single-use plastic packaging by 2025.

The global urgency of current environmental concerns seems to dismiss outright the aspirations of previously underdeveloped countries to finally start sharing in the bounty of consumption and overconsumption lavishly enjoyed in the West. Growth restrictions imposed on them for the good of all would once more appear to follow a familiar pattern, the more powerful seen to impose their will over all others. However, a possible and welcome trade-off and compensation for indiscriminate consumption might be a better and fairer repartition of world resources to help resolve health problems and social conflicts. The field is almost unlimited, as science provides the means to address many of our woes, notably in the fields of disease prevention, water treatment and food production.

These attempts could be seen as the ultimate proof of our self-centred approach to our environment, since we would naturally be the first beneficiaries of their success. This would ignore the sincere connection we have with our land and the urgency of our attempt to come to terms with a better management of the environment benefiting all species. The "partnership ethic," as proposed by Caroline Merchant, professor of environmental history at the University of California Berkeley, relies on a sustained relationship between human and non-human communities and includes considerations of economic and ecological exchanges. "It is an ethic in which humans act to fulfil both humanity's vital needs and nature's needs by restraining human hubris." It draws from the 1992 Rio Declaration's "global partnership to conserve, protect, and restore the health of the earth's ecosystems," and incorporates other humanistic considerations that should guide the selection of technologies to sustain both natural and human environments.

In *Faust,* Goethe warned, "What you have inherited from your ancestors, earn it, so as to own it." The effort now is to recognize the toxic effect of physical and moral pollution on the human and natural environments and reflect upon the measures that might allay its consequences: equity between human and non-human communities; moral considerations for both humans and other species; respect for both cultural diversity and biodiversity; inclusion of women, minorities, and nonhuman nature in the code of ethical accountability; and an ecologically sound management consistent with the continued health of both the human and the nonhuman communities. We need to resolve the moral dissonance of damage done to perpetrators and the insidious harm done to society.

Ours is the only species that has imposed its will on all that surrounds it. Now we stand accused of fatal insouciance towards the future, selfishness, smugness, immediate greed, disregard of the impact of our actions, mismanagement and a sense of entitlement over the environment. Such accusations should incite us to reconsider whether our modes of thinking and acting towards animals and nature have evolved over time. Have we progressed from absolute lords and masters of all we saw to a more sensitive position of responsibility and enlightened stewardship, attempting to right our wrongs—or are we stubbornly blind and deaf to anything but self-interest?

CHAPTER TEN

REFLECTIONS ON GOOD AND EVIL

IF I HAD ANY PRECONCEIVED IDEA when I started wondering in earnest about the part good and evil play in our behaviour and the forms taken by the order and dissonance we generate around us, it might have resembled the one eventually achieved by Dr. Seuss's Sneetches—"That day they decided that Sneetches are Sneetches / And no kind of Sneetch is the best on the beaches." Their initially biased world view was changed by experience and reason (with a little outside help) to conclude that we are all intrinsically the same and should be treated as equals. Mine was an uncomplicated view tending to belief in easy self-improvement guided by one's 'better' instincts—one that had, surprisingly, not evolved significantly since the teachings received in early childhood.

Where I ended, a year and a half later, was much closer to Pogo, the clear-eyed possum of the 1950s comic strip, who soberly realized, "We have met the enemy and he is us." His is the pithier recognition of our condition already presented by Cicero in the first century BCE: "The enemy is within the gates; it is with our own luxury, our own folly, our own criminality that we have to contend."

The challenge then may be to wonder whether, if we are indeed our own enemies, could we not also be our own allies and take the lead in our own salvation? This question was naturally based on many others. What are the certainties on which we base our judgement? Are we doomed to repeat our mistakes or can we learn from them? Why do we knowingly continue to make the same ones?

Who among us are best equipped to take the lead in attempting to gain the physical, intellectual and moral high ground?

My research caused my loss of innocence, but I hoped it would also hold some of the answers to these questions. I proceeded by taking stock, reviewing the disintegration of our current environmental and moral situation and the ensuing dooms threatened by scientists and humanists alike; next, by considering the various ways we apprehend the world and guide our actions; and finally by wondering about an unlikely coalition of potential leaders on a path to sustainability and perhaps eventual recovery.

THE WORLD ASUNDER

The few lines in Genesis relating to the Creation and the Fall raise many questions, notably about the omnipotence and goodness of God, man's dominion over the earth, the nature of man, the acceptance of evil, free will and blind trust. These questions have caused much anguish and are the source of philosophical and literary reflection that attempts to address our contradictory impulses and accommodate them within a balanced life.

Too much may have been expected from us from the start. Through a flaw in our nature, we lost the trust of God. Had we not stupidly infringed one single interdiction, our life might have been like one long day at the spa, exempt from strife and concern, free of doubt. No toiling, no exertion. No cumbersome clothes. No painful childbirth. No punishment from the One who had instilled that very flaw within us. And so the myth goes—with the Fall, we sealed our fate and were left to deal with the mess we created.

Most of all, what struck me about Genesis was the sense of being abandoned by God as man expressed his feeling of despair and helplessness in the presence of evil:

> How long, Lord, must I call for help, but you do not listen? Or cry out to you, 'Violence!' but you do not save? Why do you make me look at injustice? Why do you tolerate

wrongdoing? Destruction and violence are before me; there
is strife, and conflict abounds. Therefore, the law is para-
lyzed, and justice never prevails. The wicked hem in the
righteous, so that justice is perverted. (Habakkuk 1:2-4)

Again I looked and saw all the oppression that was taking
place under the sun: I saw the tears of the oppressed—and
they have no comforter; power was on the side of their
oppressors. And I declared that the dead, who had already
died, are happier than the living, who are still alive. But
better than both is the one who has never been born,
who has not seen the evil that is done under the sun."
(Ecclesiastes 4:1-3)

Through Adam and Eve's disobedience and God's gift of free choice,
we are constantly faced with the temptations of the seven deadly
sins, the presumed source of all evil thoughts and actions—lust,
gluttony, greed, sloth, wrath, envy and pride. I knew this from the
age of seven, which is the age of reason in the Catholic Church.
Today, I would rate greed and wrath as the top contenders, sometimes in combination with others such as envy and pride. I would
also add fear and venality, even though not included on the list, as
they affect the intensity and nature of the damage done, both to the
victim and the perpetrator. Given this wellspring of nastiness and
corruption within our souls, and our ambiguous feeling about it,
how have we adapted to today's world?

After World War II, we thought we had witnessed the ultimate
effects of what we assumed to be evil incarnate, for which we could
find no reasonable explanation. Today, we realize that we have not
recovered and that some of the same breakdown still exists in many
forms. We see it in armed conflicts where civilians, and particularly
children, bear the consequences of decisions made out of ineptitude,
greed or ideological hatred. We see it in the waves of unwanted refugees confined in camps. We see it in the daily violence of our lives
where women are still afraid to walk alone at night, families live

in slums, people go from precarious jobs to food banks. We also see it in our casual disregard of future consequences, and a sense of entitlement over a seriously mismanaged environment. We no longer even call these evil and see them as mere excesses, difficult to overlook but lacking clear solutions.

It is a common saying among criminologists that their subjects belong to one of the three categories: the bad, the sad and the mad. Such a characterization presumes that these people deviate from a generally good, happy and sane norm. One might wonder where criminologists live if such is actually their conception of the world. The reality is that criminals perform actions ranging along a spectrum artificially defined as unacceptable. Some individuals may have lost their moral compass, others may have become part of an ineluctable series of events and are hopelessly caught like cogs in moving pieces of machinery, some may experience enjoyment in cruelty, others may be able to dehumanize their victims. All perform actions that are antagonistic to the good working order of the group, defined at that precise moment in that specific place. They offend the rules for living harmoniously in society: respect of traditions, particularly taboos; promotion of orderly actions; and abhorrence of dissonant ones. Even milieus that boast of defying formalized etiquette must obey their own sets of rules, sometimes even more demanding and restrictive than those observed by the general population. Gangs, for instance, boast of lawlessness but are governed by even stronger rules intended to confirm power-based hierarchies.

To that limited extent, we can then believe that 'bad' actions merely contradict man-made laws and are relative to their time and place—without perhaps being essentially evil. Some practices we deem detestable today, such as cannibalism or incest, have had their legitimate and ritual places in other cultures at other times. Within our own society some actions once deemed criminal (homosexuality, for example) are now widely accepted, some common business practices (such as slavery) have been criminalized, and former nuisance behaviours (including bullying and harassment) are now punishable offences. We are obviously operating on shifting grounds where time and place mostly seem to determine the spiritual value of our actions.

Generally speaking, anthropologists have shown us that actions cannot be superficially transposed from one culture to another and interpreted according to extrinsic values. What matters is the coherence of cultures and whether actions are seen as contributing to the good order of things or as producing destructive dissonance within their particular context. For instance, we believe that we must not kill other humans, unless values higher than human life are at stake. Yet this seemingly lofty justification once urged Christians to kill witches and infidels, and the Inquisition burned and maimed at will in the name of God. In wars, both sides often pray for victory to the same God and are assured that His benevolent protection verifies and supports the righteousness of their contradictory causes.

But some broad notions of right and wrong supersede specific cultural contexts. We are surrounded by problems that offend more universal human values:

- Cases of extremist and fanatical behaviours (racist, homophobic, sexist, religious) are in evidence all over the world, both as solitary acts and organized manifestations. Poverty, homelessness and drug addiction run rampant in our cities.

- Huge profits are continuously being made from the manufacturing and sales of arms and narcotics; from hard pornography, gambling and prostitution; from the depiction of violence and murder.

- Social media, intended to give a voice to everyone and enhance everyday communication, have become the primary means of disseminating fake news, vacuous thoughts, conspiracy theories, discrimination and atrocious harassment.

- The gap between rich and poor has widened to unconscionable levels, most of the world's wealth being held by a handful of families. The number of billionaires is increasing all the time while, at the other end, multitudes subsist on $1.25 a day or less (the World Bank definition of extreme poverty). Multinationals rule the economy, trapping us in a deadly loop of advertising and overconsumption.

- Millions are now on the move, mostly from a devastated Africa, some aspiring to better lives but most driven by war, famine or desertification. Scientists surmise the numbers of climate refugees may reach 140 million by 2050.

- Social unrest has become rife in previously stable countries, partly driven by genuine needs, partly prodded along by politics or ill will, partly caused by terrorism or crime. The hope of a European Union with common aspirations and unified means may be slowly disintegrating. Latin America could be gradually sinking into economic and political chaos. No one knows who will eventually own the wealth of Africa.

- The objectives of accords and agreements on attempted climate control have lost ground, even if the terms of the 2015 United Nations Climate Change Conference in Paris (to reduce greenhouse gas emissions to below 2 percent) were ratified in Katowice in 2018.

The picture seems bleak and solutions, if they are to be found, must rely on the coordinated efforts of like-minded individuals able to transcend ethnic, cultural, religious, educational and political differences. But how similar are we? And how much can we rely on our commonality?

OUR UNCOMMON REALITY

We generally believe that our senses provide us with enough contextual input to form opinions on what we perceive and that sight, hearing, smell, touch and taste give tangible shape to the puzzle of our environment. After an apprenticeship served in early childhood,

REFLECTIONS ON GOOD AND EVIL

and with the exception of hallucinogenic drug use in shamanistic quests or modern subcultures, or conditions such as synesthesia (where sensations overlap), we generally trust our senses to be reliable and faithful to a concept we call reality.

Since our bodies are roughly alike, we tend to assume that all humans share the same sensory experience of the world. In reality, we interpret the sensations we receive through a cultural filter and do not classify everything alike, even concrete phenomena. For instance, in our culture we sort colours according to hue, brightness and saturation. Goethe, in *The Theory of Colours*, mostly saw our perception of colour as a scientific dialectic between light and darkness; we would be tempted to agree and think it a universal proposition. But the Hanunóo of the Philippines would have once been at a loss to understand the significance of colour charts at our paint shops. Their eyes may have perceived the same hue, brightness and saturation as ours, but the colours they saw only had meaning when considered through the prism of their cultural relevance and worldview. In this case, the meaning was related to the colours' moisture content, surface texture, lightness, association with plant life and probably other connections that we would never associate with colour. From this and other examples, we might then challenge any assumption that we all apprehend the physical world in the same way—an apprehension that is itself the gateway to formulating opinions.

Going beyond our individual interpretation of sensory perceptions, what can we say about the way we understand whole situations, either taken out of context or given a specific slant? We know how easily our attention can be distracted and how unreliable our accounts are. Among selective attention tests, the so-called 'disappearing gorilla' is famous—instructed to count how many times a volleyball is passed among players, most spectators are oblivious to a man dressed in a gorilla suit walking slowly among the players, then taking a small bow before walking away. Their eyes may have peripherally perceived the 'gorilla,' but their minds, focused on another task, did not acknowledge his passage.

In this particular case, nobody tried to influence the spectators. In other instances, we may witness scenes whose specific context may have to be explained to us, about which we may be given partial information, for which we may have already formed an opinion based on our cultural values—all of which may cause difficulty in assessing and classifying what we witness. How much of our opinion is based on reliable sources and how much manufactured by our prejudices and ability to draw conclusions? Charles Darwin, for instance, relates in his *Voyage of the Beagle* the visit he paid to a Chilean mine in 1837. He calculated at more than 200 pounds the load carried by the miners, the Apires, whom he described as "truly beasts of burden…not allowed to halt for breath":

> Although with a knowledge that the labour was voluntary, it was nevertheless quite revolting to see the state in which they reached the mouth of the mine; their bodies bent forward, leaning with their arms on the steps, their legs bowed, their muscles quivering, the perspiration streaming from their faces over their breasts, their nostrils distended, the corners of their mouth forcibly drawn back, and the expulsion of their breath most laborious. Each time they draw their breath they utter an articulate cry of "ay-ay," which ends in a sound rising from deep in the chest, but shrill like the note of a fife. After staggering to the pile of ore, they emptied the "carpacho;" in two or three seconds recovering their breath, they wiped the sweat from their brows, and apparently quite fresh descended the mine again at a quick pace. This appears to me a wonderful instance of the amount of labour which habit, for it can be nothing else, will enable a man to endure.

Today, anyone witnessing such a scene would have no doubt that these men were slaves—not because they were acknowledged as such but because the conditions of their work made them so. The outrages of slavery were well known in 1837, the Slavery Abolition Act having been passed in 1833 in the United Kingdom. Yet, Darwin (whose genius at drawing naturalistic and evolutionary conclusions shines in the last sentence) had been told their work was voluntary and, in spite of his description of their labours, he believed that these men, "excepting from accidents…are healthy and appear cheerful." Similar conclusions might have been drawn from the singing of black slaves picking cotton in southern plantations.

Today men, women, even children work for long hours at repetitive, mind-numbing, physically demanding tasks, often for a pittance. Some of them may do so voluntarily because bodies need food and a minimum of protection from the elements, but not calling them slaves is a stretch of our standards. While we should continue to maintain that some types of work are unacceptable, our assumptions, like Darwin's, could well be matters of perception. Some may find pride in toiling the hardest soil, fishing in the most dangerous waters, pitting themselves against a harsh nature in conditions that most of us, having forsaken rough physical labour for two or three generations, simply no longer understand. Perhaps the Apires derived a sense of superiority and much prestige from the excessive weight they were able to carry, that made them stand out among their peers. Values vary from group to group and from time to time, and when we do not know how embedded they are in a cultural context we may not understand, how can be sure of the validity of our interpretations and moral assessments? Only the Apires and those around them knew how the Apires stood in their social order, and whether they were abused slaves or competitive free workers.

The impact of culture on what may seem right and what is deemed wrong is particularly pronounced when applied to artistic pursuits. Certain musical and pictorial systems appear totally discordant to the classically trained ear or eye, yet are accepted as valid and praiseworthy by others: abstract painting, rap music, Chinese opera and modern dance are only some examples. There is, for instance, a Quarter of

Discord in Barcelona that displays examples of deliberately dissonant architecture of the *Modernista* movement, where all previous rules have been abandoned or broken. Yet the very combination of their discordance leads them to constitute a coherent whole.

Other art forms come to a crossroad where tradition is challenged and replaced by innovative disorder. One such event occurred on the French stage, on February 25, 1830, with the opening of *Hernani,* a radical romantic play by Victor Hugo. Until then, classical theatre had strictly adhered to conventions of time, location and action. In the clash of old and modern, later known as the Battle of *Hernani,* opponents and supporters came to blows. Change prevailed—the rules had been broken, the limits tested and French theatre was never the same afterwards.

If our beliefs and actions are based on such fragile and unreliable impressions, are all things in fact relative to their places, times and cultural contexts? If our perceptions of the real world are so different, are there any incontrovertible and consensual positions on the nature of the human condition that we can share? If asked, we would show the conventionally good side of our nature and tritely point to generally agreed human rights: that all humans deserve clean water and clean air, that people must have sufficient and appropriate food and shelter, that everyone should feel safe in the conduct of daily activities, that children should be educated to benefit from the wisdom of their tribal group (ranging from proficiency in traditional hunting techniques to doctorates in astrophysics), that individuals should be free to make their own decisions provided they are not detrimental to their community, that people should be able to worship as they choose and obey the ritual laws of their faith as long as they do not lead to violent conflicts with others.

In spite of their blatant idealism, such self-evident claims are essential and reasonable. Yet we are daily confronted with the proof that, for most of the world, few of these aspirations can be met. If we (Westerners enjoying the benefits of modern comforts and conveniences) are honest, we must acknowledge our part in helping to create an unjust world. So, if fair treatment remains out of our reach because the necessary commitment exceeds our common will, are there at least gradually achievable goals that could perhaps be unanimously negotiated?

THE HUMAN CONDITION

As he accepted the Nobel Prize for Literature, William Golding expressed the wish that writers, through "devotion, skill, passion and luck" reflect what many people are thinking. One person speaking to another, then to many, until the ripple becomes a tide, and eventually nation speaks to nation. Then:

> …we may learn to be temperate, provident, taking no more from nature's treasury than is our due…We need more humanity, more care, more love. There are those who expect a political system to produce that; and others who expect the love to produce the system. My own faith is that the truth of the future lies between the two and we shall behave humanly and a bit humanely, stumbling along, haphazardly generous and gallant, foolishly and meanly wise until the rape of our planet is seen to be the preposterous folly that it is.

"For," he concluded, "we are a marvel of creation." The year was 1983, merely three and a half decades ago. Golding's plea seemed natural then. He came from a tradition where literary works had a considerable influence on people's thinking; *Gulliver's Travels, Uncle Tom's Cabin, Oliver Twist, The Grapes of Wrath, Silent Spring,* to name a few, have affected people's views on narrow-minded politics, slavery, poverty, the environment. More generally, the nineteenth-century works of Dickens and Balzac's *La Comédie humaine* depicted the human condition and its inherent vices and virtues. Other art forms also had their traditional part to play in alerting and shaping public opinion: Picasso's *Guernica* revealed in its time the horrors of war, as did war artists of the twentieth century sketching routine scenes of confusion, filth, suffering, and sorrow—unlike earlier painters, notably David and Delacroix, who glorified war and patriotism.

Today, however, Golding's plea seems old-fashioned and lacking the urgency the situation merits. Far more than in 1983, our "marvel of creation" is giving every sign of dissonance, prodded on by greed and indifference. What is required is no longer the slow-moving progress of germinating ideas (at least not on their own) but the immediate putsch of coordinated action.

Many contemporary commentators have a grim vision of the future and our increasing disconnection from what once constituted a familiar natural and social environment. American commentator (and Presbyterian minister) Chris Hedges believes that we are squandering our future "through acts of colossal stupidity and hubris." With the slashing of the budgets of various American organizations dealing with climate change, he believes that "hurricane after hurricane, monster storm after monster storm, flood after flood, wildfire after wildfire, drought after drought will gradually cripple the empire draining its wealth and resources and creating swaths of territory defined by lawlessness and squalor."[1]

He may be correct. However, previous predictions, equally dire, have later proved to be overstated or even mistaken. Paul R. Ehrlich's influential book, *The Population Bomb* (1968) set the tone for the decade with this warning: "The battle to feed all of humanity is over." According to his forecast, hundreds of millions (sixty-five of them Americans) would starve to death in the following decade, overcrowded India would be doomed and England would cease to exist by the year 2000. Instead, in the ensuing decades, birthrates actually fell below long-term replacement numbers, notably in Japan, the industrialized West and even India, China, Southeast Asia and Latin America, entirely disproving the 'scientific' overpopulation vision of the 1960s. More recent concerns result from the anticipated population downturn. In *The Coming Population Crash and Our Planet's*

---

1. Chris Hedges, *America, The Farewell Tour* (New York: Simon & Schuster, 2018), 244.

Surprising Future (2010), Fred Pearce surmises that, rather than overpopulation, the earth's true problem is overconsumption—the overuse of available resources and its effects on climate change.

Overconsumption is inextricably linked to globalization, a phenomenon British historian and philosopher Roger Scruton sees as one of the causes for our irresponsible behaviour. We have evolved from transactions with local businesses to anonymous dealings with multinational corporations that neither produce nor sell products but merely brand them. As local stores and local producers are bought up or driven out of business by anonymous chains, goods seem to be moving around the world without anyone being responsible for them. As the distance between product and consumer increases, the disconnection extends even further:

> The cost of producing soy beans in Brazil—the cost in terms of environmental damage, devastation of the landscape, aesthetic and biological pollution—is not witnessed by consumers in the United States nor controlled by US legislation (itself responsible to lobbying from consumers). It is a cost that can be, as it were, left in Brazil and left to the future generations who will have to bear it.... The real cost of producing packaged food on the supermarket shelf includes the enormous long-term cost of non-biodegradable packaging... This cost is not borne by the supermarket or its suppliers. It is borne by all of us, and by our descendants over the next one thousand years or so.[2]

In response to this trend, some companies and organizations are moving toward a 'triple bottom line' model that, at least conceptually, includes environmental and social results along with financial performance—people and the planet are added to profits to create a 'triple P' approach. Businesses of all sizes now routinely share information about their charitable activities, manufacturing processes, supply chains and hiring practices on their websites and in their marketing materials as modern consumers, especially the

2. Roger Scruton, *Where We Are* (London, Oxford, New York: Bloomsbury, 2017), 152–55

much-coveted millenials, increasingly integrate social responsibility into their purchasing decisions. The Nielsen Global Survey on Corporate Social Responsibility (2014) found that up to 55 percent of consumers are willing to pay more for goods and services committed to social and environmental sustainability; mobile apps give shoppers access to objective information about a company's track record while making purchasing decisions. The same spirit of innovation that created the problem may yet help correct it—provided that public demand continues to support it. Yet, according to Michael Gecan, social media is partially responsible for the social dissolution occurring in thousands of communities throughout America:

> Everywhere the tightknit worlds of a dozen or so blocks—where workplace, church, neighbourhood, recreation, tavern, and political filiation were all deeply entwined—have given way to exurban enclaves, long commutes, gathered congregations, matchmaker websites, and fitness clubs filled with customers who don't know one another. A world where local news was critically important and closely followed...has been replaced by the constant flow of real and fake news arriving through social media.[3]

In spite of this apparent disengagement, a sense of community has not entirely disappeared. The traditional barn raising of pioneering days, for instance, has made way for Habitat for Humanity and similar organizations. There are countless examples of people coming together in times of emergency or grief and providing moral support and practical assistance to one another, and those examples reassure and nourish us. We are social animals and the need to feel part of a common group can still override narrow personal interests and reinforce our sense of belonging.

"The grass still grows and the birds still sing in Auschwitz." We are both indignant that nature should continue to establish

---

3. Michael Gecan, 'Back of the Yards: Lesson from a Community Organizer on Building Political Power,' *Boston Review*, January 4, 2017

its perennial rights, blind to the horrors of the past, yet reassured that those events have not forever destroyed our sense of hope and renewal. As the Franco-Russian writer Andreï Makine observes in *Au delà des Frontières* (2019):

> Every year throughout the world more than a million women are raped or murdered—3,000 a day; six million children die of hunger—one every five seconds. Do you know how many shots are fired? 800 billion each year, about one hundred per person on earth, without including bombs and missiles. All that, simultaneously with everyday life, holidays, sports, elections, overspending.

The main character in Walker Percy's dystopian novel *Love in the Ruins* (1971) wonders—as we might all do—where it all went wrong:

> Was it the nigger business from the beginning? What a bad joke: God saying, here it is, the new Eden, and it is yours because you are the apple of my eye; because you the lordly Westerners, the fierce Caucasian-Gentile-Visigoths, believed in me and in the outlandish Jewish Event even though you were nowhere near it and had to hear the news of it from strangers. But you believed and so I gave it all to you, gave you Israel and Greece and science and art and the lordship of the earth, and finally even gave you the new world that I blessed for you. And all you had to do was pass one little test, which was surely child's play for you because you already had passed the big one. One little test: here's a helpless man in Africa, all you have to do is not violate him. That's all. One little test: you flunk!

When confronted with the evil at the source of his condition, man, who has been given so much, fails to pass the final test of his humanity. It is a test he failed more than once through his history, repeatedly in fact, and in many forms—many of which have been related here.

Believing this to be the human condition does not preclude us from attempting to control our instincts. We should take heart that there continues to be a spark of brotherly love, a sense of humanity, a generosity of spirit even in the very midst of evil. Those among Nazi concentration and death camp survivors who agree to talk tell the same tales of horror and inhumanity, yet some also speak of receiving comfort and sustenance from others as abused as themselves; of listening to songs, instrumental music, or poetry recited or played by those who could bring a little beauty and pleasure into a place so devoid of them; of basic medical care given by those without means; of pieces of clothing generously offered, of bits of food generously shared among the starving.

The notion of evil is only bearable because we also know of the existence of good. Without this knowledge we would be doomed souls, instead of knowing that hope and redemption are possible. Humans can be remarkably idealistic, considering how universally destructive they have also been—they can rally as swiftly to a call for help as they can hound someone whose attitude or looks they dislike. This idealism has led to the constitution of a large variety of international organizations playing a major part in improving lives. Among them (but certainly not limited to them) are the Red Cross and the Red Crescent, UNICEF, the World Bank, Amnesty International and Médecins sans Frontières.

The International Red Cross, founded in 1863 and joined in 1919 by the Red Crescent, constitutes a movement in which some ninety-seven million people participate. Both started in response to what was witnessed on battlefields (Solferino in 1859 and conflicts between the Russian and Ottoman Empires from 1876 to 1878) and have mostly been associated with helping wounded soldiers. Their stated principles have remained the same: humanity, impartiality, neutrality, independence, voluntary service, unity and universality. Through the work done by its international organization and numerous national branches, the Red Cross has been rewarded with four Nobel Peace Prizes: its founder Henri Dunant received the first in 1901, in 1917 it was for work on behalf of soldiers, in 1944 for work done to help prisoners of war, and in 1963 in celebration of its first century.

The devastation of World War II led to the creation of several non-governmental organizations that all aimed at compensating for the moral bankruptcy and physical violence that had been the hallmarks of the first half of the twentieth century. The United Nations International Children's Emergency Fund (UNICEF) was created in 1946 to provide emergency food and healthcare to children in countries devastated by the war: "UNICEF works in 190 countries and territories to save children's lives, to defend their rights, and to help them fulfil their potential, from early childhood through adolescence."

Amnesty International, created in London in 1961, focuses its efforts on human rights, investigating claims of wrongdoing (to underline the severe shortcomings evident in most parts of the world, 2018 was declared The Year of Human Rights). The United Nations peacekeeping Blue Helmets are routinely sent to distressed areas to prevent a conflict from escalating into full-fledged war. Their presence may sometimes be more symbolic than effective, but their very presence brings the conflict to the attention of the world.

Médecins sans Frontières/Doctors without Borders started in France as non-governmental organization in 1971 to provide international humanitarian and medical care—notably in conflict zones and in countries with few resources to address endemic diseases. It is ever-present in the midst of turmoil and is often the last humanitarian group to leave a war-torn country.

The World Bank's low-interest loans have transformed many lives, particularly those of women involved in local economy. Their work is based on sustainable development goals that address several aspects of the perceived needs: working at reducing poverty (improving malnutrition, sanitation, education, and health care), mitigating and containing the negative impact of human activity (expanding marine protection, transitioning to renewable energy sources), and promoting private markets that generate jobs and higher incomes.

With the exception of the Red Cross, which was founded in the nineteenth century, all these organizations are by-products of the global confrontation with evil and turmoil of the twentieth century. As we applaud their continuing success and efficiency, we must bear in mind that they arose from the depths of our immorality and that, unfortunately, their work continues to be of paramount importance for those forever without shelter, food, care, safety, hope. We may feel pleasantly altruistic as we see them at work, perhaps supporting them ourselves, but they only reflect the sad reality faced by a large proportion of mankind. Along with good will and practical assistance, this is the message these organisations should carry and where their focus should remain—that the needs are enormous and always growing and the people assisted are not responsible for their fate but are usually the victims of circumstances over which they have no control.

The face of charity has thankfully evolved from alms and personal contact and gracious largesse. Once, a lady with some means and her daughters might visit the poor with baskets of food and words of comfort sometimes barely disguising an admonition; it taught well-born girls social responsibility and was intended to generate gratitude in the bosom of the needy. Ladies' organizations also took care of orphans, single mothers, derelicts and prisoners, often in a highly moralistic way. Yet charity, even in this superior and ineffective form, had a recognizable human face. Such is no longer the case as solid rationalization of efforts and greatly superior means have taken its place.

The focus of philanthropy and sponsorship has now broadened to include the values and leaders of Silicon Valley, Wall Street and Davos (meeting place of the World Economic Forum). Noteworthy among individuals actively engaged in humanitarian fields, Bill and Melinda Gates's foundation (started in 2000) has reputedly devoted around

$50 billion to the goals of promoting access for children to healthcare and education, giving people the tools to lead healthy and productive lives and the means to lift themselves out of poverty, delivering the latest in science and technology to the neediest, changing public policies and attitudes, working in partnerships at the local level. It also partnered with billionaire Warren Buffet to start The Giving Pledge—to date, more than 150 other billionaires have committed to giving away at least half their fortunes to philanthropic causes.

Other initiatives have brought significant benefit with fewer resources and more personal participation. For instance, Spread the Net, started by two Canadian media personalities, engaged school children across the country and raised enough money to provide Liberia and Rwanda with 500,000 insecticide-treated mosquito nets, distributed through UNICEF to protect people against malaria.

In addition to fundraising initiatives, motivated groups and individuals continue to take direct action. Among individuals who have marked the world by their humanity are those who put their lives at risk to save Jewish children (up to 10,000 of them) and adults from Nazi concentration camps in the 1930s and during World War II. The state of Israel created Yad Vashem in 1953, the Shoah Martyrs and Heroes' Remembrance Authority, to recognize and commemorate "the Righteous among the Nations." In other fields, Greenpeace's *Rainbow Warrior* protested whaling and nuclear testing until she was sunk in New Zealand in 1985 by French agents, and the *Phoenix* sailed the Quaker Action Group to North Vietnam in 1957 in an attempt to bring in medical supplies and drugs. Ordinary people continue to go out of their way, donating time and occasionally taking risks to follow their conscience.

These efforts demonstrate that we have an enormous capacity for addressing what we see as the consequences of rampant evil (war, poverty, disease, discrimination, misfortune, abuse) particularly when we recognize that we have brought them upon ourselves and those close to us.

However, those who oppose liberal activities are also garnering their own forces to counteract peaceful efforts and democratic interventions. They may cause violent counter-manifestations, threats and obstruction, and their presence is expected almost as a matter of course. Sometimes they are on the official side of law and order in countries that harshly control their citizens. Elsewhere, they may only consist of ragtag citizens parading with tiki torches, wearing armbands or white robes and conical hoods. Whoever they are, they are constant reminders that humanity is multiple in its beliefs and that no single model is going to satisfy everyone.

TOMORROW'S LEADERS

If we are to win our battle against passive acceptance of the self-destructive status quo, we will need a new breed of leaders. The generous and vigilant humanism we need today may well come from the traditionally disenfranchised—indigenous groups, women and children constitute powerful elements that, if united and organized, could substantially influence both politics and the economy.

The traditional values espoused by indigenous people, whatever their cultures, are essential to reconstituting our own. They once took from the earth only what they needed without waste, a concept almost alien to us today, and their potential to reintroduce a more holistic worldview has not yet been tapped.

At first, aboriginal people's efforts were mostly through conventional channels and participation in the United Nations Indigenous Decade (1995–2004) whose goals were "to strengthen international cooperation for the solution of problems faced by indigenous people in the areas of human rights, culture, the environment, development, education and health." While language difficulties and time constraints prohibited significant progress, 68 percent still expressed satisfaction with the outcome of the exchanges of experience and contacts among indigenous organizations.

Experience showed that informal contacts, generated by

indigenous groups themselves rather than promoted under the United Nations aegis, were what actually worked. Some groups already existed. The Arctic Winter Games, a biennial competition that includes both ancestral and modern events, have brought together participants from Alaska, northern Canada and Greenland, as well as the Sami people of Scandinavia and the Okrug people of Russia. New connections are now being interwoven among Maori, Canadian First Nations, Indians of the Amazon and other groups who see their survival—and that of the planet—linked to values mostly fallen into disregard.

Having seen the failure of governments to protect them, indigenous groups are ready to take matters into their own hands, particularly with regard to the Amazonian forest. The combined effects of legal and illegal deforestation, the activities of mercenaries, the unwillingness of exploiters and their governments to put an end to catastrophic environmental abuses, the slow response to human losses and the destruction of South American native cultures have led Amazonian tribes to reach out to international communities from the United Nations to other traditional indigenous nations. In the latter, they find understanding and models of self-assertion and governance that might be adapted to their own situation.

At the national level, indigenous groups continue to be underrepresented, but their political influence is growing. In Western Canada, notably, the political influence of First Nations has recently been demonstrated in decisions bearing on politics, the economy and the environment. Moreover, they have achieved symbolic precedence; civic occasions and events hosted on their ancestral lands now begin with an acknowledgement of the fact.

The International Native Tradition Interchange Inc. is, among others, an organization dedicated to the advancement of the rights of indigenous people and the protection of the earth through striving "to enhance indigenous capacity and legitimate participation based on traditional knowledge and a holistic vision of the work in

cooperation with the international community." Whatever the effi-
cacy and results of this particular organization, such objectives are
valid and ought to inspire further emulation.

From the start, women have been earmarked as disrupters—it
was Eve who offered the apple to Adam, not the other way around.
Of all creatures described in Genesis, woman is the sole derivative,
created from Adam's rib. This otherness, so long a hindrance, might
now be a source for change.

We may wonder about the type of power women actually yield
today, given their continuing fight to be recognized as equals. Much
of their work remains uncompensated (worldwide, the value of this
unpaid labour would amount to some $10 trillion), they are gener-
ally not paid at the same rate as men and they are mostly excluded
from senior management positions. However, women vote, work
and belong to unions. A 2015 BMO Report shows them holding
52 percent of management and professional positions in the United
States, being the primary breadwinners in over 40 percent of households, having outnumbered men in higher education since the
1970s, and controlling more than half of the total personal wealth
(or US$14 trillion, expected to climb to 22 trillion in 2020).

Most of all, in the western world women generally control the
purchasing choices made by their households—in a society devoted
to consumerism, this is power indeed. Even though most of the
products and services they purchase are still produced by companies
founded and directed by men, they are said to control about 85 percent of consumer spending in the United States, having a decisive
voice in the choice of automobile, home, furnishings, vacations,
entertainment and clothing for the whole family.

It would be an error to think of women as a homogeneous group
(witness the 'Women for Trump' signs at American political rallies)
but, when their common interests are obviously at stake, they can
come together in significant numbers. In 411 BCE, Aristophanes
wrote the bawdy tale of an Athenian woman by the name of

Lysistrata who, to end the Peloponnesian War, convinced all women to withhold sex, forcing their desperate husbands to negotiate a peace. In our time, the #MeToo movement has led to the recent and ongoing downfall of hundreds of predatory men who had sexually exploited women of inferior status. Women probably did not suspect how overwhelming their success would be and should be emboldened to realize the power they hold when united.

Women have achieved such success before: the English girls and women who created the Matchgirls' Union in 1888 to fight off the use of lethal phosphorus at the Bryant & May match factory in Bow; Carrie Nation and her fellow activists campaigning for Prohibition; and the five Canadian women of the Persons Case in 1928-29, who sought with less drama but equal determination to have women recognized as people under the law; the women who fought for access to medical schools, Olympic sports, private clubs and other male bastions.

When psychologist William Moulton Marston introduced Wonder Woman in 1941—only twenty-one years after women gained the right to vote in America—it was to produce the image of a free and courageous woman who would serve as a model to young girls. Most powerful women of the past (queens, empresses, tsarinas) and more recent politicians such as Margaret Thatcher have displayed what we mostly see as manly characteristics. Today's veteran female politicians (such as Hillary Clinton) may be tainted by their antecedents and, because of their age, will not inhabit the future they would seek to improve. Effective powerful politicians such as Angela Merkel are at the end of their career. The political scene for women is changing. A new breed of young politicians who will live with the long-term consequences of their policies (such as Alexandria Ocasio-Cortez from the US or New Zealand's Jacinda Ardern) is required to carry the appropriate momentum.

On February 14, 2018 seventeen students and staff were shot to death and another seventeen were wounded at Marjory Stoneman

Douglas High School in Parkland, Florida. Once more, the rest of the world—constantly astonished as such hopeless recurrence—heard the same words iterated in the same defeated tones of voice. We heard the same sorrow expressed and the same vague and ineffective promises made by politicians and adults in position of power. But, this time, the loudest voices were those of the surviving children and, unlike the usual adult voices, they have not been muted and their speakers have not passed on to other things. Rather, they have coordinated their efforts to achieve even greater coherence and purpose.

These students came from a culture of violence, practising all their school lives for the eventuality of such senseless attacks. When one finally came to them and the usual futile adult words had been uttered, their rallying cry became "We Call BS." The National Rifle Association and its powerful lobbies have been powerless against them and, unlike the adults, they believe that something can actually be done. Within days of the shooting, they started their own lobby aimed at representatives in the Florida state capital and in Washington. They created #NeverAgain (of similar intensity to the women's #MeToo). One month after the shooting, they led demonstrations supported by more than a million students across the US and, on March 24, they organized the March for Our Lives, rallying huge crowds outside the Capitol. Since then, they have formed alliances with similar groups (Good Kids Mad City, the Peace Warriors), other survivors of mass shootings and individual survivors of violence, racism, and sexism in many states, their main focus always on preventing free access to guns. While still unable to vote, they have conducted themselves as responsible citizens, reminding politicians that most of them would be eligible to cast their ballots in the next election. One year after the events, the students have matured and become experienced speakers and effective agitators; more to the point, sixty-seven gun-related bills were enacted in twenty-six states and Washington, DC, in 2018.

The unusual persistence of #NeverAgain and similar groups comes from a deeper sense of peril than the ones experienced so far, best expressed by one volunteer and student at UCLA, Natalie Rotstein:

> I'm surrounded by friends who don't want to have kids because they don't feel like they can in good conscience put children into the imminent apocalypse that looks like our future right now. It's such an everyday, grinding kind of acceptance that there's probably going to be an apocalypse within our lifetime, and nobody is really doing anything to stop it, so it's the young people who feel the need to save our own futures because no one else is doing it.

The young people behind #NeverAgain are part of an international youth movement determined to take matters into their own hands, having seen the failure of adults to make any significant progress in securing their future. Their current actions are not without precedents. In 2014, seventeen-year-old Malala Yousafzai was honoured with the Nobel Peace Prize for her personal suffering and her activist stance on girls' education. In 2018, at the United Nations Climate Change conference in Katowice, Poland it was sixteen-year-old Greta Thunberg's turn to stand out, saying unequivocally: "So we have not come here to beg the world leaders to care for our future. They have ignored us in the past and they will ignore us again. We have come to let them know that change is coming, whether they like it or not."

School children have taken to the streets in Australia, Finland, Germany, Ireland, Switzerland, but nowhere more than in Belgium where, on January 31, 2019, 35,000 marched in Brussels alone. Up to 70,000 school children are regularly marching each week in 270 towns and cities worldwide. The numbers kept growing and, by March 2019 they were marching in about 1,700 cities in more than 100 countries. The children continue to march every Friday, to the detriment of their education but following their convictions and carried along by momentum propagated through such social media hashtags as #fridaysforfuture and #YouthStrike4Climate.

Scientists have rallied behind them. On February 15, 2019, 224 British scientists signed a letter of support, quoting Nelson Mandela, "Our children are our greatest treasure. They are our future. Those who abuse them tear at the fabric of our society and weaken our nation," adding "human planetary abuse is, in a very real sense, child neglect." In New Zealand alone, more than 1,500 academics have issued a similar statement. Across Germany, Austria, and Switzerland, more than 12,000 scientists are urging governments to comply to the 2015 Paris climate accord, backing the young people's actions they see as "justified and supported by the best available science."

Fred Vargas, mostly known as a successful mystery writer but also a researcher who worked for fifteen years with the Centre National de la Recherche Scientifique in Paris, added her voice with *L'humanité en peril*, published in 2019. The title is self-explanatory and the guilty parties are soon identified—criminally greedy billionaire industrialists and multinationals responsible for wilful misinformation and holding governments hostage.

Vargas points out that the two degree Celsius temperature increase that many governments see as a desirable target represents an average that includes the cooler oceans and polar ice caps. Two degrees are actually closer to five degrees on the continents and—again, should no drastic action be taken—the increase could reach four degrees (ten on the continents) by 2080. Since the beginning of the industrial era, the world's temperature has risen by a little over one degree. We now stand at 1.1 degree and could reach 1.5 by 2035. Vargas claims that at 1.5 degrees, half the world population will die of hunger, thirst, and epidemics, and that at two degrees, such will be fate of three quarters of the world population.

Fred Vargas, an elderly woman, has naturally been accused of being hysterical. However, scientists do not appear to have dismissed her numbers or conclusions. The question remains with each fraction of degree of increase—what will mankind eat, drink and breathe?

In the most welcome congruence of our times, scientists and children are coming together to act upon the last observation in the 2018 Living Planet Report 'Aiming Higher': "We are the first generation that has a clear picture of the value of nature and our impact on it. We may be the last that can take action to reverse this trend." Following the latest environmental reports and the impetus created by Greta Thunberg and other school children, the head of the European Commission announced in February 2019 that one fourth of the European Union expenditures between 2021 and 2017 would go towards mitigating climate change.

Indigenous people, women and children can build enormous momentum if united and effectively organized. No doubt, time and complacency would eventually turn them as well into their own worst enemies, for such is human nature. But, so far, they offer an optimistic alternative to the power structures that have led us to our current situation and we have little choice but believe that the best results can only be achieved when politicians act on the basis of scientists' findings with the backing of involved citizens.

I BEGAN BY EXAMINING DEEDS THAT implied some wrongness in their conception, realization or consequence—ill will either overtly or covertly present. Contrary to proverbial belief, I found that the road to hell was not, for the most part, paved with good intentions. This may happen once in a while by miscalculation, but the rule of thumb is that evil deeds result from bad intentions lucidly chosen for their immediate benefits. We cannot plead innocence.

Even if context has much to do with rating evil in different societies, reviewing its manifestations in our own society and in our times did not leave me unscathed. Body snatching for profit or creepy charivari did not particularly affect me—either they were too far in the past or their effects seemed more petty than cruel.

At that point in my research, I still wondered whether we might progress over time, either by miraculous grace or natural evolution, hoping to see some improvement through the Renaissance, the Age of Enlightenment and our modern humanism, despite mankind's ever-present temptation (from Adam to Faust) to sell its soul to the Devil in exchange for knowledge and power.

However, by the time I was reading about massacres, my spirits were sinking and I was questioning the wisdom of pursuing my project. I was at an all-time low when I read about the Rape of Nanking. One of my sources, Donald Dutton, wrote, "I was so shocked, revolted and numb that I could not function for some time." I also learned that Iris Chang, who had written on the same topic in 1997, subsequently suffered from severe depression. While this did not help, it explained the cumulative effect these several months of reading had on me.

In a sense, I was reassured by these painful reactions—they were appropriate and proved that we are not individually impervious to the harm we cause collectively. If I could feel such revulsion at our misdeeds, if reflecting upon our greed, irresponsibility and mindless cruelty could actually cause me such discomfort, it had to be a positive and hopeful sign. We know that we have already dissipated much of our inheritance and have allowed violence to run rampant, we realize that we might end up owning a world of physical devastation and moral dissolution if we go on undeterred on the same path, but—beyond these selfish concerns—we continue to grieve for the loss of innocence.

There is a generally heavy-hearted acknowledgement of failure in much of what is written today. Far from being "generous and gallant," as Golding thought we might be, we have become even more disconnected. Many feel like Chris Hedges:

> The single-minded pursuit of happiness, with happiness equated with hedonism, wealth, and power, creates a population consumed by anxiety and self-loathing... Building a society

around these goals is masochistic. It shuts down any desire for self-knowledge because the truth of our lives is unpleasant. We fill the spiritual vacuum with endless activities, entertainment, and nonstop electronic hallucinations. We flee from silence and contemplation. We are determined to avoid facing what we have become.[4]

What we believed to have been earlier existential threats (nuclear annihilation, overpopulation) were only possibilities. By contrast, climate change and its consequences are already occurring and are measurable. As we accept the reality and urgency of our situation, we need to act by empowering those who appreciate the immensity of the task. Politicians are often hampered by special interest groups, party discipline, election cycles and, most importantly, by the passivity or partisanship of voters. So, it is perhaps outside the field of politics that we may find help, among idealists who show imagination and fearlessness, and are energized by an imminent and realistic sense of purpose. Real adventurers are called for, conscientious objectors to excesses of all sorts. This is why this book is dedicated in part to my great-grandchildren, the generation on whose shoulders rests the burden of carrying on with what other children have already started, vocal girls and determined boys, only a few years older.

There will be scientists among them, political leaders, passionate ecologists, strict disciplinarians of excesses, moral guides, artists and philosophers. Inevitably, there will also be spendthrift consumers, fighters in unfair wars, righteous moralizers and immoral profiteers. The next wave of humanity will still be fighting the battle of good and evil, but perhaps a little wiser, less self-absorbed than the last few generations, and more aware of the dangers facing our future on earth.

---

4. Chris Hedges, *America, The Farewell Tour* (New York: Simon & Schuster, 2018), 244.

ACKNOWLEDGEMENTS

SEVERAL PEOPLE HAVE PARTICIPATED IN THE construction of this book, from its initial form of dictionary of malefaction to more developed essays on the banality of evil and our deep distrust of dissonance.

Lynn Duncan, my editor, has challenged me many times to dig a little deeper whenever she suspected indolence or laziness on my part. I appreciate the long hours she spent on my text, the keenness of her observations and her constant support. Kilmeny Jane Denny put in the final touches and created the cover and its saturnine evocation. I am grateful for their interest in the project and their belief that this book had something to say about our errant way of life.

John Layton resumed once more the onerous task of endlessly carting library books back and forth and being made to listen to obsessive monologues across the dinner table. As usual, I cannot thank him enough for his support and forbearance.

Elvi Whittaker and Lee Southern have for more than forty years put up with my vagaries and confusion, and, as with my previous books, provided encouragement, advice, and reading material. I thank them for their grace, their endurance, and their friendship.

I also thank Ken McLeod and Meg Hickling for their encouragements and useful comments and am much obliged to someone who wishes to remain anonymous for time spent researching and sharing with me Scriptural arguments on the matter of good and evil.

Saving the foundations for last, I must mention the many writers who have done the groundwork from which I have borrowed so liberally. A collective thank you is due to those listed in the bibliography—and to others whose real influence is less tangible than that contained in a footnote.

Vancouver, 2019

INDEX

'Dulce et Decorum Est' 174. *See also* Owen, Wilfred
Dumont, Louis 28, 34
   Homo Hierarchicus: The Caste System and Its Implications
Dutton, Donald 234

E

Ecce Homo: How One Becomes What One Is 157. *See also* Nietzsche, Friedrich
Economic Power Excessive Concentration Elimination Law (1947) 65
Ecrit en Chine 37. *See also* Voisins, A.G. de
Ehrlich, Paul R. 218
   The Population Bomb
Emerson, Barbara 161 .
Emma Bovary 125–126
End of Sex and the Future of Human Reproduction, The 115. *See also* Greely, Henry
Etudiant noir, L' 62
Evelyn, John 186
Execution by Hunger: The Hidden Holocaust 163. *See also* Dolot, Mirion

F

Faceless Killers 24. *See also* Mankel, Henning
Fair Trade Law (1947) 65
Family Britain 1951–1957 30. *See also* Kynaston, David
Fanon, Frantz 63
   The Wretched of the Earth (*Les damnés de la terre*)
Faust 206, 234. *See also* Goethe, Johan Wolfgang von
Ferguson, Niall 180
Fichte, Johann 11
Finkielkraut, Alain 193
Forum of China–Africa Cooperation (FOCAC) 66
14th Amendment, Equal Protection Clause 35
Frankenstein, or the Modern Prometheus 90. *See also* Shelley, Mary Wollenscraft
Freud, Sigmund 13, 120
Fromm, Erich 171
Funk & Wagnalls Standard Dictionary of Folklore and Mythology 119

G

Galen of Pergamon 103, 118
Gambler, Clive 154
Gandhi, Mahatma 74, 198
Gaskill, Malcolm 122
Gecan, Michael 220
   'Back of the Yards: Lesson from a Community Organizer on Building Political
   Power,' *Boston Review* 220
General History of the Robberies and Murders of the Most Notorious Pyrates, A 146. *See also* Defoe, Daniel
Gentleman's Magazine 91
ghettos 31, 39–42
Gilbert, Martin 41
Gilbert, W.S. 94
   'The Yarn of the Nancy Bell'
Global Wealth Report (2017) 50
Globe and Mail, The 113. *See also* Motluck, Alison

K

Kant, Immanuel 11, 19
Kids, Crime and Chaos. A World Report on Juvenile Delinquency 152–153. *See also* Tunley, Roul

King Lear 22. *See also* Shakespeare, William
Kipling, Rudyard 52–53
'The White Man's Burden'
Koestler, Arthur 49
Darkness at Noon 49
Kristeva, Julia 14
Kubrick, Stanley 157, 159–160
Kumar, Krishan 60
Kynaston, David 30
Family Britain 1951–1957

L

La Landelle, Gabriel de 137
Lapérouse, Comte de 58
Larsson, Stieg 24
The Millenium Trilogy 24
Law for the Prevention of Defective Progeny 34–35
Leavitt, Judith 129
Le Bon, Gustave 172
Lee, Stan 178
Légende des siècles, La 158. *See also* Hugo, Victor
Legras, Judge Claire 111
Lively, Penelope 130
Living Planet Report (2018) 201, 233
Lord of the Flies, The 12. *See also* Golding, William
Love in the Ruins 221. *See also* Percy, Walker
Lovelock, James 192
Lu Yu 38
Songs of the Frontiers

M

Machiavelli, Niccoló 10
The Prince
Makine, Andreï 221
Au delà des Frontières
Making Oscar Wilde 80. *See also* Mendelssohn, Michele
Malleus Maleficarum 123, 133
Mankell, Henning 24
Faceless Killers
Margulis, Lynn 192
Masefield, John 140
Sea Life in Nelson's Time
Médecins sans Frontières 222–223
mellahs *See* ghettos
Melville, Herman 143
White Jacket
Mendelssohn, Michele 79–80
Making Oscar Wilde

BIBLIOGRAPHY

van Acker, Rene, Motior Rahman and S. Zahara H. Cici. 'Pros and Cons of GMO Crop Farming.' *Environmental Science*, October 2017. Oxford Research Encyclopedias. https://oxfordre.com.

Adam, Ahmed H. 'Are We Witnessing a New Scramble for Africa?' *Al Jezeera*, March 26, 2018.

Avery, Catherine B. *The New Century Classical Handbook*. New York: Appleton-Century-Crofts Inc, 1962.

Bahree, Megha. 'Your Beautiful India Rug was Probably Made by Child Labor,' *Forbes*, February 5, 2014.

Baker, Jane and D. Scharie Tavcer. *Women and the Criminal Justice System: A Canadian Perspective*. Toronto: Emond Montgomery, 2018.

Ball, Philip. 'The Science Behind a Fertility Revolution,' *The Guardian Weekly*, October 25, 2018.

Barth, Brian. 'For Gas and Diesel,' *Modern Farmer Media*, October 2, 2017.

Bates, Stephen. 'The Hidden Holocaust,' *The Guardian*, May 13, 1999.

Baynham, Henry. *Before the Mast. Naval Ratings of the 19th Century*. London: Hutchinson & Co., 1971.

———*From the Lower Deck: The Old Navy, 1789-1840*. London: Arrow Books, 1972.

Beaglehole, J.C., ed. *The Journals of Captain Cook. The Voyage of Resolution and Discovery. 1772-1775*. Cambridge: Cambridge University Press for the Hakluyt Society, 1969.

Beck, Horace. *Folklore and the Sea*. Middleton, Connecticut: Wesleyan University Press, 1973.

Beckett, Lois. 'Parkland's Activities Gear Up For a 2020 Youth Revolution,' *The Guardian Weekly*, February 15, 2019.

Bielski, Zosia. ' 'Gender transgression': Why women cheat,' *The Globe and Mail*, October 2, 2018.

Blanco, Silvia. 'Spain Struggles with Surrogate Pregnancy Issue,' *El País*, February 24, 2017.

Bogousslavsky J. and L. Tatu. 'French Neuropsychiatry in the Great War: Between Moral Support and Electricity,' *Journal of the History of Neuroscience*. Vol. 22, No. 2 (2013).

Bohigas. Oriol, 'Architecture in the Emerging Metropolis,' *Homage to Barcelona: The City and its Art 1888-1936*. London: Thames and Hudson, 1986.

Boseley, Sarah. 'Child Labour Rife in Tobacco Industry,' *The Guardian Weekly*, June 29, 2018.

Botwin, Carol. *Tempted Women. The Passions, Perils, and Agonies of Female Infidelity.* New York: William Morrow and Company, 1994.

Boyer, Paul and Stephen Nissembaum. *Salem Possessed.* Cambridge, Mass.: Harvard University Press, 1974.

Brabbs, Derry. *Hadrian's Wall.* London: Frances Lincoln Limited, 2008.

Bradley, Anthony. 'Second-Hand Clothing Undermines Africa's Economy.' *Acton Institute Powerblog,* April 12, 2017. https://blog.acton.org.

Braudel, Fernand. *Civilization & Capitalism, 15th-18th Century. The Wheels of Commerce.* London: Willliam Collins, 1983.

Brendon, Piers. *The Decline and Fall of the British Empire. 1871-1997.* London: Vintage Books, 2007.

Bristow, William. 'Enlightenment.' *The Stanford Encyclopedia of Philosophy,* edited by Edward N. Zalta, (Fall 2017).

British Broadcasting Corporation. *'Shell Shock.'* Inside Out Extra, March 3, 2004. http://www.bbc.co.uk/insideout/extra/series-1/shell_shocked.shtml

Brown, Anthony G. 'The Nore Mutiny—Sedition of Ships' Biscuits. A Reappraisal.' *The Mariners' Mirror* 92, no.1 (February 2006)

Brown, Elizabeth A. 'Widely Misinterpreted Report Still Shows Catastrophic Animal Decline.' *National Geographic,* November 1, 2018.

Browning, Christopher. *Ordinary Men: Reserve Police Battalion 101 and the Final Solution in Poland.* New York: HarperPerennial, 1992.

Buranyi, Stephen. 'The Turn of the Tide.' *The Guardian Weekly,* November 23, 2018.

Burls, Frank. 'Is PMS Real?' *Slate,* November 28, 2016.

Burns Kingsbury, Kathleen. 'Financial Concerns of Women.' *BMO Wealth Institute,* March 2015.

Burt, Mary and WT Chapin, ed. *Kipling Stories and PoemsEvery Child Should Know.* Boston: Houghton Mifflin, 1909. Project Gutenberg

Byrne, Emma. *Swearing is Go•d f•r You. The Amazing Science of Bad Language.* Toronto: House of Anansi Press, 2017.

Camus, Albert. *The Plague.* Translated by Stuart Gilbert. New York: Vintage, 1991.

Carrington, Damian. 'Why Air Pollution is a Global Health Emergency.' *The Guardian Weekly,* November 9, 2018.

Carrington, Damian and Jonathan Watts. 'Humanity Has Wiped Out 60% of Mammals, Birds, Fish and Reptiles Since 1970.' *The Guardian Weekly,* November 9, 2018.

Castleman, Michael. ' 'Hysteria' and the Strange History of the Vibrator.' *Psychology Today,* March 2013.

Center for Biological Diversity Report (CBD). *A Deadly Toll: The Gulf Oil Spill and the Unfolding Wildlife Disaster.* https://www.biologicaldiversity.org/. April 2011.

Césaire, Aimé. *Discourse on Colonialism.* Translated by J. Pinkham. New York and London: Monthly Review Press, 1972.

Chaline, Olivier. 'Les mutineries de 1979 dans la Navy'. *Histoire, Economie & Société* 1, (2005)

Chang, Iris. *The Rape of Nanking. The Forgotten Holocaust of World War II.* New York: Basic Books, 1991.

Chiu, Elizabeth. 'The Legacy of Rehtaeh Parsons.' CBC News, April 5, 2018. https://newsinteractives.cbc.ca/longform/five-years-gone

Chrisafis, Angélique. 'French Pressured to Remember WWI Soldiers Executed for 'Cowardice' ' *The Guardian,* October 1, 2013.

———'French Skinheads Go on Trial Over 2013 Death of Anti-fascist Activist.' *The Guardian,* September 2018.

Colleu, Michael. 'The Songs of French Sailors.' *Musical Traditions,* no. 9, (Autumn 1991).

Compassion in World Farming (CIWF). *The Life of Dairy Cows.* Updated September 2012. https://www.ciwf.org.uk/media/5235185/The-Life-of-Dairy-cows.pdf.

Conklin, H. C. 'Hanunóo Color Categories.' *Southwestern Journal of Anthropology,* 11 (1955).

Cook, Tim. 'The Long Shadow of War.' *The Globe and Mail,* November 10, 2018.

Cooke, Michèle. 'Repartee From Ridicule.' *The Guardian,* June 15, 2018.

Cordingly, David, ed. *Pirates, Terror on the High Seas from the Caribbean to the South Seas.* Atlanta: Turner Publishing, 1996.

———*Women Sailors and Sailors' Women. An Untold Maritime History.* New York: Random House, 2001.

———*Pirate Hunters of the Caribbean.* New York: Random House, 2011.

Corntassel, Jeff. 'Partnership in Action? Indigenous Political Mobilization and Co-optation During the First UN Indigenous Decade (1995-2004).' *Human Rights Quarterly,* 29 (2007).

Criminal Code of Canada. 1985. http://laws-lois.justice.gc.ca. Last amended June 21, 2018.

Cunningham, Matt. *10 Disadvantages of Biofuels.* Howstuffworks. https://auto.howstuff-works.com/fuel-efficiency/biofuels/10-disadvantages-of-biofuels.htm. 2019.

Dallaire, Roméo, with Brent Beardsley. *Shake Hands with the Devil. The Failure of Humanity in Rwanda.* Toronto: Vintage Canada, 2003.

Darwin, Charles. *A Naturalist's Voyage Round the World. The Voyage of the Beagle.* London: John Murray, 1913. Project Gutenberg.

Day, Michael. 'Mafia crime wave in Naples.' *Independent,* September 9, 2015.

Dean Michelle. 'The Story of Amanda Todd.' *The New Yorker,* October 18, 2012.

Dee, Robert. 'The Massive Cost and Burden to Society and the Environment of the Internal Combustion Engine (ICE).' *CleanTechnica,* October 23, 2017.

Delacy, Justine. 'How French Women Got that Way – And How to Handle Them'. *The New York Times,* January 13, 1971.

Diagne, Souleymane. 'Negritude.' *Stanford Encyclopedia of Philosophy.* Edited by Edward N. Zalta, (Spring 2016).

Diamond, Jared. Collapse. *How Societies Choose to Fall or Succeed.* New York: Viking, 2005.

Dickens, Charles. *David Copperfield.* (1850). London: Heron Books, 1967.

Dinapoli, Jessica and Mark Bendeich. 'Green Groups Target Consumer Goods Companies at Davos Over Plastic Waste.' *The Globe and Mail,* January 28, 2019.

Douglas, Mary. *Purity and Danger. An Analysis of Concept of Pollution and Taboo.* (1966). New York: Routledge Classics, 2002.

Dostoevsky, Fyodor. *Crime and Punishment* (1866). Translated by Constance Garnett. 2007. Project Guttenberg.

Dr. Seuss. *The Sneetches and Other Stories.* New York: Random House, 1953.

Duckworth, A. R. 'Leopold Sedar Senghor's Concept of Negritude,' The Motley View. *Journal of Films, Art and Aesthetics,* February 8, 2010.

Duffin, Jacalyn. *History of Medicine. A Scandalously Short Introduction.* Toronto: University of Toronto Press, 1999.

Dumont, Louis. *Homo Hierarchicus: The Caste System and Its Implications.* (1970). Translated by Mark Sainsbury, Louis Dumont, and Basia Gulati. India: Oxford University Press, 1999.

Dunleavy, Brian. 'Life in the Trenches of World War I.' *History,* April 23, 2018.

Dutton, Donald G. *The Psychology of Genocide, Massacres, and Extreme Violence. Why 'Normal' People Come to Commit Atrocities.* Westport, Connecticut: Praeger Security International, 2007.

Endler, Norman S. 'The Origins of Electroconvulsive Therapy (ECT).' *The Journal of ECT* 4, no. 1 (1988).

Faith, Karlene. *Unruly Women. The Politics of Confinement and Resistance.* Vancouver: Pressgang Publishers, 1993.

Fanon, Frantz. *The Wretched of the Earth.* New York: Grove Weidenfeld, 1963.

————*Towards the African Revolution,* New York: Grove Press, 1964.

Ferguson, Niall. *The Pity of War.* London: Penguin Books, 1998.

Finkielkraut, Alain. *Des Animaux et des Hommes.* Paris: Stock, 2018.

Fishwick, Carmen. 'What is Female Genital Mutilation?' *The Guardian,* May 17, 2014.

Fixico, Donald L. 'When Native Americans Were Slaughtered in the Name of Civilization.' *History,* March 2, 2018.

Flaubert, Gustave. *Madame Bovary.* (1857). Translated by Eleanor Marx-Aveling. 2016. Project Gutenberg.

Forshaw, Barry. *Nordic Noir. The Pocket Essential Guide to Scandinavian Crime Fiction, Film & TV.* Harpenden: Old Castle Books, 2013.

Freedland, Jonathan. 'Swaggering Machismo Rules Global Politics.' *The Guardian Weekly.* October 5, 2018.

Frost, Jack, ed. *Grog: A Collection of Lyrics and Pictures of Sea Shanties from Olden Times.* ZBooks, 2015. Kindle Edition

Frykman, Niklas. 'The Mutiny on the Hermione: Warfare, Revolution, and Treason in the Royal Navy.' *Journal of Social History* IV no. 1 (Fall 2010).

Gambler, Clive. *Time Walkers. The Prehistory of Global Colonization.* Cambridge, Mass.: Harvard University Press, 1993.

Garin, Virginie. 'Chine: Une Ferme de 100,000 Vaches Pollue les Nappes Phréatiques.' *RTL,* December 27, 2016. https://www.rtl.fr/actu/debats-societe/chine-une-ferme-de-100-000-vaches-pollue-les-nappes-phreatiques-7786462404

Gaskill, Malcolm. *Witchcraft. A Very Short Introduction,* Oxford: Oxford University Press, 2010.

Gecan, Michael. 'Back of the Yards: Lesson from a Community Organizer on Building Political Power.' *Boston Review,* January 4, 2017.

George, Michael. 'Relations between English Settlement and Indians in 17th Century New England.' Diploma Thesis. Masaryk University, 2016.

George, Rose. *Ninety Percent of Everything: Inside Shipping, the Invisible Industry That Puts Clothes on Your Back, Gas in Your Car, and Food on Your Table.* New York: Henry Hold, 2013.

Gilbert, Ben. 'A Visit to Israel's Wall with Palestine.' *Business Insider*, July 21, 2018.

Gilbert, Martin. *In Ishmael's House. A History of Jews in Muslim Lands.* Toronto: McClelland & Stewart, 2009.

Goeschel, Christian and Nikolaus Wachsmann. *The Nazi Concentration Camps 1933-1939.* Lincoln: University of Nebraska Press, 2012.

Golding. William. *The Lord of the Flies.* New York: Faber and Faber, 1954.

———'Nobel Lecture' (1983). *Nobel Lectures, 1981-1990.* Edited by In Tore Frängsmyr. Singapore: World Science Publishing, 1993.

Goni, Uki. '40 Years Later, the Mothers or Argentina's 'Disappeared' Refuse to Be Silent. *The Guardian*, September 18, 2018.

Gordon, Dave. 'Shouting Match.' *The Globe & Mail*, November 17, 2018.

Greenblatt, Stephen. *The Rise and Fall of Adam and Eve.* New York: WW Norton & Company, 2017.

Greer, John Michael. 'A Conversation with Nature.' *Ecosophia*, February 20, 2019.

Grooten, M. and R.E.A. Almond, eds. *Living Planet Report: Aiming Higher.* Glared, Switzwerland: World Wide Federation, 2018.

Gutman, Rachel. 'The Three Most Chilling Conclusions from the Climate Report.' *The Atlantic*, November 25, 2018.

Haberman, Clyde. 'The Unrealized Horror of Population Explosion'. *The New York Times*, May 15, 2015.

Hanania, Jordan, Braden Heffernan, James Jenden, Kailyn Stenhouse, and Jason Doney. 'Access to Non-Solid Fuel.' *Energy Education.* University of Calgary. https://energyeducation.ca/encyclopedia/Access_to_non-solid_fuel. Accessed March 30, 2019.

Hersch, Seymour M. *'The Scene of the Crime. Letter from Vietnam.'* The New Yorker, March 30, 2015.

Hilowitz, Janet. 'International Programme on the Elimination of Child Labour.' *International Labour Organization.* https://www.ilo.org/public//english/standards/ipec/publ/policy/papers/labelling/part2.htm. Updated October 18, 2000.

History.com Editors. 'Armenian Genocide.' A&E Television Networks. https://www.history.com/topics/world-war-i/armenian-genocide. October 1, 2010, updated September 20, 2018.

Ingle, Sean. 'Football Hooliganism, Once the English Disease, Is More Like a Cold Sore Now.' *The Guardian*, November 4, 2013.

Johnson, Christen A. and K.T. Hawbaker. '#MeToo: A Timeline of Events.' *Chicago Tribune*, September 19, 2018.

Hall, Nigel. 'Argentina and 'Los Desaparecidos'.' *International Federation of Social Workers*, April 23, 1918.

Hall, Paul. *Cities in Civilization.* New York: Pantheon Books, 1998.

Hankel, Gerd. 'Leipzig War Crimes Trials.' *International Encyclopedia of the First World War, 1914-1918 Online.* https://encyclopedia.1914-1918-online.net/home.html. October 2016.

Hanson, Erin. 'Reserves.' *First Nations Indigenous Studies.* The University of British Columbia, 2009.

Hanson, Neil. *The Custom of the Sea.* London, New York: Doubleday, 1999.

Harari, Yuval Noah. *Sapiens. A Brief History of Humankind.* Toronto: McClelland & Stewart, 2014.

Harper, Kyle. *The Fate of Rome. Climate, Disease, and the End of the Empire.* Princeton and Oxford: Princeton University Press, 2007.

Harris, Marvin. *Cows, Pigs, Wars, and Witches. The Riddles of Culture.* New York: Vintage Books, 1989.

Hayward, Arthur L., ed. *Lives of the Most Remarkable Criminals.* (1735). New York: Dodd Mead, 1927.

Hedges, Chris. *America, The Farewell Tour.* Alfred A. Knopf: Summit Study, 2018.

Himmelfarb, Gertrude. 'The Victorian Ethos: Before and After Victoria.' in GM Young, *Victorian England.* London: The Folio Society Series: A History of England, 1999.

Hobsbawn, E.J. *The Age of Empire. 1875-1914.* London: Abacus, 1987.

Holy Bible, containing the Old and New Testaments. Authorized King James Version.

Houdebine, Louise-Marie. 'Impacts of Genetically Modified Animals on Ecosystems and Human Activities.' *Global Biotics,* 25 no. 1 (March 2014).

Hoyt, Charles Alva. *Witchcraft.* Carbondale: Southern Illinois University Press, 1989.

Howell, Tom. *The Rude Story of English.* Toronto:McClelland & Stewart, 2013.

Hughes, Geoffrey. *Swearing. A Social History of Foul Language, Oaths and Profanity in English.* Oxford: Basil Blackwell, 1991.

Hugo, Victor. *La Lègende des Siècles* (1888). 2005. Project Gutenberg.

Huizinga, J. *The Waning of the Middle Ages.* Garden City: Doubleday Anchor Books, 1954.

Huxley, Aldous. *The Devils of Loudon.* New York: Harper & Row, 1952.

Irvine, William B. *A Slap in the Face. Why Insults Hurt and Why They Shouldn't.* Oxford: Oxford University Press, 2013.

Islahi, Amin Ahsan. *Good and Evil. Lectures.*Translated by Saeed Ahmad. Al-Mawrid, A Foundation for Islamic Research and Education. http://www.al-mawrid.org/index.php/articles/view/good-and-evil-1-views-of-the-philosophers. January 1998.

Jan, Michel. *The Great Wall of China.* Translated by Josephine Bacon. New York: Abbeville Press Publishers, 2001.

Jones, Edgar. 'Shell Shocked.' *American Psychological Association* Vol. 43, no 6. (June 2012).

Joyce, Fraser. 'Prostitution and the Nineteenth Century. In Search of the 'Great Social Evil'.' *Reinvention: A Journal of Underground Research* vol. 1, no. 1 (2008).

Judt, Tony. *Reappraisals. Reflections on the Forgotten Twentieth Century.* New York: Penguin Press, 2008.

Kaho, Todd. 'Fuel from Plants. The Basics of Biofuel.' *Mother Earth News,* Summer 2012.

Kassam, Ashifa. 'Canada's Indigenous Women Were Coerced Into Sterilizations, Lawsuit Says.' *The Guardian,* October 27, 2017.

Kayembe, Danielle. 'The Silent Rise of the Female-Driven Economy.' Refinery29. https://www.refinery29.com/en-us/2017/12/184334/rise-of-female-driven-economy-feminist-economics Accessed December 20, 2017.

Kirk, W. Robert. *History of the South Pacific since 1513.* Denver: Outskirt Press, 2011.

Kristeva, Julia. *Powers of Horror. An Essay on Abjection.* Translated by Leon S. Roudiez. New York: Columbia University Press, 1982.

Kumar, Krishan. *Visions of Empire. How Five Imperial Regimes Shaped the World.* Princeton: Princeton University Press, 2017.

Kumar, Sashi N. and Arun Kumar Jain. 'E-waste: Health Impacts in Developing Countries.' *EHS Journal,* July 9, 2014.

Kynaston, David. *Family Britain, 1951-57.* London: Bloomsbury Publishing, 2009.

Lanchester, John. 'The Deadly Legacy the Babyboomers Have Left the Young.' *The Guardian Weekly,* February 15, 2019.

Latowsky, Anne A. *Emperor of the World. Charlemagne and the Construction of Imperial Authority. 800-1229.* Ithaca: Cornell University Press, 2013.

Lavery, Brian. *Nelson's Navy. The Ships, Men, and Organisation, 1793-1815.* London: Conway Maritime Press, 1989.

Layton, Monique. 'Streetwalkers and the Ambiguities of the Law'. *Chitty's Law Journal* 27, no. 4 (1979).

———*Street Women and the Art of Bullshitting.* Vancouver: Webzines of Vancouver, 2010.

———*Notes from Elsewhere. Travel and Other Matters.* iUniverse, 2011.

Leach, Maria, ed. *Funk and Wagnalls Standard Dictionary of Folklore Mythology and Legends.* Vol. 2 (J-Z), 1950.

Lee, Stan. *Stan's Soap Box. The Collection.* Los Angeles: The Hero Initiative, 2008

Legras, Claire. 'Why Has France Banned Surrogate Motherhood?' *Law/Politics,* February 23, 2015.

Leonard, George. 'Climate Change and the Ocean: A Stark Message From the IPCCC.' Blog. https://www.chicagomanualofstyle.org/tools_citationguide/citation-guide-1. html#cg-social. Accessed October 11, 2018.

Lever, R.J.A.W. 'Whales and Whaling in the Western Pacific.' *South Pacific Bulletin,* April 1964.

Levine, Allan. 'The Quintessence of a Minority.' *The Globe and Mail,* November 3, 2018.

Lévy-Strauss, Claude. *Origin of Table Manners.* (Mythologiques, Vol. 3). Translated by J. & D. Weightman. Chicago: University of Chicago Press, 1978.

Libaek, Ivar. 'The Red Cross: Three-Time Recipient of the Peace Prize.' The Nobel Prize. https://www.nobelprize.org/prizes/themes/the-red-cross-three-time-recipient-of-the-peace-prize/ October 30, 2003.

Liles, Heino. 'Circle Sentencing: Part of the Restorative Justice Continuum.' International Institute of Restorative Practices. https://iirp.edu/news/circle-sentencing-part-of-the-restorative-justice-continuum. August 9, 2002.

Linder, Douglas O. 'My Lai Massacre Courts Martial: An Account.' Famous Trials. UMKC School of Laws, 1995. http://law2.umkc.edu/Faculty/projects/ftrials/ftrials.htm.

Llamas, Jewel. 'Female Circumcision: The History, the Current Prevalence and the Approach to the Patient.' *Virginia School of Medicine,* April 2017.

Llewelly, Julia. 'Why Are So Many Married Women Having Affairs?' *The Telegraph,* November 22, 2010.

Lloyd, Christopher and Jack L.S. Coulter. 'Life at Sea in Nelson's Navy.' In Lieut.-Cmdr P.K. Kemp. *History of the Royal Navy.* New York: G.P. Putnam's Sons, 1969.

Lombardo, Paul. 'Eugenic Sterilization Laws.' Image Archive on the American Eugenics Movement. http://eugenicsarchive.org/html/eugenics/essay8text.html. Accessed February 14, 2019

Machiavelli, Niccoló. *The Prince*. Planet EBook.

Maine, Rachel P. *The Technology of the Orgasm*. Baltimore: Johns Hopkins University Press, 1999.

Makine, Andrei. *Au delà des Frontières*. Paris: Grasset, 2019.

Mankel, Henning. *Faceless Killers*. Translated by Steven Murray. New York: Vintage Books, 2003.

Mariott, McKim. 'Stratification. Homo Hierarchicus. Essai sur le Système des Castes. Louis Dumont.' American Anthropologist 71 (1969).

Mark, Joshua. 'Wall.' Ancient History Encyclopedia. September 2009.

Marriott, Kathy. 'The Second Scramble for Africa.' *Geopolitics,* November 20, 2014.

Marwah, Sonal. 'Canada and the Global Compact on Refugees' *The Ploughshares Monitor* 39, no. 4 (Winter 2018).

Marx, Jennifer G. 'The Golden Age of Piracy' and 'The Pirate Round.' In D. Cordingly, ed. *Pirates, Terror on the High Seas from the Caribbean to the South China Sea*. Atlanta: Turner Publishing, 1996.

Masefield, John. *Sea Life in Nelson's Time*. London: Conway Maritime Press, 1984.

Mendelssohn, Michele. *Making Oscar Wilde*. Oxford: Oxford University Press, 2018.

Merchant, Carolyn. *The Death of Nature: Women, Ecology, and the Scientific Revolution*. San Francisco: Harper & Row, 1980.

———'The Violence of Impediments: Francis Bacon and the Origins of Experimentation.' *Isis* 99 (2008).

———'Environmentalism: From the Control of Nature to Partnership.' Based on the Bernard Moses Lecture. Berkeley: University of California, May 4, 2010.

Mohr, Melissa. *Holy Sh•t: A Brief History of Swearing*. Oxford: Oxford University Press, 2013.

Montagu, Ashley. *The Anatomy of Swearing*. London: McMillan and Collier, 1973.

Moran, Michael. *Beyond the Coral Sea. Travels in the Old Empire of South-West Pacific*. London: HarperCollins Publishers, 2003.

Moss, Laura. 'The 13 Largest Oil Spills in History.' *Mother Nature Network*, July 16, 2010.

Motluck, Alison. 'How Canada Became an International Surrogacy Hotspot.' *The Globe and Mail,* October 6, 2018.

McKie, Robin. 'The Rising.' *The Guardian Weekly,* December 7, 2018.

New York Times Editorial Board. 'Yes, It's Genocide.' *New York Times,* June 3, 2016.

Nguyen, Truc. 'Green Is the New Black.' *Bay Street Bull,* Winter 2018.

Nittle, Nadrá. 'What the Rana Plaza Disaster Changed About Worker Safety.' *Racked,* April 13, 2018.

Naipul, V.S. *An Area of Darkness*. London: André Deutsch, 1964.

Nietzsche, Friedrich. *The Portable Nietzsche*. Edited by Walter Kauffman. New York: The Viking Press, 1954.

Olsen, Jack. *Silence on Monte Sole*. New York: G.P. Putnam's Sons, 1968.

Orwell, George. *Down and Out in Paris and London.* (1939). Australia: Penguin Books, 2013.

Otsubo, Shigeru T. 'Post-war Development of the Japanese Economy.' Economic Development Policy and Management Pogram. Nagoya University, Japan. https://www.gsid.nagoya-u.ac.jp/sotsubo/Postwar_Development_of_the_Japanese%20Economy(Otsubo_NagoyaU).pdf

Overy, Richard. *The Twilight Years. The Paradox of Britain Between the Wars.* New York: Viking, 2009.

O'Loughlin, Ed. 'Ireland's Catholic Church-run Mother and Baby Homes Gave Children's Bodies to Medical School for Dissection.' *The New York Times,* April 18, 2019.

Palmer, Roy. *The Oxford Book of Sea Songs.* Oxford: Oxford University Press, 1986.

———*The Sound of History. Songs and Social Context.* Oxford: Oxford University Press, 1988.

Parker, Laura. 'We Made Plastic. We Depend on It. Now We're Drowing in It.' *National Geographic,* June 2018.

Peck, Scott M. *People of the Lie. The Hope for Healing Human Evil.* New York: Simon and Schuster, 1983.

Pelchat, André. 'Sorcery in New France.' *Canada's History,* 2016.

Philbrick, Nathaniel. *In the Heart of the Sea. The Tragedy of the Whaleship Essex.* Penguin Books, 2000.

Phillips, Tom. 'The Cultural Revolution: All You Need to Know About China's Political Convulsion.' *The Guardian,* May 11, 2016.

Picard, André. 'Canada's New Prostitution Laws May Not Make Sex Work Safer: Research.' *The Globe and Mail,* July 27, 2018.

Pilklington, Ed. 'Trapped in a Hoax: Survivors of Conspiracy Theories Speak Out.' *The Guardian,* January 24, 2019.

———'Going Viral: The Victims of Online Conspiracy Theories.' *The Guardian,* January 28, 2019.

Piñero, Claudia. 'Argentina's Women Will Not Be Defeated' *The Guardian Weekly,* August, 17, 2018.

Plimsol, Samuel, M.P. *Our Seamen. An Appeal.* London: Virtue & Co., 1873. Digitized by Google from the collections of the University of Virginia.

Poccia, Cheryl. 'A Look at the Israeli Westbank Barrier Wall.' *State of the Planet,* Earth Institute, Columbia University. August 30, 2017.

Poonam, Snigdha. 'Five Million Indian Women Built the Right Kind of Wall.' *The Guardian Weekly,* January 11, 2019.

Poteranski, Waclaw. *The Warsaw Ghetto.* Warsaw: Interpress Publishers, 1968.

Radcliffe-Brown, A.R. 'Joking Relationships.' *Africa: Journal of the International African Institute* Vol 13, no. 3 (July 1940).

Redicker, Marcus. *Between the Devil and the Deep Blue Sea.* Cambridge: Cambridge University Press, 1987.

———'Libertalia. The Pirate's Utopia.' In D. Cordingly, ed. *Terror on the High Seas from the Caribbean to the South China Sea.* Atlanta: Turner Publishing, Inc., 1996.

———*Villains of All Nations: Atlantic Pirates in the Golden Age.* Beacon, Massachusetts: Beacon Press, 2004.

Rochman, Chelsea et al. 'Anthropogenic Debris in Seafood: Plastic Debris and Fibers from Textiles in Fish and Bivalves Sold for Human Consumption.' *Scientific Report* 5 (September 2015).

Rouffranche, Marguerite. 'The Oradour-sur-Glane Massacre. The Story of Survivor Madame Marguerite Rouffranche.' *Official Publication of the Military Tribunal of Bordeaux*, 1953.

Rounding, Virginie. *Grandes Horizontales. The Lives and Legends of Four Nineteenth-Century Courtesans.* New York: Bloomsbury USA, 2003.

Rosenberg, Kenneth Paul. *Infidelity. Why Men and Women Cheat.* New York: Da Capo Press, 2018.

Rousseau, Jean-Jacques. *Discourse on the Origin and Basis of Inequality Among the French* (1775). Penguin Books, 1989.

Rummel, R.J. 'Exemplifying the Horror of European Colonization: Leopold's Congo.' University of Hawaii. http://www.hawaii.edu/powerkills/COMM.7.1.03.HTM. 2001 and 2003.

Safi, Michael and Dominic Rushe. 'Rana Plaza, Five Years On: Safety of Workers Hangs in Balance in Bangladesh.' *The Guardian*, April 24, 2018.

Sartre, Jean-Paul. *Saint Genet. Actor and Martyr.* Translated by Bernard Frechtman. New York: George Braziller, 1963.

Scharf, Rafael F. *In the Warsaw Ghetto: Summer 1941.* New York: Aperture Foundations, 1993.

Scruton, Roger. *Where We Are.* London: Bloomsbury, 2017.

Shelley, Mary Wollenscraft. *Frankenstein, or the Modern Prometheus* (1818). Planet EBook.

Shakespeare, William. *The Complete Works.* The University Society. Philadelphia: John D. Morris & Company, 1901.

Slejokava, Nadezda. 'Marriage and Adultery in Tolstoy's Anna Karenina.' M.A. Thesis, McGill University, 1973.

Spade, Paul Vincente. 'Medieval Philosophy.' *The Stanford Encyclopedia of Philosophy.* Edited by Edward N. Zalta. (Summer 2018).

Sputeri, Melanie. 'Sentencing Circles for Aboriginal Offenders in Canada: Furthering the Idea of Aboriginal Justice Within a Western Justice Framework.' M.A. Thesis, University of Windsor, 2001.

Steel, Peta. *The Spithead and Nore Mutinies of 1797. An Account of Rebellious Activities in London, the South East, and East of England in the Eighteenth Century.* London: Sertuc, 2013.

Stevenson, Robert Louis. *The Strange Case of Dr. Jekyll and Mr. Hyde.* New York: Vintage Books, 1991.

Stone, Dan. *Concentration Camps.* Oxford: Oxford University Press, 2017.

Tambiah, S.J. 'Review of Homo Hierarchicus: An Essay on the Class System.' *American Anthropologist* 74 (1972).

Tanguy, Joelle. 'Global Health and Humanism.' Speech delivered at Stanford University. March 27, 2000.

Tatu, L. and Julien Bogousslavsky. 'World War I Psychoneuroses: Hysteria Goes to War.' *Frontiers of Neurology and Neuroscience*, June 26, 2014.

Tavcer, Scharie and Jane Baker. 'Finding a Middle Ground on Prostitution.' *Policy Options Politiques,* May 4, 2018.

Taylor, Kate. 'A Shocking Look at Humanity's Footprint.' *The Globe and Mail*, October 1, 2018.

Taylor, Matthew and Sandra Laville. 'Why Study For a Future We Might Not Have?' *The Guardian Weekly,* February 15, 2019.

Thrasher, Frederick M. 'What is a Gang?' In *Classics of Criminology,* edited by Joseph E. Jacoby, Long Grove, Illinois: Waveland Press, 1979.

Tolstoy, Leo. *Anna Karenina* (1879). Translated by Constance Garnett. Project Gutenberg.

Topping, Alexandra. 'Up, Up and Away. Mass Protests Planned Against Trump.' *The Guardian Weekly,* July 13, 2018.

Trigger, Bruce G. *Natives and Newcomers. Canada's 'Heroic Age' Reconsidered.* Montreal: McGill-Queen's University Press, 1985.

Trueman, C. 'World War One Executions.' *The History Learning Site,* March 31, 2015.

Tuchman, Barbara W. *A Distant Mirror. The Calamitous 14th Century.* New York: Alfred A. Knopf, 1979.

Tunley, Roul. *Kids, Crime and Chaos. A World Report on Juvenile Delinquency.* New York: Dell Publishing, 1964.

United States Holocaust Memorial Museum. 'Ghettos.' https://www.ushmm.org/. Accessed January 6, 2019.

Vargas, Fred. *L'humanité en Péril. Virons de Bord, Toute!* Paris: Flammarion, 2019.

Vidal, John. 'How Developing Countries Are Paying a High Price for the Global Mineral Boom.' *The Guardian,* August 15, 2015.

Virdi, Jaipreet. 'Canada's Shame: The Coerced Sterilization of Indigenous Women.' *New Internationalist,* November 30, 2018.

Visser, Margaret. *Much Depends on Dinner. The Extraordinary History and Mythology, Allure and Obsessions, Perils and Taboos, of an Ordinary Meal.* Toronto: McClelland & Stewart, 1986.

———*The Rituals of Dinner. The Origins, Evolution, Eccentricities and Meaning of Table Manners.* Toronto: HarperCollins Publishers Ltd., 1991.

———*The Way We Were.* Boston and London: Faber and Faber, 1994.

Wallace-Wells, David. 'What Are We Going to Do Now?' *The Guardian Weekly,* February 8, 2019.

Warren, Matthew. 'Thousands of Scientists are Backing the Kids Striking for Climate Change.' *Nature International Journal of Science,* March 14, 2019.

Wengraf, Lee. 'The New Scramble for Africa.' *International Socialist Review,* July 2008.

Wente, Margaret. 'Why Are the Swedes So Disgruntled?' *The Globe and Mail,* September 11, 2018.

Wilde, Oscar. *The Picture of Dorian Gray.* London: Oxford University Press, 1974.

Willis, Sam. *In the Hour of Victory. The Royal Navy at War in the Age of Nelson.* London: Atlantis Books, 2013.

Wilson, Philip K. 'Eugenics.' *Encyclopedia Britannica.* https://www.britannica.com/science/eugenics-genetics

Withey, Lynne. *Voyages of Discovery. Captain Cook and the Exploration of the Pacific.* Berkeley: University of California Press, 1989.

Witt, Emily. 'From Parkland to Sunrise: A Year of Extraordinary Youth Activity.' *The New Yorker,* February 13, 2019.

Wolfenden, Sir John. *The Report of the Department Committee on Homosexual Offences and Prostitution. London.* 1957. https://www.ncbi.nlm.nih.gov/pmc/articles/PMC1962139/

Wohlleben, Peter. *The Hidden Life of Trees*. Translated by Jane Billinghurst. Vancouver: Greystone Books Ltd., 2015.

———*The Secret Wisdom of Nature. Trees, Animals, and the Extraordinary Balance of All Living Things*. Translated by Jane Billinghurst. Vancouver: Greystone Books, 2017.

World Health Organization. (WHO) 'Female Genital Mutilation.' Report. January 31, 2018. https://www.who.int/news-room/fact-sheets/detail/female-genital-mutilation.

Wulf, Andrea. *The Invention of Nature. Alexander von Humboldt's New World*. New York: Vintage Books, 2016.

Zhangm Chen, Robert Wohehueter and Han Zhang. 'Genetically Modified Foods. A Critical Review of their Promise and Problems.' *Food Science and Human Wellness* Vol. 5, no. 3 (September 2016).

FILMS AND TELEVISION DOCUMENTARIES

Avrich, Barry. *The Reckoning: Hollywood's Worst Kept Secret*. Documentary Film. Directed by Barry Avrich. Melbar Entertainment Group, 2018.

Bern, Stéphane. 'Les Reines de Paris.' Television Episode. Directed by David Janikowski and David Perrier. Secrets d'Histoire, 2014.

Bracher, Julia. *Filles de Joie et de Misère*. Documentay Film. AB Productions. 2016.

Dabner, Jack. *The Silent Scream*. Presented by Dr. B. Nathanseon. American Portrait Films, 1984.

Devillers, Jean-Pierre and Adrien Soland. 'La Grande Librairie'. Television Episode. Hosted by François Brusnel. Rosebud Productions, 2019.

Frears, Stephen. *Philomena*. Feature Film. The Weinstein Company, 2013

Giroux, Aube. *Modified*. Documentary Film. Directed by Aube Giroux, 2017

Karel, William and Blanche Finger. *Jusqu'aux Derniers. La destruction des Juifs d'Europe*. Television Series. Zadig Productions and LOOKSfilm, 2014.

Klovborg, Søren. ' Maid in Hell.' Television Episode. *The Passionate Eye*, 2018.

Kubrick, Stanley and Arthur C. Clarke. *2001: A Space Odyssey*. Feature Film. Directed by Stanley Kubrick. Metro-Goldwyn-Meyer, 1968.

Rankin, Ian. *Ian Rankin's Evil Thoughts*. Television Series. BBC and BFI, 2010.

Suzuki, David. 'The Genetic Revolution.' Television Episode. *The Nature of Things*. Canadian Broadcasting Corporation, 2018.

Weilhammer. Françoise. 'Rescapées de la Prostitution.' Television Episode. *Le Temps Présent. Magazine de Reportages*, 2018.

ABOUT THE AUTHOR

MONIQUE LAYTON is the former Associate Director of the Centre for Distance Education (Criminology Programs) at Simon Fraser University and resides in Vancouver. She was raised in North Africa and educated in France and Britain. After moving to Canada, she obtained degrees in comparative literature (MA) and cultural anthropology (PhD). Layton is the author of a number of non-fiction works and translated Claude Levi-Strauss's *Structural Anthropology Volume 2* (University of Chicago Press).

www.moniquelayton.com